Home Field

AN ILLUSTRATED HISTORY OF
120 COLLEGE FOOTBALL STADIUMS

Richard Pennington

EAKIN PRESS ⚜ Fort Worth, Texas

This book is dedicated to the late Ed Eakin.

ALL RIGHTS RESERVED. No part of this book may be reproduced in any form without written permission from the publisher, except for brief passages included in a review appearing in a newspaper or magazine.

Copyright © 2003
By Richard Pennington
Published By Eakin Press
An Imprint of Wild Horse Media Group
P.O. Box 331779
Fort Worth, Texas 76163
1-817-344-7036
www.EakinPress.com
ALL RIGHTS RESERVED
1 2 3 4 5 6 7 8 9
ISBN-10: 1-57168-674-6
ISBN-13: 978-1-57168-674-9
Library of Congress Control Number 2002117359

Contents

Foreword by Craig James	vii
Preface	ix
Harvard Stadium (Harvard)	1
Dodd Stadium (Georgia Tech)	3
Yale Bowl (Yale)	5
Scott Field (Mississippi State)	7
Schoellkopf Field (Cornell)	9
Nippert Stadium (Cincinnati)	11
Camp Randall Stadium (Wisconsin)	12
Lewis Field (Oklahoma State)	14
Husky Stadium (Washington)	16
Memorial Stadium (Kansas)	19
Neyland Stadium (Tennessee)	21
Stanford Stadium (Stanford)	24
Ohio Stadium (Ohio State)	26
Rose Bowl (UCLA)	27
Franklin Field (Pennsylvania)	30
Memorial Stadium (Illinois)	32
Memorial Stadium (Nebraska)	34
Spartan Stadium (Michigan State)	36
Memorial Stadium (California)	38

Los Angeles Memorial Coliseum (Southern California) ..	40
Folsom Field (Colorado)	42
Michie Stadium (Army)	45
Ross-Ade Stadium (Purdue)	47
Royal–Memorial Stadium (Texas)	49
Tiger Stadium (Louisiana State)	52
Memorial Stadium (Oklahoma)	54
Ryan Field (Northwestern)	55
Memorial Stadium (Missouri)	57
Michigan Stadium (Michigan)	59
Kenan Stadium (North Carolina)	61
Legion Field (Alabama–Birmingham)	63
Bryant-Denny Stadium (Alabama)	65
Arizona Stadium (Arizona)	67
Wade Stadium (Duke)	69
Sanford Stadium (Georgia)	70
Kinnick Stadium (Iowa)	73
Peden Stadium (Ohio)	75
Carter Stadium (Texas Christian)	77
Kyle Field (Texas A&M)	79
Florida Field (Florida)	81
Notre Dame Stadium (Notre Dame)	83
Skelly Stadium (Tulsa)	86
Scott Stadium (Virginia)	87
Floyd Stadium (Middle Tennessee)	90
Spartan Stadium (San Jose State)	91
Williams-Brice Stadium (South Carolina)	93
Citrus Bowl (Central Florida)	95
Martin Stadium (Washington State)	97
Glass Bowl (Toledo)	99
Orange Bowl (Miami)	101
Reynolds Razorback Stadium (Arkansas)	102
Waldo Stadium (Western Michigan)	105
Jordan-Hare Stadium (Auburn)	107
Rubber Bowl (Akron)	108
Robertson Stadium (Houston)	111
Vaught-Hemingway Stadium (Mississippi)	113
Memorial Stadium (Clemson)	115
Jones SBC Stadium (Texas Tech)	117

War Memorial Stadium (Wyoming)	120
Casey Stadium (Baylor)	121
Byrd Stadium (Maryland)	123
Rice Stadium (Rice)	125
Campbell Stadium (Florida State)	128
Fouts Field (North Texas)	130
Reser Stadium (Oregon State)	132
Alumni Stadium (Boston College)	134
Sun Devil Stadium (Arizona State)	136
Navy–Marine Corps Memorial Stadium (Navy)	139
University Stadium (New Mexico)	142
Beaver Stadium (Penn State)	143
Memorial Stadium (Indiana)	146
Falcon Stadium (Air Force)	148
Dowdy-Ficklen Stadium (East Carolina)	150
Sun Bowl (Texas–El Paso)	151
Edwards Stadium (Brigham Young)	153
Liberty Bowl (Memphis)	155
Lane Stadium (Virginia Tech)	158
Huskie Stadium (Northern Illinois)	160
Mackay Stadium (Nevada)	161
Perry Stadium (Bowling Green)	163
Carter-Finley Stadium (North Carolina State)	164
Qualcomm Stadium (San Diego State)	167
Autzen Stadium (Oregon)	169
Ball State Stadium (Ball State)	171
Romney Stadium (Utah State)	173
Groves Stadium (Wake Forest)	174
KSU Stadium (Kansas State)	176
Hughes Stadium (Colorado State)	178
Aillet Stadium (Louisiana Tech)	180
Dix Stadium (Kent State)	181
Rynearson Stadium (Eastern Michigan)	183
Bronco Stadium (Boise State)	185
Cajun Field (Louisiana–Lafayette)	187
Kibbie Dome (Idaho)	188
Veterans Stadium (Temple)	191
Boyd Stadium (Nevada–Las Vegas)	193
Kelly-Shorts Stadium (Central Michigan)	195

Commonwealth Stadium (Kentucky)	197
Indian Stadium (Arkansas State)	199
Aloha Stadium (Hawai'i)	201
Trice Stadium (Iowa State)	202
Louisiana Superdome (Tulane)	205
Roberts Stadium (Southern Mississippi)	208
Malone Stadium (Louisiana–Monroe)	209
Aggie Memorial Stadium (New Mexico State)	211
Mountaineer Field (West Virginia)	213
Carrier Dome (Syracuse)	215
Bulldog Stadium (Fresno State)	217
Vanderbilt Stadium (Vanderbilt)	219
Humphrey Metrodome (Minnesota)	221
Yager Stadium (Miami [Ohio])	224
Marshall University Stadium (Marshall)	226
UB Stadium (Buffalo)	228
Rutgers Stadium (Rutgers)	230
Papa John's Cardinal Stadium (Louisville)	233
Rice-Eccles Stadium (Utah)	235
Princeton Stadium (Princeton)	237
Ford Stadium (Southern Methodist)	238
Heinz Field (Pittsburgh)	240
Rentschler Field (Connecticut)	243

Foreword

I was recently on the campus of Southern Methodist University and reflecting back on the good old times. I had a great experience during my days at SMU. The friendships, the games, the challenges of growing up are all part of the things I will always remember.

SMU had just recently moved into brand-new and beautiful Gerald Ford Stadium. It sits on the exact site of the old Ownby Stadium. I was standing at midfield with some of my old teammates and was flooded with memories of the many days of working out at Ownby Stadium. Doak Walker, Kyle Rote, and Don Meredith were just a few of the former Mustangs who grew up on the turf. While thoroughly impressed with the new digs, I left that day glad that I knew the history of the site on which I was standing.

As many of you know, I am a huge college football fan. Richard Pennington's book does a terrific job of telling us how most of college football's stadiums came about. Being from the Southwest, I was particularly interested to learn how TCU's Amon Carter Stadium came into existence. I knew it was old, but I did not realize that it opened in 1930, nor why Mr. Carter's name was placed on the stadium, nor how the seating capacity has changed. I was reminded of some of the players and teams that had participated there.

During my days with ESPN, I had a chance to see Michigan play on campus and wish I had known more about the history of Michigan Stadium. The Big House is beautiful and full of memories for a lot of people. I would have thrown Lee Corso a big curve if I had spouted off on the air how the stadium sits on the site of an underground spring that caused construction problems, once sinking a crane which remains below ground even today.

There is no doubt that we have entered a new era for college football. New facilities are being constructed, and many of our kids will not be able to sit in the stands at some of these old gems. I am thankful for *Home Field: An Illustrated History of 120 College Football Stadiums*. It has great pictures and history to boot. Enjoy!

—CRAIG JAMES

Preface

Like many people, I find college football stadiums not merely interesting but compelling. At various times in the last three decades, I have been in Lexington, Boulder, Lubbock, Baton Rouge, Ann Arbor, Knoxville, Palo Alto, Durham, Fayetteville, Oxford, and El Paso, and I always made a special effort to see where the local team played; in these cases, it was at Commonwealth Stadium, Folsom Field, Jones SBC Stadium, Tiger Stadium, Michigan Stadium, Neyland Stadium, Stanford Stadium, Wade Stadium, Reynolds Razorback Stadium, Vaught-Hemingway Stadium, and the Sun Bowl. It hardly mattered that no game was being held or that I sometimes did not get inside, only that I might gaze at the building and imagine all that must have happened within its walls. I pondered the unsung heroes who planned and constructed these stadiums, the emotional highs and lows of fans, players, and coaches over the generations, and most of all, the stadiums' significance to their respective universities. There is no way to quantify what a successful football program means to an institution. Whether it inspires generosity from alumni or help in recruiting students is debatable. But I do believe that the roar of a stadium can unite a campus community unlike anything else.

In this book, I have chosen to focus on 120 stadiums, those of the 115 NCAA Division I-A members, plus five Ivy League schools (Harvard, Yale, Cornell, Pennsylvania, and Princeton) that dominated in the game's early years. In some instances, stadiums that have been razed are of greater import than those now in service. Some schools have invested heavily to update or expand their stadiums, while others have done little to modernize. More than a few have made the painful choice of moving off campus or selling the name of their stadium to the highest bidder.

The word "stadium" derives from *stade*, a Greek unit of length, approximately 192 meters, the distance of the first Olympic footrace. It later came to refer to the running area and eventually the terraced rows on which spectators sat and cheered. Whether on the grounds near the Temple of Zeus in the eighth century B.C. or on today's Internet-wired college campus, such facilities have served the twin purposes of great social gatherings and spirited competition. With all due respect to professional arenas like Lambeau Field, Fenway Park, and Madison Square Garden, college football stadiums hold sway as America's most revered playing fields. No sports venue is more colorful, festive, or exalted on a fall weekend or can conjure such feelings for alumni who return to campus. To these fans, the stadium of their alma mater is hallowed ground.

Fear that commercial entertainment had begun to dwarf the core mission of higher education propelled the founding of the Ivy League and caused the University of Chicago (another early-day powerhouse) to drop the sport altogether. If its evolution from student-run enterprise to big business offends our sensibilities, we accept that nonetheless. College football is now in the midst of a mammoth building boom, an arms race that is only accelerating. In the 1990s alone, more than $2 billion of taxpayer-subsidized facilities were built, the most visible symbols of an athletic system that has grown dramatically. With the help of a floodtide of corporate and television dollars, college football stadiums are becoming more and more like their National Football League counterparts. Advertising, both visual and auditory, is now common. Furthermore, most of the schools' athletic departments are paying disproportionate attention to their high-end clientele, with club seating, luxury boxes, and other perks.

While I leave trenchant criticism of big-time college sports to authors like Murray Sperber, I cannot help feeling a measure of discomfort, too. The gap between haves and have-nots is growing, and it is questionable how much the haves really have, since so many athletic programs (especially in the Title IX era) are awash in red ink. Still, attendance is better than ever; more than 30 million people went to I-A games in the 2000 season. With all its problems and ominous trends, college football remains the greatest game around. From Tuscaloosa to South Bend, from the maize and blue to the orange and white, from the Bruins to the Tar Heels, there is nothing like walking into a stadium on a Saturday afternoon and sharing this communal experience with thousands of others. College football, which has a history of more than 130 years, has changed with the times and will surely remain an important part of our cultural heritage.

—RICHARD PENNINGTON
Austin, Texas

Home Field

Harvard Stadium (Harvard)

Harvard, the oldest university in the United States, was also involved in the country's first intercollegiate sports event—a rowing contest with Yale in 1852. The Crimson football team, which got started in 1874 and won several early-day national championships, played at two spots on campus and at the South End Grounds in nearby Boston before finding a home across the Charles River on Soldiers Field. It was named for Harvard grads who had fought in the Civil War.

Despite its qualms about the growing popularity of the game, Harvard enacted a bold plan. The class of 1879 did most of the heavy lifting in a drive that netted $310,000 to construct a new 22,000-seat stadium. Architects Charles McKim and George Bruno de Gernsdorff designed a horseshoe facility patterned after the one in Greece that had hosted the 1896 Olympics. Harvard Stadium, a massive reinforced-concrete structure built in four months, was regarded as an engineering marvel and a sign that American college athletics was here to stay. The stadium was dedicated on November 14, 1903, in a game against Dartmouth, but the Indians took an 11–0 victory. The season ended on a sour note the following Saturday when Yale came to Cambridge and laid another shutout on the Crimson.

Harvard Stadium was just three years old when the rules committee of the newly formed National Collegiate Athletic Association sought ways to alleviate the brutality of football, which had caused an alarming number of injuries and deaths. The committee considered either increasing the width of the field by forty feet or allowing the forward pass. The latter option was chosen because it would open up the game but also because much-admired Harvard Stadium could scarcely have been altered in such a drastic manner. Thus passing joined running and kicking as means of moving the ball downfield.

Wooden bleachers were added in the north end shortly thereafter, as was the colonnade, a set of Parthenon-style pillars wrapping around the top of the stadium. A new press box was built on the west side, and university groundskeepers began growing ivy up the exterior facade. Jim Thorpe and the Carlisle Indians played and lost at Harvard Stadium in 1908, and the U.S. Olympic track and field trials were held there in 1920 and 1924. With steel stands in the north end, the stadium had a seating capacity of 36,000, although some Harvard-Yale games were reputed to draw crowds as large as 57,000.

After coach Robert Fisher led the Crimson to the 1919 national crown (and a Rose Bowl win over Oregon), Harvard never again got near the mountaintop. Athletic director William Bingham briefly had visions of remaking Harvard football; he scheduled games against such schools as Indiana, Penn State, Michigan, Army, Purdue, North Carolina, and Texas and even advocated tearing down Harvard Stadium and replacing it with one seating 80,000 fans. But Bingham, who kept the job for twenty-five years, was swimming against the current. Attendance declined as Harvard retreated from the world of big-time college football. There was no longer any need for seats in the north end. Like its brethren of the Ivy League (a term first used in the 1930s but not made a reality until 1956), Harvard chose to pursue broad-based "sensible athletics," eschewing scholarships for jocks.

In 1968, the stadium was the site of a famous game in which both Harvard and Yale came in with 8–0 records. The Bulldogs seemingly had things in hand until Harvard scored 16 points in the final 42 seconds to tie it 29–29 when Pete Varney scored on a two-point conversion. The New England Patriots of the NFL called the stadium home in 1970 while erecting one of their own in Foxboro. Harvard Stadium, used by the Crimson's football, lacrosse, and field hockey teams, has never been lighted or given artificial turf. The track was removed, the seating area was modernized, and some basic steel-and-concrete work was done prior to a series of Olympic soccer games in 1984. World Cup soccer was played there in 1994, and the school's 350-year celebration was held there in 1986. The Murr Center, an 89,000-square-foot multi-use facility, was built in the north end in 1998, enclosing the stadium. On a campus full of historic buildings, Harvard Stadium remains a classic sports venue, a landmark of aesthetics and old-time charm.

Dodd Stadium (Georgia Tech)

While both Harvard and Pennsylvania claim to have the oldest college stadium in the U.S., the Ivy Leaguers have not played big-time football for decades. The oldest facility among NCAA Division I-A schools belongs to Georgia Tech, dating back to 1913.

— Courtesy of Georgia Tech sports information department

4   HOME FIELD

As early as 1905, the Yellow Jackets had played some home games at a spot in the southeast corner of campus dubbed "the flats." Eight years later, John W. Grant, an Atlanta merchant and member of the Board of Trustees, gave $15,000 to build some concrete stands on the west side of the field; the work was performed by a crew of Georgia Tech students. Named for Grant's deceased son, it could hold 5,600 patrons. Three years after the stadium opened, it was the scene of a game that would live in infamy. Coach John Heisman (of Heisman Trophy fame) was determined to avenge a baseball loss to Cumberland College, and Georgia Tech proceeded to drub the visitors from Tennessee 222–0.

Grant Field, which hosted baseball in its early years and track meets as late as the 1980s, grew to 18,000 seats in 1924 with the construction of east-side stands, and a horseshoe in the south end a year later brought it to 30,000. It was perhaps the biggest stadium in the South at the time. The press box and west stands were rebuilt and enlarged in 1948, stands in the north end zone came ten years later, and second decks were built in the east in 1962 and the west in 1967, bringing Grant Field to its largest seating capacity, 58,121, although the 1973 Georgia game was played before 60,316 fans.

From 1904 to 1966, the white and gold had just three head coaches—Heisman, Bill Alexander, and Bobby Dodd, each of whom won one national championship (1917, 1928, and 1952, respectively) during their tenures. Dodd was still in charge when Georgia Tech, a charter member of the Southeastern Conference, withdrew in 1964 in a dispute over scholarship limitations, beginning fourteen years as an independent before joining the Atlantic Coast Conference. While Georgia Tech's pigskin success dropped off for a while, the coaching staff had the moxie to start Eddie McAshan, a black quarterback, from 1970 to 1972, when some of their fellow Deep South colleagues were still toying with token integration. Things picked up again in 1990 when coach Bobby Ross brought another national championship trophy to Atlanta.

The stadium continued to evolve. Artificial turf was used at Grant Field from 1971 to 1994, and the sixty-year-old south stands were demolished in 1986, making way for the $12 million Wardlaw Center, a six-level facility that includes the visitors' locker room and twelve luxury boxes. That did, however, result in a 12,000-seat drop in seating capacity. The Moore Center was built in 1992 on the west side of the stadium, serving both GT academics and athletics and adding another thirty-two luxury boxes.

The Yellow Jackets' venerable stadium was renamed in 1988 in honor of Bobby Dodd. An all-America quarterback at Tennessee, he spent fifty-eight years at Georgia Tech as an assistant coach, head coach, athletic director, and fundraiser. A nearby street, Bobby Dodd Way, also preserves the memory of a charismatic coach who never earned more than $25,000 a year and still won 71 percent of his games. Although the tree-lined stadium was not used as a venue during the 1996 Atlanta Olympics, the Georgia Tech campus was the site of the Olympic Village and hosted boxing and aquatic events.

After Georgia Tech sold out the final four games of the 1999 season, the process was begun in which the facility—too small and showing signs of age—would be expanded and renovated. At a cost of $63 million, the university is adding more luxury boxes, plus seating in the south and north ends, with two tiers in the north. In 2003, Dodd Stadium will have room for 55,000 fans, and they will be able to see the games in considerably more comfort.

Yale Bowl (Yale)

"What Washington was to his country, Walter Camp was to American football—the friend, the founder and the father," said John Heisman, whose name is appended to the most prized trophy in college sports. Camp, captain of the Yale team in 1878 and 1879, later compiled a 67–2 record as coach of the Bulldogs. He is credited with limiting the number of players to eleven per side, use of the quarterback, set plays, and first downs. Yale, the dominant football power at a time when the East ruled, played in an ad hoc facility. So the university purchased an apple orchard two miles west of campus and erected Yale Field. That wooden stadium would serve as home to the blue for thirty years and sometimes held crowds as big as 33,000.

Shortly after Yale's last national championship (1909), the stadium's inadequacy became apparent. Archrival Harvard had

6 HOME FIELD

—Courtesy of Yale sports information department

erected a big new stadium a few years earlier, and one was needed in New Haven, too. It would not do for Yale, the school of Walter Camp, boola-boola cheers, and the fictional Frank Merriwell, to have a decrepit stadium. A committee of twenty-one football-minded alums chose a spot adjacent to Yale Field and had Charles Ferry design an elliptical bowl that covered twelve acres and measured 933 feet long and 744 feet wide. Majestically scaled and built with fan comfort in mind, the Yale Bowl cost $750,000 and had room for 60,617 people, plus 249 in the large and commodious press box. Intentionally or not, it dwarfed Harvard Stadium. The grand opening came in the final game of the 1914 season versus Harvard. On a sunny November afternoon, an overflow crowd of 71,000—then the largest in the history of American athletics—descended upon New Haven, and they witnessed a 36–0 thumping by the visiting Crimson. Even with expansion around the perimeter a few years later to a seating capacity of 70,869, it was not uncommon for the Yale Bowl to sell out; an estimated crowd of 80,000 attended the 1923 Yale–Army game. The Rose Bowl, Michigan Stadium, and Notre Dame Stadium would be patterned after the Yale Bowl, a great compliment indeed.

Before the Dartmouth game in 1928, the recently deceased

Camp was honored. The field was named after him, as was a memorial gateway composed of a series of lofty stone pillars. It included tablets with the names of over 500 football-playing colleges and secondary schools, testimony to Camp's legacy. A couple of Yalies, Larry Kelley and Clint Frank, won the Heisman Trophy in the mid-1930s, but little changed there over the next several decades. A large scoreboard was added in 1958, and a new press box went up in 1986. Other alterations in 1994 reduced seating capacity to 64,269. The Yale Bowl served as home for the NFL's New York Giants in 1973 and 1974 while Yankee Stadium underwent renovation and prior to the construction of Giants Stadium. Most recently, luxury boxes on the upper promenade and a hospitality village outside the main gate give it the veneer of modernity, although nearly nine decades have passed without an extensive restoration.

Some good teams and players—by Ivy League standards—competed during the thirty-two-season (1965–96) career of Yale coach Carmen Cozza. The most notable pro success was running back Calvin Hill, who went on to a fine career with the Dallas Cowboys, Cleveland Browns, and Washington Redskins. It is debatable whether the years have been kind to the cavernous Yale Bowl, where huge throngs once gathered. Today, with the main exception of the Harvard game in odd-numbered years, attendance is a problem. Despite vigorous marketing and ticket giveaways, sometimes fewer than 4,000 fans gather at the old stadium, home to a football program with 800-plus victories.

Scott Field (Mississippi State)

Mississippi A&M College became Mississippi State College in 1932 and finally Mississippi State University in 1958, and the Aggie mascot gave way to the Bulldog in 1961, but modern names will be employed throughout here. A land-grant school in the east-central region of the Magnolia State, MSU was winless its first two seasons of college football, quit the sport for the next four, and finally achieved victory in 1901, over Ole Miss. The team had played home games inside a horseracing track at the Starkville

8 HOME FIELD

— Courtesy of Mississippi State sports information department

Fairgrounds and a spot on campus when coach W. D. Chadwick became athletic director and had a stadium of sorts built in 1914. Available records do not indicate how substantial New Athletic Field (a football field enclosed by a 440-yard cinder track) was, but in all probability the stands were small and made of little more than wood and nails. Six years after the stadium's construction, the student body passed a referendum naming it Scott Field in honor of former football star and Olympic sprinter Don Scott.

The Bulldogs' new stadium notwithstanding, they regularly had home games out of town in such places as Columbus, Tupelo, Clarksdale, Greenwood, Meridian, Aberdeen, and the state capital of Jackson. Agreements with other southern teams led to games in neutral sites like Memphis, Birmingham, Montgomery, Shreveport, Houston, Dallas, Atlanta, and Jacksonville. It went to such absurd lengths that several times, as late as the 1981 season, just two games took place at Scott Field.

Those fair-haired lads from upstate, the Mississippi Rebels, had lost twelve straight times to MSU until a 7–6 win in Starkville in 1926. When celebrating Ole Miss fans tried to tear down the goal posts, they met with resistance from their Bulldog counterparts, and a wild brawl ensued. Two years later, the wooden bleachers at Scott Field were taken out and replaced with a 3,000-seat structure costing $15,000. Despite coaching turnover, poor facilities, a history of losing, and its remote campus, Mississippi State was invited to join the Southeastern Conference, which began play in 1933. The maroon and white faithful, who loved to ring cowbells during football games, got an enlarged stadium in 1936 as Scott Field's seating increased to 26,000, then up to 35,000 in 1948. The 1940 squad, coached by Allyn McKeen, went 10-0-1, beat Georgetown in the Orange Bowl and may have been MSU's best team of the pre-integration era. But there would not be another bowl game for twenty-one years.

Bleachers in the north end zone were removed in 1983, and the stadium got lights and a west-side upper deck to match that on the east in 1986, up to 40,656 seats. That year, a record crowd of 42,700 filled the place when Mississippi State and Alabama met; it was the Crimson Tide's first visit to Starkville since 1962. The Turman Fieldhouse was erected in the south end of the stadium in 1990, providing locker rooms and a center to display MSU's athletic heritage.

Artificial turf has never besmirched the Bulldogs' home, which was renamed Davis Wade Stadium at Scott Field in 2000 to honor the alumnus who gave a significant portion of the $21 million needed to expand the stadium again to around 52,000 seats, including fifty luxury boxes on the east side. It is still among the smallest facilities in the SEC, so MSU and Vanderbilt will continue to bring up the rear in league attendance. Larry Templeton, athletic director since 1987, and Jackie Sherrill, coach since 1991, have gotten Mississippi State away from the weak position of playing erstwhile home games off campus, as every home game for the past decade has been played at Scott Field.

Schoellkopf Field (Cornell)

Madness reigned at Percy Field in the early part of the twentieth century. Cornell's football, baseball, and track teams practiced and played there, often simultaneously. It was also a twenty-minute walk from campus, so some alumni persuaded the university to set aside a portion of its domain for a suitable athletic facility. Glenn "Pop" Warner, a former Cornell player, had just fin-

— Courtesy of Cornell sports information department

ished a brief tenure as head coach before moving on to greater fame at Georgia, Iowa, Carlisle, Pittsburgh, Stanford, and Temple. He left Ithaca during a ten-year period of striving and pleading for donations. Finally, enough money was raised to pay the Turner Construction Company to build a gymnasium in 1911 and a football stadium on its south side in 1915. Both were named for the Schoellkopf family, which had sent many sons to Cornell and given liberally of its treasure.

Schoellkopf Field could hold 9,000 fans, and in its inaugural season, the Big Red went undefeated (administering Harvard's first defeat in almost four years). They won the first of three national championships in an eight-year span. A set of barely adequate lights was installed in 1920, and the stadium grew considerably four years later. Architect Gavin Hadden designed the distinctive "crescent" on the east side, increasing capacity to 21,500. Just after World War II, the west side finally got some permanent seating—twenty-five rows (4,467 seats) and a press box.

Cornell was still competitive enough in 1951 to beat Michigan at home before a record crowd of 35,300, which was possible with temporary end-zone seating. But the Big Red soon joined the

Ivy League and stopped making noise nationally except for the career of running back Ed Marinaro. He was the first player to gain more than 4,000 yards and finished second in Heisman Trophy voting in 1971.

That was the first year in which Schoellkopf Field had artificial turf (and a rubber track, because it has been a dual-purpose facility from the start). Cornell invested $3.6 million in a 1986 renovation that included a new press box and lights. What was Schoellkopf Fieldhouse in the north end has long since been converted into Schoellkopf Hall, home of the school's athletic department.

Nippert Stadium (Cincinnati)

Every school needs an Arch Carson. As a freshman in 1885, he put together the University of Cincinnati's first football team, of which he was captain and de facto coach. Within ten years, he had

— Courtesy of Cincinnati sports information department

become the physical education director and had a plan to build a stadium for the Bearcats. Wooden bleachers on the surrounding hillside were erected in 1902, and it was dubbed Carson Field. Construction of a brick-and-concrete facility began in 1916 and proceeded at a snail's pace. It took a tragedy to complete UC's stadium. In the last game of the 1923 season, James Nippert sustained a fatal injury. His grandfather, James Gamble (of Procter & Gamble, then and now among the Queen City's largest companies), donated $250,000 to finish the 12,000-seat, horseshoe-shaped stadium. Dedicated on November 8, 1924, Nippert Stadium was the first in the Midwest to be equipped with lights.

Seating capacity doubled in 1936 when the field was lowered twelve feet, and an upper deck on the east side in 1954 gave it a total of 28,000 seats. That happened largely because of the Bearcats' heyday when they were coached by Sid Gillman. From 1949 to 1954, he led them to a 50–13–1 record with two bowl games. The Cats were thrice champions of the Mid-American Conference before Gillman left for a Hall-of-Fame career in pro football.

Other than the introduction of artificial turf in 1970, no significant changes were made to Nippert Stadium until 1990. It was closed that season for renovation, so UC played at Riverfront Stadium, home of the Cincinnati Bengals. Some $10 million was spent on a three-tier press box on the west side, a new scoreboard and lights, and expansion of the upper deck. With room for 35,000 fans, the stadium is big enough for Cincinnati. A record crowd of 32,117 attended the 1998 game against Indiana, a 48–14 victory by the Hoosiers.

Camp Randall Stadium (Wisconsin)

No facility in American college athletics can claim a deeper and richer history than Wisconsin's Camp Randall Stadium. Its fifty-three acres served as the Wisconsin State Fairgrounds until the outbreak of the Civil War in 1861. Named to honor a wartime governor, Camp Randall became the state's primary military training center as more than 70,000 men marched, drilled, and otherwise prepared for the rigors of combat. Some 1,400

An Illustrated History of 120 College Football Stadiums 13

— Courtesy of Wisconsin sports information department

Confederate prisoners were held there before the war's conclusion. The area reverted to fairgrounds, and President U. S. Grant hailed it as "a symbol of beating the spears of war into the plowshares of peace." But the fair moved from Madison, the state capital, to Milwaukee, leaving Camp Randall in disuse and in threat of commercial development, which a group of Civil War veterans protested as a "sordid sacrilege." They urged the Wisconsin legislature to buy the land and present it to the university as a memorial athletic park. This was done in 1893, and Camp Randall was retained as its name.

While the Badger football team practiced there occasionally, games were held elsewhere on campus until 1913, when some wooden stands were built beside the statue of a Civil War vet. But during the 1915 game against Minnesota (UW–UM is the longest-running rivalry in college football), a section collapsed, injuring twenty fans. A $15,000 appropriation from the legislature allowed the school to erect a concrete structure on the west side of the football field. It was dedicated on homecoming day 1917, a 10–7 defeat of Minnesota's Golden Gophers.

Wisconsin had a veritable plethora of all-Americans in the next few decades, but few titles. They played in the Big 10, the toughest conference in the U.S., dominated by Michigan, Minnesota, and Ohio State. UW went through a forty-year drought before winning a championship and representing the league in the Rose Bowl in 1953. In the meantime, the Badgers' stadium grew steadily. The east-side stands and a north-end horseshoe in the 1920s brought seating capacity to 38,293. A fieldhouse for the Badger hoopsters was built in the south end in 1930. Although Wisconsin averaged less than 20,000 in home attendance, about twenty-five rows were added to the west (1936) and east (1941) stands, and with growing demand, to the north end (1951). At that point, UW had a perfectly symmetrical stadium capable of holding 51,000 fans. In 1958, the track, an original feature of the stadium, was taken out, the field was lowered ten feet, and total seating increased to 63,435.

Another major change came in 1966 when the Wisconsin athletic department spent $2.8 million for a west-side upper deck and five-level press box. In 1969, Camp Randall Stadium became the third college-only facility (behind Washington's Husky Stadium and Tennessee's Neyland Stadium) with artificial turf. Fourteen luxury boxes were added in 1984, for a total of 76,129 seats. A computerized scoreboard and message center went up in 1992, and permanent lighting was added three years later.

Challenging for national honors was an infrequent occurrence in Madison, the main exception being the 1954 Heisman Trophy won by running back Alan Ameche. In the late 1980s, on the heels of five straight losing seasons, the athletic department was in debt, average attendance at Camp Randall Stadium hovered around 40,000 (the lowest since World War II), and apathy abounded. The Barry Alvarez era began inauspiciously with a 1–10 record, but he reversed the tide; his Badgers have won three Rose Bowls, and Ron Dayne brought another Heisman to campus and in the process broke the college career rushing mark once held by Ameche.

Lewis Field (Oklahoma State)

Just as the Mississippi A&M Aggies outgrew their old name and mascot, so did the Oklahoma A&M Aggies, who became the

AN ILLUSTRATED HISTORY OF 120 COLLEGE FOOTBALL STADIUMS 15

—Courtesy of Oklahoma State sports information department

Oklahoma State Cowboys. They had been playing football in Stillwater for a dozen years before a patch of campus ground was given the generic title of Athletic Field in 1913. The student body voted to rename it Lewis Field to honor Dr. Laymon Lewis, the dean of veterinary medicine, science, and literature and the acting president. The Cowboys competed there for eight seasons before the erection of some wooden grandstands capable of holding 8,000 fans, and thus 1920 is considered the stadium's first year. Unfortunately, OSU was 0–7–1 and finished last in the Southwest Conference (prior to a thirty-two-year affiliation with the Missouri Valley Conference and then joining the Big 8 in 1957). The orientation of the field was changed from north-south to east-west at that time to minimize the effect of prevailing winds, a fortuitous move given the approaching Dust Bowl days.

Lewis Field was first expanded in 1924 with a 5,000-seat reinforced concrete section on the south side and again in 1929 on the north side for a seating capacity of 13,000. Attendance grew thanks largely to Bob Fenimore, one of the first runners to exceed 1,000 yards in a season. He led the way in 1944 and 1945 as the Cowboys twice went undefeated and took victories in the Cotton Bowl and Sugar Bowl; they also beat their in-state rival, Oklahoma, for the last time until 1965. So more rows were added to the south side in 1947 and the north side in 1950, for a seating capacity of 39,000, including end-zone bleachers. The stadium's first permanent press box was built atop the south stands at the same time.

The stadium remained essentially unchanged until 1971, when $2.5 million was spent to lower the field by twelve feet, eliminate the running track, install artificial turf, and add more rows (for a total of seventy-three on both north and south sides), as Lewis Field grew to its present capacity of 50,440 seats. Prior to the 1978 season, Oklahoma State built the Coaches Building in the east end zone to house its football staff, the AD's office, and a varsity club lounge. A new press box was built in 1980, and Lewis Field finally got lights five years later. The athletic department has plans to renovate the stadium, enhance its exterior to cover up scaffolding beneath the stands, and expand seating in the west end zone.

Although Stillwater has never been the center of the college football world (the Cowboys have an overall sub-.500 record), fans of the orange and black can point to Barry Sanders, who had a dazzling 1988 season, running for an NCAA-record 2,628 yards and winning the Heisman Trophy.

Husky Stadium (Washington)

Seven different locations in downtown Seattle served as home for the Washington football team before the school moved five miles northeast. There, on land vacated by the Alaska-Yukon-Pacific Exposition, Denny Field was built. Coach Gil Dobie led the team to a thirty-nine-game winning streak which, admittedly, included some non-collegiate competition; his success was the beginning of high expectations for the purple and gold. Denny Field had become inadequate even before the 1919 California game, witnessed by a crowd of 16,000, with many more turned away for lack of seating.

Darwin Meisnest led a group of energetic UW students who devised the idea of raising money to build a modern stadium, and the alumni and business community concurred. Simultaneous with a statewide campaign (which would be subsequently noted and fol-

—Courtesy of Washington sports information department; photo by Mary Levin

lowed by many other schools) to collect $350,000, the design, dredging, and construction of a 30,000-seat U-shaped stadium took place. The architectural company Bebb & Gould studied stadiums at Yale, Michigan, Harvard, Princeton, and Cornell and included a Tudor Gothic motif that would be shelved due to its cost; nevertheless, the university could congratulate itself on having a monument of imposing dignity. It was originally dubbed Washington Field but soon became Husky Stadium when the school mascot was changed from the Sun Dodger to the Husky. Placement of the stadium was done carefully to minimize the glare of the sun for players and to allow fans a view of Lake Washington and Mt. Rainier. Completed in just over six months, the stadium had a track with a 220-yard straightaway and was the pride of the Emerald City. Given that the U.S. was still recovering from the effects of World War I, a rather ambitious plan had come to fruition. With lavish ceremonies that included a seventeen-gun salute, it was dedicated on the final game of the 1920 season, a 28–7 loss to Dartmouth before 24,500 fans.

Husky Stadium has never contained players' locker rooms. They were originally situated in an adjacent dormitory and then, in 1927, in Hec Edmundson Pavilion (home of UW basketball and twice the site of the NCAA Final Four), connected by a 362-foot tunnel. There had been just eight sellouts in fifteen years, and it was the middle of the Great Depression when the athletic department decided to expand by adding thirteen rows all around the stadium for a seating capacity of 40,000. That grew to 55,000 in 1950 when "Cassill's Castle" went in on the south side. So named for AD Harvey Cassill, it was a steeply pitched upper deck with a cantilever roof from which hung a new press box, all at a cost of $1.7 million. On the strength of Pac-8 titles in 1959 and 1960 followed by Rose Bowl wins, UW pondered erecting a matching upper deck on the north side but backed off due to ominous dollar figures. Relatively minor improvements were made, such as artificial turf and a rubber track in 1968, lights in 1969, and new scoreboards at both ends in 1976. That was the year the NFL arrived in Seattle, and the Seahawks, playing in the downtown Kingdome, caused a temporary 10 percent decline in attendance. The long-contemplated, long-delayed upper deck on the north side was built in 1987, despite a harrowing construction accident. It cost $13 million and included a glass-enclosed reception area known as the Tyee Center, which ran the length of the field. Husky Stadium's capacity grew to 72,500, largest in the Pacific Northwest. Another $3.7 million was spent in 1989 to shore up the infrastructure of the seven-decade-old edifice.

Driven by coach Don James and defensive lineman Steve Emtman, the Huskies went 12–0 and won a share of the 1991 national championship. Four years later, a record crowd of 76,125 attended the game against Army. The Kingdome, which went from architectural marvel to civic eyesore in just twenty-four years, was demolished in 2000, forcing the Seattle Seahawks to rent the collegiate stadium for two seasons at a cost of $305,000 per game.

Even when the home team was winning, people have been inclined to divert their eyes from the field to the placid beauty surrounding them. With both alpine and maritime qualities, Husky

Stadium is truly an unparalleled setting, one in which some 5,000 fans dock their boats or yachts nearby before walking to the game.

Memorial Stadium (Kansas)

McCook Field had served the University of Kansas well. Built in 1892 on the northern edge of campus, it was the scene of many feats of speed, skill, and daring in both football and track, and crowds as great as 10,000 were known to gather in Lawrence to watch the Jayhawks. But it was in a state of advancing deterioration in 1920 when an epochal event in KU history occurred. Coach Forrest "Phog" Allen rallied his team from a 20-point deficit to tie Nebraska. Allen, also the school's athletic director, was in the middle of a basketball career that would encompass 771 victories, and that was his only year to head the football program. At any rate, he urged a convocation of faculty, students, and alumni to raise money for a new stadium, a memorial to KU students who had made the supreme sacrifice in World War I. In the so-called

—Courtesy of Kansas sports information department; photo by Thad Allton

"million-dollar drive," however, considerably less than that was pledged and even less collected. There was no going back after a university holiday in May 1921 when 4,000 students demolished McCook Field, adjacent to the site where the new stadium was being erected.

Designed by KU civil engineering professor C. C. Williams, it had forty rows on the east and west sides and could hold 22,000 fans. A quarter-mile running track meant it would be a multi-purpose facility. Memorial Stadium cost $375,000 and was ready by the 1921 season, although its dedication was delayed a year. In the first game, Kansas beat Kansas State 21–7 before a disappointing crowd of 5,160. In 1925, both sections of the stadium were extended south and locker rooms were constructed. Two years later, a connecting north-end horseshoe was built, bringing seating capacity to 35,000. It also cost $325,000, exacerbating a debt problem. The stadium had been poorly financed from the beginning, which would be a major headache until 1947. That season, the Jayhawks, coached by George Sauer and co-captained by Don Fambrough (a future KU coach) and Otto Schnellbacher, won the Big 6 crown and played in the Orange Bowl. Thus the twenty-seven-year debt was finally paid off.

The Herculean effort to reach solvency may explain why the stadium did not change for more than three decades. Its fame derived as much from track and field as from football due to the Kansas Relays and such Jayhawk greats as Wes Santee, Jim Ryun, and Al Oerter. Finally, in 1963, twenty-six rows and a new press box were added to the west side, and a matching extension on the east in 1965 brought seating capacity to 51,500. But the cost/benefit ratio was dubious since KU's enlarged stadium did not have a sold-out home game until 1973.

Aluminum seats, artificial turf, and a rubber track were added in the 1970s, and the south end-zone bleachers were removed in 1987 and later put back, which reduced seating to 50,250. The stadium was barely half full for the final game of the 1991 season when Tony Sands set an NCAA record by running for 396 yards against Missouri. That was reason enough for the fans to employ their strange "Rock Chalk Jayhawk" chant.

Memorial Stadium underwent a $26 million renovation in

1998 and 1999 that included extensive repairs, a new press box, a large videoboard in the south end, and thirty-six "scholarship suites." Future plans include permanent lighting (temporary lights were first used there in 1931), removal of the track, and lowering the field to gain extra seating.

Neyland Stadium (Tennessee)

Even the most towering redwood trees began life as acorns, and Neyland Stadium had modest beginnings, too. Originally just a rustic section of stands in a boggy ravine, it grew, over eight

— Courtesy of Tennessee sports information department

decades and through repeated expansions, into one of the most impressive facilities in college sports.

The Tennessee Volunteers had played home football games at tiny Wait Field since 1908, but the university had its eye on a seven-acre plot of land a mile away. There, it was hoped, students would someday have a fitting physical education/athletic field. Progress was slow until a benefactor emerged. Knoxville banker and UT trustee W. S. Shields bought the land and gave it to the university in 1919. In gratitude, the Board of Trustees named the new playground Shields-Watkins Field to honor him and his wife. Then, at a cost of $20,000, a set of seventeen rows of concrete stands (capable of holding 3,200 fans) was built west of the field, which remained a muddy mess. In the spring of 1921, virtually every able-bodied male student and professor used picks, shovels, and wheelbarrows to make a crude football field, baseball diamond, and quarter-mile cinder track. Facilities for the latter two sports soon moved out of Shields-Watkins Field to make way for King Football. The stadium was inaugurated on September 24, 1921 when UT beat Emory and Henry 27–0.

It is amusing to think of Vanderbilt lording it over the University of Tennessee, but such was the case in the early 1920s, when the Commodores routinely won—sometimes by large margins—and could boast of their new 20,000-seat Dudley Stadium. That was reason enough to expand Shields-Watkins Field with matching stands to the east. The Vols and their visitors also got locker rooms and thus no longer had to use those in the nearby YMCA gym. A new drainage system helped alleviate the dreary mud all too familiar at UT football games. In 1926, the coaching reins were turned over to Bob Neyland, who would lift the program to national prominence and become the dominant figure in Tennessee athletic history. He was not just a football coach but a graduate of West Point who would twice leave for active army duty, rising from captain to major to brigadier general. When Neyland's first three teams went 25–1–2, plans were drawn up for an extension of the original west stands for a seating capacity of 17,860. The athletic department then envisioned long-range growth of the stadium up to 40,000 or perhaps even 50,000.

Shields-Watkins Field took another big jump in 1938 with the addition of over 12,000 seats on the east side and 64 dormitory rooms underneath. Neyland's teams were best known for the single-wing offense, but their defense was stout, too, especially in 1939 when they held every regular-season opponent scoreless before losing to Southern Cal in the Rose Bowl. Neyland was back in Knoxville in 1946 after his second military hiatus, and soon the stadium had a 15,000-seat horseshoe (holding more dorm rooms) in the south end zone, close to the Tennessee River. The General's 1951 team won the national championship shortly before he retired from coaching.

He stayed on as UT's athletic director until his death in 1962 and was posthumously honored when the stadium was named after him; although Shields-Watkins Field remains a part of the name, it has fallen into disuse. The 1960s saw several changes to Neyland Stadium, including a new press box and upper decks on the west and east sides, which boosted its capacity to almost 60,000. The "Volunteer Navy" (fans who arrived by boat) made its first appearance, as did the distinctive orange-and-white checkerboard end zones. Artificial turf was installed, followed twenty-six years later by a reversion to grass.

In the 1970s, nighttime football (which Neyland had disdained) was introduced in Knoxville, and two sections on the upper deck added nearly 16,000 seats. Surging attendance happened despite a decline in the Vols' performance as they sometimes struggled to reach .500. They failed to win the Southeastern Conference crown between 1969 and 1985.

Construction costs were going up, but with standing-room only the norm at Neyland Stadium, UT filled in the north end in 1980 and later built a seven-level press box, which included forty-two luxury boxes. By that time, Tennessee had a monster facility (seating capacity: 91,249), third in size to Michigan Stadium and the Rose Bowl. Yet the sellouts continued, eventually leading to more dizzying growth. In 1996, it became a complete double-decker all the way around. Luxury boxes on the east side boosted its total to over 104,000 seats. With the play of Peyton Manning, UT's most decorated football star, and the 1998 squad winning the national championship, there are still more fans than seats available in this huge stadium, which has grown piecemeal since 1921.

Stanford Stadium (Stanford)

Just as today, Stanford's main rival eight decades ago was its neighbor on the other side of the bay, the University of California. The two schools wanted to see who could be the first to erect a big new stadium, and Stanford won by a comfortable two-year margin. Engineering professors Charles Wing, Charles Marz, and William Durand designed a sixty-six-row horseshoe with a seating capacity of 60,000. Construction by Baker & Carpenter (who also did Cal's stadium) took just four months and $200,000. Stanford Stadium was ready in time for the final game of the 1921 season. But Stanford's opponent, the Golden Bears of California, inflicted a 42–7 defeat.

Some 10,200 seats were added in 1925, partially closing the open end to the south but leaving room for a long track runway. The 1926 team, coached by Glenn "Pop" Warner, won every regular-season game and tied Alabama in the Rose Bowl, which led to the Indians and Crimson Tide sharing the national crown. Capitalizing on that success, the university built fourteen more rows around the top of the stadium in 1927, making room for 85,500 fans. The following year, a memorable non-athletic event happened at Stanford Stadium. Herbert Hoover (manager of the first Stanford football team back in 1891) gave a speech accepting the Republican nomination for president, and he went on to become the nation's thirty-first commander in chief. The biggest crowd in the stadium's history, 94,000, witnessed the 1935 Stanford-Cal game.

Several superb quarterbacks have played on "the farm," an informal name for the lush campus in Palo Alto. They include Frankie Albert (whose 1940 team used the T-formation offense to go 10–0), John Brodie in the mid-1950s, 1970 Heisman Trophy winner Jim Plunkett, and possibly the greatest of all, John Elway, who won two NFL titles with the Denver Broncos. No significant changes were made to Stanford Stadium for three decades before a new press box was built on the west side in 1960, just in time for the U.S. Olympic track and field trials. Another big meet occurred there in 1962 when the Americans and

Soviets faced off with national pride and Cold War tension in the air.

For many years, crowds at Stanford Stadium had been entertained by Prince Lightfoot, a Native American who rode horseback on the field. But with changing times and attitudes, he was retired along with the Indian mascot. The university administration decreed in 1972 that the singular Cardinal had been chosen as a replacement.

The East-West Shrine Game, a college all-star contest held in San Francisco each January since 1925, was moved to Stanford Stadium in 1974 and stayed for a twenty-six-year run. A rubber track and north and south scoreboards were new features in 1978, and the locker rooms and press box were modernized prior to the Super Bowl in January 1985 when the San Francisco 49ers beat the Miami Dolphins. A series of important soccer matches have been held at Stanford Stadium including the 1984 Olympics, the 1994 World Cup, the 1996 Olympics and the 1999 women's World Cup.

Except for odd-numbered years when Cal visits, Stanford Stadium is seldom anywhere near sold out; the typical game has 30,000 or more empty seats. Still, Stanford spent $34 million in 1994 to renovate its venerable facility. The concourses were widened, wooden benches were replaced with aluminum, and the restrooms (which appeared not to have been touched since Hoover's famous speech in 1928) were upgraded. The prime giver in that campaign was insurance executive Louis Foster, and for such generosity, the field was named in his honor.

Stanford made headlines in 1999 with the announcement of a new policy removing ads from the stadium and Maples Pavilion, home of the Cardinal basketball teams. President Gerhard Casper called it a mandate in response to the mass commercialization of college sports. It was a noble gesture, one worth $2.5 million per year, and one that few other schools would attempt. Most cash-strapped athletic departments have no choice but to adorn their facilities with logos of whoever is willing to pay. Stanford, however, has a huge endowment and generous donors—another reason why revenue-producing luxury boxes have not yet been built at the stadium.

Ohio Stadium (Ohio State)

Since the era of the horse and buggy, Ohio State had played football at Ohio Field on the east side of campus. That stadium, twice expanded, could hold crowds of 14,000, but many more wanted to see the Buckeyes, with their 157-pound all-America running back Charles "Chic" Harley. While some people later called Ohio Stadium "the house that Harley built," plans for a new and bigger home had been in the works several years before he played. OSU, newly admitted to the Western Conference (predecessor to the Big 10), had won the 1920 championship but lost to California in the Rose Bowl.

As a result, the stadium idea picked up steam in Columbus. Professor Thomas French, president of the OSU Athletic Board, pushed for it, and AD Lynn St. John did, too. A fundraising drive aimed for $600,000, but it netted almost twice that. And while some people urged that a reasonably sized (35,000-seat) stadium be built, they were overruled. Architect Howard Smith designed a horseshoe-shaped double-decker with room for 66,210 fans. In August 1921, ground was broken in former pastureland on the east bank of the Olentangy River. The E. H. Latham Company took fourteen months to erect Ohio Stadium, one of the grandest facilities in college football. While the naysayers insisted it would never be filled, more than 71,000 people were there on October 21, 1922. The dedication game between those dear enemies, Ohio State and Michigan, was won by the Wolverines.

The following year, a six-lane cinder track was added, one on which the wondrous Jesse Owens would soon run and jump. Average attendance bottomed out at 22,000 in the early years of the Great Depression, but lots of people showed up for the 1935 season finale, then known as the greatest game ever played. The scarlet and gray allowed Notre Dame to score twice in the last minute and take an 18–13 win. Coach Paul Brown and Les Horvath, the first of five OSU Heisman Trophy winners, brought home the 1942 national championship. In the years after World War II, field and box seats were built, giving Ohio Stadium more than 70,000 seats, and semi-permanent stands in the south end took it over 80,000. Since 1949 (when the NCAA began keeping such records) until 1973, the Buckeyes led the nation in attendance twenty times. With Woody Hayes raging along the sidelines, OSU also took national crowns in 1957 and 1968. The latter team was one of the greatest of all time, with players like Rex Kern, Jack Tatum, Jim Stillwagon, and John Brockington. Coach Jim Tressel led the Buckeyes to another title in 2002 with a dramatic double-overtime defeat of Miami in the Fiesta Bowl.

Artificial turf was installed at Ohio Stadium in 1971 and would be replaced by grass nineteen years later. A $2.6 million scoreboard appeared in the south end in 1984, and portable lights allowed the first night game in school history. Another 5,000 end-zone seats in 1991 gave the stately old arena a seating capacity of 89,841, although crowds as big as 95,000 were sometimes shoehorned in.

They had gone without a national championship for nearly thirty years, but the Buckeyes won at least ten games four straight seasons, proving they were still a powerhouse. Then, in 1998, the decision was made to expand and renovate Ohio Stadium in a four-year project which cost a staggering $187 million. Athletic director Andy Geiger, who also oversaw the construction of OSU's $110 million basketball arena, said: "This is as big a project as you can imagine, with a huge, huge price tag, and we're working as hard as we possibly can to pay for it."

The stadium was made compliant with the Americans with Disabilities Act, and other structural problems were fixed. The field was dropped fourteen feet and the track was removed, which allowed for ten new rows of seats. Nineteen rows were built around the top of the stadium, with a new press box on the west side. Revenue-producing luxury boxes, a new scoreboard, permanent seating in the south end, and new locker rooms were part of the package. Permanent lighting, curiously enough, was not. Ohio Stadium, on the Register of National Historic Places and formerly a rather tired and dismal facility, has been preserved and turned into a shiny and modern one seating some 98,000 fans.

Rose Bowl (UCLA)

By 1920, crowds for Pasadena's post-season east-west football game had grown too large for Tournament Park. William

— Courtesy of UCLA sports information department

Leishman, president of the Tournament of Roses, wanted a stadium similar in look and scale to the Yale Bowl. The location he chose, theretofore a home for bootleggers and rusted-out cars, was in the foothills of the San Gabriel Mountains. Leishman, architect Myron Hunt, and builder William Taylor were most responsible for erecting a 57,000-seat horseshoe. Costing $272,000, the stadium was deeded to the city following its completion. A press agent for the Tournament of Roses called it the Rose Bowl, and the name stuck. What would become the most famous college football stadium of all was first used on October 28, 1922, when Southern Cal and California played; the first Rose Bowl game following that season featured USC and Penn State. The Trojans were one of the premier football programs on the West Coast, and they would have a new home of their own in 1923 when Memorial Coliseum opened adjacent to the USC campus. So the citizens of the Los Angeles area constructed two large stadiums in the span of a year.

The history and tradition of the Rose Bowl grew with time, partly because of its picturesque setting and the pageantry surrounding the New Year's Day game. While it was the oldest, most prestigious, and best-paying bowl game, much of that popularity derived from the legendary stadium, which was first expanded in 1929 when the south end was enclosed. Further alterations raised seating capacity to 83,677 in 1938, 100,807 in 1949, and 104,696 in 1972. Subsequent changes have dropped that number to 92,000. The Rose Bowl, which has never had artificial turf, features over 79,000 square feet of plush grass. It has also been a remarkably underused facility until recently. Some events of the 1932 Olympics were held there, and the Junior Rose Bowl (an ostensible junior college national championship game featuring California's top team versus a challenger from out of state) began in 1946 and lasted until the late 1960s. No pro football team has called the stadium home, although it has hosted the Super Bowl five times—following the 1976, 1979, 1982, 1986, and 1992 seasons. Soccer has played a prominent role in the past two decades with the 1984 Olympics, the 1994 men's World Cup, and the 1999 women's World Cup, made memorable by Brandi Chastain scoring the game-winner followed by a lusty display of her sports bra. The Los Angeles Galaxy of Major League Soccer has played at the Rose Bowl since 1996.

UCLA was of little consequence when the Rose Bowl was built. The original branch of the Berkeley-based University of California only began playing football in 1919, and most home games were held at Moore Field for the first decade. In 1929, two significant events transpired. UCLA moved to a new campus in the Westwood section of town, and the Bruins started sharing Memorial Coliseum with USC. The two rivals would split time at that facility for more than a half-century. In the late 1930s, Woody Strode, Kenny Washington, and Jackie Robinson accelerated integration of Pacific Coast Conference athletics. The 1954 UCLA team, coached by Henry "Red" Sanders, won every game and a share of the national title. And quarterback Gary Beban won the 1967 Heisman Trophy, an honor that barely eluded Troy Aikman in 1988 and Cade McNown in 1998. Linebacker Jerry Robinson and defensive back Kenny Easley were both three-time all-Americans, and many other greats wore blue and gold. They played in the Rose Bowl seven times between 1942 and 1975.

Prior to the 1982 season, the Oakland Raiders moved to Los Angeles for what turned out to be a rather brief sojourn, taking over Memorial Coliseum on Sundays. Proximity to USC's campus had always made it more of a Trojan place than a Bruin place, so the UCLA athletic department responded when the Rose Bowl was made available. In preparation for that move, the press box was refurbished and 50,000 chairback seats replaced wooden benches. Terry Donahue's teams made themselves right at home, winning the Pac-10 crown in 1982, 1983, and 1985, beating Michigan, Illinois, and Iowa, respectively, in the fabled January 1 game.

Regular-season sellouts are few and far between for UCLA, as attendance averages 60,000, which leaves more than 30,000 empty seats. In 1992, in anticipation of another Super Bowl, the stadium got a new press box and thirty-six luxury suites. But more of those money-makers were needed, so a $22 million project is now ongoing. To the horror of purists, the city of Pasadena (technically the Rose Bowl Operating Company) has listened to corporate offers regarding naming rights. It is conceivable that this historic stadium, a shrine to college football, which sits amid 3,000 rosebushes of 100 varieties, may not always be known as the Rose Bowl.

Franklin Field (Pennsylvania)

One wonders what Benjamin Franklin would have said about this. Philadelphia's most famous citizen and founder of the University of Pennsylvania (in 1740) is the person for whom its fabled football and track stadium is named. The Quakers have played there, just west of the Schuylkill River, for over a century. But while the location has not changed, the facility has—twice, which raises questions about Penn's claim, backed by the NCAA, to having the oldest stadium in the U.S.

A $100,000 facility was built in 1895, the year the red and blue went 14–0 with ten shutouts and won the national championship.

But as much as a home for football, Franklin Field was the site of the Penn Relays, America's longest-running and foremost track and field carnival. The stadium had wooden stands and was the first to feature a scoreboard. It could not accommodate the number of fans who wished to see Penn or the Army-Navy game (held there sixteen times between 1895 and 1934), so the stands were torn down in 1903 and replaced with a concrete horseshoe stadium at the same time Harvard was erecting one in Cambridge. The second version of Franklin Field had a seating capacity of approximately 30,000 and was state of the art at the time. But it, too, would have a short life.

Since the stadium did not lend itself to expansion, it was razed after the 1921 season and the Turner Construction Company erected a much larger steel and concrete horseshoe that could hold 54,000. Franklin Field, the third and current version, hosted the first football game to be broadcast on radio in 1922 and the first to be televised in 1940, a 51–0 defeat of Maryland. For $750,000, a second tier was added in 1925 (the year Red Grange ran for 331 yards in an Illinois victory), bringing seating capacity to 78,205, which made it the biggest in the East. The Quakers led the nation in attendance every year from 1938 to 1942, drawing 1,780,000 fans.

The 1947 team was perhaps the best in modern Penn history, going 7–0–1. It was headed by running back Anthony "Skip" Minisi and linemen George Savitsky and Chuck Bednarik. Bednarik, one of the last of the true two-way men, stayed right there for professional football; he played twelve years with the Philadelphia Eagles, who made Franklin Field home. It would remain so until 1971 when Veterans Stadium was built.

Athletics had been a big source of revenue at Penn for many years and helped fuel a lively social life. But changes were afoot. Even in the 1930s, there were efforts to extricate the university from the big time, although such a move had to be finessed to avoid offending alumni and other fans. It was the one school of the emerging Ivy League that had the most trouble initially adhering to the rules of no scholarships, no recruiting, no spring training, and a genuine focus on academia. The athletic department was in debt, and it had become clear that Penn's days as a football powerhouse were over. In 1953, the president (Harold Stassen) resigned, the athletic director (Franny Murray) was fired, and the coach (George Munger) quit, resulting in what was considered an academic coup d'état. Thus, Pennsylvania was a bona fide member of the Ivy League.

The stadium's seating capacity was reduced to 60,546 (and later to 52,593) when the stands in the west end were demolished because Penn's attendance figures no longer warranted such a big facility. Artificial turf and a rubber track were installed in 1969 and lights in 1970. In the mid-1990s, it underwent an extensive renewal program that addressed infrastructure problems and added modern amenities. Like its campus neighbor, the Palestra, a classic old-style basketball fieldhouse, Franklin Field is regarded fondly by generations of fans who have witnessed track, college football, and pro football over the years.

Memorial Stadium (Illinois)

In 1920, Illinois hosted Ohio State in a game that would determine the Big 10 crown. Nearly 20,000 fans overflowed the Illini's old wooden stadium—and witnessed an OSU victory—but AD George Huff was dismayed because he could have sold 50,000 tickets if the seats were available. With the idea of creating a memorial to UI alums who had died in World War I, Huff, university president David Kinley, and coach Bob Zuppke launched a fundraising drive which netted $1.7 million. Huff had hoped for more, envisioning a palace with a seating capacity of 75,000, expandable to 120,000. What he got was not at all bad, however. Memorial Stadium, situated in a former hayfield, was a 57,000-seat structure with east and west stands, both of which had "balconies," aka upper decks. Architect James White gave it a red brick and bedford stone exterior with a tower at each corner and 200 limestone columns bearing the names of those who had fought and died in Europe.

Due to construction delays, Memorial Stadium was not quite ready for its first game, a 7–0 defeat of Chicago on November 3, 1923. Heavy rains caused a huge mudbath, albeit one seen by 60,032 patrons. The dedication game did not come until nearly a year later. Following the requisite parades and speeches, the Illini (defending national champs) played Michigan in their new stadium in Champaign, and it was one of the most famous games in the history of college football. As more than 67,000 fans looked on, all-American Red Grange ran for five touchdowns and passed for a sixth, humbling the Wolverines. As significant a 1920s sports figure as Babe Ruth or Jack Dempsey, Grange went on to a fine career with the Chicago Bears and helped legitimize the National Football League.

Zuppke, who coached UI for twenty-nine years and for whom the field would later be named, had three outstanding teams from 1927 to 1929. So the athletic department ponied up $500,000 to build a south-end horseshoe which raised seating capacity to 67,000. In the almost three-fourths of a century since, Memorial Stadium has not had another significant expansion.

For decades, there was a minimum of glory for the Illini, who struggled to stay competitive. Linebacker Dick Butkus led them to a conference title and Rose Bowl win in the 1963 season, finishing third in the nation. But the years were taking a toll on the

—Courtesy of Illinois sports information department

stadium, and cosmetic changes (aluminum seats, a new press box, artificial turf, and removal of the 400-meter track) could not conceal the deterioration. At home football games, fans in the balconies claimed they could feel the stadium move. The local media aggressively pursued the story, which raised public awareness in the early 1980s. But this did not prevent Illinois from having its two highest home attendance averages (over 76,000) in 1985 and 1986.

A civil engineering firm hired to assess the condition of Memorial Stadium concluded that it would soon be "nonfunctional" if major infrastructure work were not implemented. What also got the Board of Trustees' attention was the estimated price tag of $115 million for a new stadium. There have been three phases of a comprehensive renovation project over the last twenty years, costing approximately $40 million. A historic building worthy of preservation, Memorial Stadium has seen its seating capacity drop from 78,000 to 70,904, including elimination of the north-end bleachers.

The stadium was the site of one of Willie Nelson's Farm Aid concerts and has hosted a few NFL exhibition games. Since 1985, a bubble covering the field in the winter has allowed more non-football activities. A most unfortunate moment in the stadium's life occurred in 1989 when a trio of inebriated UI students pulled a prank that got out of hand. Attempting to burn a message into the artificial turf, they saw a forty-yard swath of the field go up in smoke. Since four home games remained in the season, a company was hired and worked furiously to install a new carpet at a cost of $583,000. The Chicago Bears called Memorial Stadium home during the 2002 season while Soldier Field was undergoing a $600-million renovation.

Memorial Stadium (Nebraska)

When a fundraising campaign in the fall of 1922 brought in $430,000, the University of Nebraska wasted no time in constructing a football stadium. In just over ninety working days, a 31,000-seat facility was built, replacing one that had served since 1909. The east and west stands were gently curved with small upper

—Courtesy of Nebraska sports information department; photo by Rick Anderson

decks, and a track encircled the field. It was a memorial to honor all Nebraskans who had served in the Civil War, the Spanish-American War, and the recently concluded World War I. The four corners of the stadium were thus inscribed: "In commendation of the men of Nebraska who served and fell in the nation's wars/Not the victory but the action; not the goal but the game; in the dead the glory/Courage; generosity; fairness; honor; in these are the true rewards of manly sport/Their lives held their country's trust; they kept its faith; they died its heroes."

The first game at Memorial Stadium was on October 13, 1923, when the Cornhuskers beat Oklahoma 24–0, en route to their third straight Missouri Valley Conference title. Later in that season, they hosted and defeated Knute Rockne's Notre Dame team.

NU played in its first bowl game, the Rose Bowl, after the 1940 season, but World War II wreaked havoc on attendance at home games, which dropped to an average of 4,000 in 1944. There was really no need to expand the stadium until the mid-1960s. By then, of course, Nebraska's famous sellout streak (now over 250 games) had begun. In 1964, the south end-zone section was built, adding new locker rooms and 17,000 seats. And over the next two years, the north end zone was filled in, making Memorial Stadium a 65,000-seat bowl.

A new press box was built atop the west-side stands in 1967, and the stadium was equipped with artificial turf three years later. That was when NU decided to remove the track, making Memorial Stadium a football-only facility. And Cornhusker football was about to hit the big time, with coach Bob Devaney and offensive stars Jerry Tagge and Johnny Rodgers guiding the team to national championships in 1970 and 1971.

The south end zone was extended in 1972, raising seating capacity to 73,650, which went down to 72,700 in 1994 and back up to 74,056 in 1999. After lights were installed in 1986, the Huskers played their first night game ever in Lincoln, beating Florida State. In the midst of another run of greatness (national titles in 1994, 1995 and 1997), a pair of fancy 17' x 23' foot scoreboards were erected in the end zones.

The university honored its retired coach, Tom Osborne, by naming the field after him in 1998. The following year, Nebraska invested $36 million in forty-two luxury boxes, club seating, a lounge, a new media facility, and other improvements to the stadium, all befitting the third-winningest program in college football.

Spartan Stadium (Michigan State)

In the early 1920s, Michigan State was a modest agricultural school looking for a way to boost enrollment. The Spartans had played at Old College Field for two decades when L. Whitney Watkins, an influential state politician, led the charge for a new stadium. "Nothing appeals so strongly to the boy or girl who is just finishing high school as a college furnishing high-class athletic entertainment," he said with admirable candor. "In order to overcome this weakness, we must have a fine stadium." The legislature granted MSU $160,000, and work began on a 14,000-seat steel and concrete facility on the south shore of the Grand River. Ralph Wilson, who was also the track coach and AD, brought the green and white into the unnamed stadium for the first time on November 10, 1923, but they lost to Creighton 27–7. Dedication took place the next year when mighty Michigan came to East Lansing and won by seven.

MSU expanded the stadium in 1935 by adding a 12,000-seat horseshoe in the south end and also gave the place a name. It became Macklin Field in honor of John Macklin, who had coached the team from 1911 to 1915 and won 85 percent of his games. The east and west sides got more rows in 1948, raising seating capacity to 51,000, just in time for Michigan State's rise to national prominence. Under coach Clarence "Biggie" Munn, the Spartans put together a 28-game winning streak and won the national championship in 1951 and 1952, although in neither instance did they play in a bowl game. Such success merited an invitation to join the Big 10 in 1953. They were co-champs that first year and went on to beat UCLA in the Rose Bowl.

Munn turned it over to his assistant, Hugh "Duffy" Daugherty, who kept the Spartans in the highest echelons of college football. They were claimants to the 1955 and 1957 national titles (although Oklahoma and Auburn, respectively, were more widely recognized), and the stadium was expanded twice. A 9,000-seat addition to the north end and matching east and west upper decks made room for 76,000 fans. And there was another change in nomenclature as Macklin Field became Spartan Stadium.

Two more national championships followed in 1965 and 1966. East Lansing was the scene of a monumental game in the latter season when the two top-ranked teams, MSU and Notre Dame, faced off before a crowd of 80,011 and ended up with a 10–10 tie. Four Spartans—Charles "Bubba" Smith, Gene Washington, Clinton Jones, and George Webster—went in the first round of the NFL draft, indicative of the kind of talent Daugherty had stockpiled. Not so much was at stake late in the 1974 season when No. 1 Ohio State invaded Spartan Stadium. But when Levi Jackson streaked down the sideline for an 88-yard touchdown late in the fourth quarter to upset the Buckeyes, it was one of the most electrifying moments in Michigan State history.

Portable lights enabled the Spartans to have nighttime football in 1987, and renovations, which included dropping the field by eight feet in 1994, improved comfort and sightlines for the fans but eliminated nearly 4,000 seats. The seventy-five-year-old facility got another facelift in the late 1990s, and new scoreboards went up in the north and south ends. Attendance in recent years has been strong, but not enough to warrant further expansion of Spartan Stadium. Nevertheless, the athletic department has determined that connecting the upper decks would give a seating capacity of 105,000. Artificial turf, a feature there since 1969, was taken up thirty-two years later as MSU joined the trend back toward grass. Coupled with that was the possible sale of naming rights to the field, an issue university officials found both appealing and appalling. Spartan Stadium was the site of a rather unique event in September 2001 when an outdoor hockey rink was set in the middle of the field. Michigan State and Michigan played to a 3–3 tie witnessed by 74,554 fans, a record for that sport.

Memorial Stadium (California)

West Coast pundits called them the "wonder teams"; the California Golden Bears, coached by Andy Smith, went 44–0–2 from 1920 to 1924. That was surely the apogee in Cal football history, encompassing a national championship and two Rose Bowl victories. Demand for tickets to games at California Field was far greater than supply, which spurred a statewide campaign to build a football stadium in honor of those who had died in World War I. Fundraising ($1.4 million), design (by John Galen Howard), and construction (including 12,000 barrels of cement and 600 tons of steel) took two years. The result was Memorial Stadium, capable of holding 80,000 fans. Not only did it resemble the Colosseum in Rome, but the setting—in a beautiful area known as Strawberry Canyon, with the Berkeley hills to the east and San Francisco Bay to the west—was splendid. The inaugural game, on November 24, 1923, was a 9–0 defeat of cross-bay rival Stanford.

At Memorial Stadium once every season from 1932 to 1939, Cal engaged in the curious gambit of playing doubleheaders. Perhaps the athletic department sought to give fans in those Great Depression days extra value for their dollar, but the Bears did indeed play back-to-back games, their second opponent always being a non-collegiate team called the California Aggies. Major pushovers, the Aggies scored in only two of the eight games they played.

Relatively few changes have been made to the stadium in its long history. Renovations over the years have dropped seating capacity to 75,028, and artificial turf was installed in 1981 before a return to grass in 1995. It has never had lights.

Memories of being among the elite gnaw at alumni of the blue and gold. Their team finished in the top ten in 1948, 1949, and 1950, but never since. The days of huge crowds jammed into

— Courtesy of California sports information department

Memorial Stadium are in the past, as the Bears have not won the Pac-10 title nor played in the Rose Bowl since 1958. Their quarterback that season was Joe Kapp, a rookie coach in 1982 when Cal pulled off the wildest game-winning play in the history of the sport. Stanford, visiting Berkeley, had taken the lead by making a field goal with four seconds left. The Cardinal's band began flooding the field even as the kickoff happened. Kevin Moen received the ball at the 43-yard line and lateraled to Richard Rogers, who lateraled to Dwight Garner, who lateraled to Mariet Ford, who lateraled back to Moen, all while running past bewildered Stanford defenders and musicians. In fact, Moen flattened a Stanford trombonist as he crossed into the end zone, setting off a delirious celebration among Cal fans.

Los Angeles Memorial Coliseum (Southern California)

Although they would later become one of the proudest and winningest football progams, the Southern California Trojans were a peripatetic bunch, bouncing among six rented parks in Los Angeles. None were adequate, although Bovard Field on campus could hold 10,000 spectators. In 1919, Mayor Meredith P. Snyder gathered 100 prominent citizens at a downtown bank. Their dream was to erect a stadium in Exposition Park, just south of USC, and name it in honor of those who had given their lives in World War I. After arranging a city-county-state partnership, they secured an $800,000 loan at a reduced rate. For that matter, architect John Parkinson and the Dixon Construction Company made similar sacrifices in the spirit of civic cooperation. Groundbreaking on the site of a former racetrack was in December 1921, and Los Angeles Memorial Coliseum was completed on budget in May 1923. It was a grand structure with a seating capacity of 75,000 and room for growth. (Exposition Park later became home to gardens, museums, and the LA Sports Arena.) Even before USC played a game there, the announcement was made that the stadium would host the 1932 Olympic Games. Behind the scenes, however, disagreements over ultimate ownership and control of the facility had begun and would last for years.

At any rate, the men of Troy moved in and were evidently pleased with their new home; over the next six seasons they played just ten games outside of LA Memorial Coliseum. Coach Howard Jones' 1928 team won the national championship, the first of eight claimed by the school. Their cross-town rivals, the UCLA Bruins, liked the stadium, too. Thus began a stretch of fifty-three seasons of sharing it. Conflict was inevitable, with many instances of one team using the stadium on a Friday night and the other on Saturday afternoon.

In anticipation of the Olympics, LA Memorial Coliseum was expanded to 101,573 seats at a cost of $950,000. This also included the graceful peristyle at the south end which has become its most recognizable aspect. As if to celebrate, the Trojans won consecutive national titles in 1931 and 1932, with Rose Bowl wins over Tulane and Pittsburgh.

Lights were installed in 1944, three years before 104,953 people witnessed USC's loss to Notre Dame. That remains the largest crowd in the history of the stadium. The turf got more wear when the NFL's Los Angeles Rams began playing there on Sundays, and

— Courtesy of Southern California sports information department

it was later home to the Los Angeles Dodgers of major league baseball and the Los Angeles Raiders. Those guiding the destiny of LA Memorial Coliseum made improvements almost annually. Unless the Trojans were hosting UCLA or Notre Dame, tickets were abundantly available at the stadium. Seating capacity was reduced to 92,000 in 1964, and it has fluctuated around that level ever since. In recent years, a retractable fabric has been stretched over east and west end-zone seats, seemingly an admission that the stadium is too big. Many empty seats were in evidence when the Green Bay Packers and Kansas City Chiefs played the first Super Bowl there on January 15, 1967. Southern Cal fans will always recall the 1974 game against Notre Dame. Trailing the Irish 24–0, Anthony Davis and Pat Haden forged the mother of all comebacks, winning 55–24. The cardinal and gold was on its way to another national title.

More history was made at Los Angeles Memorial Coliseum when it hosted the opening and closing ceremonies and track and field competition for the 1984 Olympics, making it the only facility to have done so twice. The stadium got a $15 million renovation in 1993 as the field was lowered eleven feet and moved west, the track was taken out, and other much-needed changes were made. Less than a year later, however, Los Angeles was hit with an earthquake. Costs to repair the damage and to do seismic retrofitting came to a cool $93 million.

Folsom Field (Colorado)

When the University of Colorado erected a football/track facility in 1924, the era of stadium building was well underway; three times as many stadiums from the 1920s remain standing compared to those built in the following decade. The Buffaloes (better known at the time as the silver and gold) had played home games at Gamble Field for twenty years, but president George Norlin decided a new facility was needed. Even before financing was secured, Norlin had the dirt flying. He was the prime mover, along with former coach Frank Folsom, then on the CU law faculty. Splendidly adapted to the contours of a ravine, the 30,000-

— Courtesy of Colorado sports information department

seat U-shaped stadium had a minimum of steel and concrete and was made mostly of wood, which accounted for its bargain-basement price of $70,000. More than 4,000 people marched in a parade in the dedication ceremonies on November 1, 1924, before Colorado took a 3–0 win over Utah.

Until the mid-1930s, it had been common to flood the stadium in wintertime, providing CU students a delightful ice-skating rink. But resultant damage to the field brought that policy to a halt. Oddly enough, the largest stadium in the Rocky Mountain area had no official name for twenty years. It was informally called Norlin Stadium, Boulder Bowl, and Colorado Stadium. When he died in 1944, Folsom was honored for almost half a century of work as a coach, professor, and administrator.

From its inception, Folsom Field did not change until 1956, except for the addition of a scoreboard. While it had been logically predicted that the north end of the horseshoe would be closed in, that did not happen. Instead, a 15,000-seat upper deck was built, encompassing the east side and south end. It stopped rather abruptly at the goal line because of the adjacent CU fieldhouse. Nearly 1,000 tons of steel, 750 tons of native stone, and 75,000 bricks gave Folsom Field the solid look and feel that was formerly lacking. While it was a lovely setting for college football, with the Flatirons looming over the stadium, the Buffs seldom sold out, except for when Oklahoma, the Big 8 powerhouse, came to town.

Coach and AD Eddie Crowder pushed for another expansion in 1967. At a cost of $500,000, the field was lowered ten feet (necessitating removal of the track) and shifted ten yards south. This allowed construction of 6,500 prime seats. A six-level press box was built on the west side in 1968, and artificial turf was installed three years later. The creaky wooden seating throughout the stadium was replaced with silver and gold aluminum benches in 1976.

Quarterback Darian Hagan, running back Eric Bieniemy, and defensive lineman Alfred Williams led the Buffs to consecutive eleven-win seasons and the national title in 1990. A year later, the Dal Ward Center was built in the north end. This $14 million building, which included new locker rooms, had the red tile roof, stone walls, and Italianate architecture characteristic of the Boulder campus. It also gave permanence to the north-end bleacher seating, which put Folsom Field's capacity at just under 52,000.

Natural grass (along with an elaborate underground heating system) returned in 1999, and videoboards were erected in both ends. While CU has hosted a dozen night games, all required temporary lighting. In addition to football, Folsom Field has been the scene of graduation ceremonies and concerts, and each Memorial Day, 40,000 people finish the Bolder Boulder 10K by running into the stadium.

Michie Stadium (Army)

In the 1910s and early 1920s, perhaps no other school suffered such an embarrassing inadequacy of facilities as the U.S. Military Academy, better known as Army. Home games were held on "the plain," where military drilling otherwise took place. That necessitated repeatedly putting up and taking down steel stands on opposite sides of the gridiron. With the popularity of college football

— Courtesy of Army sports information department

growing in the post–World War I era, it was clear that a real stadium was needed at West Point. In December 1922, after an 8–0–2 season, things were set in motion by Douglas MacArthur, superintendent of the academy. He connected athletics and military life with these words: "Upon the fields of friendly strife are sown the seeds that upon other fields, on other days, will bear the fruits of victory."

The future general chose a meadow near the Lusk Reservoir, and the initial plan was to build a wooden—and thus temporary—stadium. But the U.S. Treasury agreed to loan half of the $300,000 needed to cover design, excavation, and construction, so a steel and concrete facility was built, an athletic amphitheater on the west bank of the Hudson River. The Newport Engineering and Construction Company put together a cozy 16,000-seat horseshoe with 5,000 temporary seats on the east side. It was named after Dennis Michie, the organizer, player-coach, and business manager of the first Cadet team in 1890 and who died in the Spanish-American War. Michie Stadium was dedicated on November 15, 1924, when Army and Columbia played to a 14–14 tie.

Running back Chris Cagle, one of the long gray line of stars, was an all-American in 1927, 1928, and 1929 when Army was among the top teams in the country. By 1932, when the Black Knights lost their first game at Michie Stadium, more rows on the west side gave it 26,491 seats. While the stadium got occasional facelifts and virtually came to represent the Cadets' ethos of duty, honor and country, it remained unchanged for the next thirty years. Army's fortunes were in decline before Earl "Red" Blaik was hired in 1941. The legendary football mentor built some powerful teams, aided during the war years by a number of all-Americans from other schools. With twin Heisman Trophy winners, Glenn Davis and Felix "Doc" Blanchard, the Cadets won national championships in 1944 and 1945, and a late-season tie with Notre Dame caused them to share the 1946 title with the Irish. Blaik kept on through a cheating scandal that decimated the 1951 team, but things were better by his last year. In 1958, he had his third Heisman Trophy winner, Pete Dawkins, and the black and gold finished 8–0–1 and No. 3. Never again has Army breached the top ten.

The east stands of Michie Stadium were made permanent in 1962, and the west side received extra rows and an upper deck in

1969, elevating seating capacity to 41,684 (since adjusted to 39,929). The $2.3 million project was performed by the U.S. Army Corps of Engineers. In 1977, a year after the first class of women was admitted to the academy, artificial turf was installed at the stadium which served a multiplicity of uses. Portable lights were first employed in 1984, and the field was named for Blaik in 1999. It was a tribute to Blaik's coaching legacy, although he always had detractors, those not pleased with how football had been overglorified at an institution meant to train soldiers. If not the dominant force they once were, the Black Knights have been more competitive in recent seasons, playing in four different bowls. In the next few years, a new press box will be built, as well as a $33 million athletic annex off the south end zone.

Michie Stadium has long been a place that could inspire people to wax poetic about college football on an autumn afternoon. In 1999, the small stadium amid the rocky hills of upstate New York was chosen as *Sports Illustrated*'s third-favorite sports venue, trailing just Yankee Stadium and Augusta National golf course.

Ross-Ade Stadium (Purdue)

David Ross, a Purdue alumnus and trustee in the early 1920s, believed athletics had traditionally been given short shrift. The prime example was Stuart Field, a little facility in the heart of campus where the Boilermakers played. So Ross joined forces with George Ade, a well-known author, playwright, humorist, and fellow alum. The pair paid $40,000 for a sixty-five-acre dairy farm just north of campus and donated it to the university. They also set up the Ross-Ade Foundation to collect funds to pay for construction of a suitable stadium. With thirty rows on the east and west sides, Ross-Ade Stadium could hold 13,500 fans, and there was standing room for another 5,000. It was dedicated on November 22, 1924, when coach James Phelan's team prevailed 26–7 over the Indiana Hoosiers.

Phelan's last year in West Lafayette was a dandy—the 1929 Boilermakers went 8–0 and featured two all-Americans, tackle Elmer Sleight and running back Ralph Welch. The gold and black

— Courtesy of Purdue sports information department

did not won another outright Big 10 championship for the rest of the century. Even in 1943, when they won all nine games (and finished No. 5 in the nation), they had to share the conference title with Michigan.

Enrollment and attendance were booming after World War II, and temporary bleachers were needed at Ross-Ade Stadium as crowds as large as 47,000 gathered to see Purdue. How so many people could fit into an 18,500-seat stadium, even with bleachers everywhere, is difficult to imagine. AD Guy Mackey, with help from the Ross-Ade Foundation, raised enough money for a major expansion of the stadium. Thirty more rows were built atop the east and west sides, and a north-end horseshoe equaled their sixty rows, for a total of 51,000 seats.

Other than the addition of a west-side press box in 1955, little changed at Ross-Ade Stadium until 1964 when the field was lowered eight feet and thirteen rows were added around the lower perimeter, which made room for another 11,000 fans. At the same time, fiberglass seating in alternating gold and black created a distinctive look. That was just in time for a glorious three-year stretch for the Boilermakers. In 1966, quarterback Bob Griese took them to the Rose Bowl, where they beat Southern Cal and ended up No. 7. Like Griese, running back Leroy Keyes was a Heisman Trophy runner-up, and Purdue had top-ten finishes in 1967 and 1968.

The press box was expanded to four levels in 1969, and fifty-five rows of steel stands were added to the south end, which had held temporary seating almost from the beginning. Many other schools were changing over to artificial turf in the early and mid-1970s, but not Purdue. A couple of faculty agronomists came up with prescription athletic turf for Ross-Ade Stadium, and it has become one of the best and most popular forms of grass in both college and the pros.

Defensive back, kick returner, and occasional wide receiver Rod Woodson was a two-time all-American and one of the Boilermakers' greatest. He was a senior in 1986 when portable lights enabled Ross-Ade Stadium to host its first-ever night game. Even with Woodson's exploits, Purdue had a decade of losing football, weak attendance, and an old stadium in dire need of upgrading. The success of coach Joe Tiller and quarterback Drew Brees (the most productive quarterback in Big 10 history, with 11,792 yards passing and 90 touchdowns), turned that around. Following the 2000 season, the first phase of a three-phase project was begun at a cost of $60 million. Much more than a Band-Aid, it involved basic structural changes, a new press box, and thirty-seven luxury boxes. The stadium got a limestone and brick facade to match the main architectural theme of the rest of the Purdue campus. All told, seating capacity was reduced by 5,000. The second and third phases are tentative, riding on continued Boilermaker victories and ticket demand; upper decks on the east side and north end would give the stadium roughly 80,000 seats.

Royal-Memorial Stadium (Texas)

Fitted with orange and white bunting for a big game, Clark Field was a charming but outdated facility for the Texas Longhorns.

So L. Theo Bellmont, athletic director, and H. J. Lutcher Stark, chairman of the Board of Regents, began a fundraising campaign for a new stadium. Despite a couple of political brouhahas, they succeeded. Rallying behind a slogan of "For Texas, I will," students and alumni contributed $275,000 for Memorial Stadium, named to honor the 198,000 Texans who had fought in World War I. Architect Herbert Greene designed and the Walsh & Burney Company built a 27,000-seat stadium for football and track. (The Texas Relays would soon be a major track and field meet.) On November 27, 1924, an overflow crowd celebrated its dedication with a 7–0 defeat of Texas A&M. UT's stadium, while modest compared to those recently built in the East, North, and West, was by far the largest in that part of the country. Memorial Stadium's construction was so significant, it helped prevent the movement of the university away from the Forty Acres to a more spacious and idyllic spot on the Colorado River.

Just two years later, the athletic department erected a north-end horseshoe with thirteen graceful exterior arches, the central one bearing an unmistakable resemblance to the facade of the Alamo. The stadium could hold 40,500 fans, but with the success of Dana Bible's teams, that was not enough. The east and west stands got twenty-six new rows and a section to the south in 1948, which made it 60,130. Lights were added in 1955, but there were problems. The stadium had not been well maintained, and in the mid-1960s, UT thought seriously about erecting a new facility in north Austin and razing Memorial Stadium. However, a prohibitive cost and the problems inherent to off-campus football soon demonstrated the folly of such an idea. It would be better to keep, and enhance, the storied stadium.

That process began in 1967 with a $200,000 facelift, and two years later, much bigger work was undertaken. Artificial turf and a rubber track were installed, and aluminum benches replaced wood throughout the stadium. Construction of a 15,000-seat upper deck on the west side required moving a street and thus cutting down a dozen old cypress and oak trees. In keeping with the tenor of the times, UT's students and hippies protested vigorously, but to no avail; the trees came down and the stadium grew to a seating capacity of 75,504. Football fans did not mind a bit, as Darrell Royal's Horns won their third national championship in eight

— Courtesy of Texas sports information department; photo by Susan Sigmon

years (1963, 1969, and 1970) and achieved a thirty-game winning streak.

A Cotton Bowl loss to Notre Dame prevented Texas and Heisman Trophy winner Earl Campbell from claiming the 1977 national title, and a fumbled punt led to the same result against Georgia in the Cotton Bowl following the 1983 season. Back in Austin, nothing major happened to Memorial Stadium until 1986 when the Neuhaus-Royal (later renamed Neuhaus-Moncrief) Complex was built in the south end. Among other things, it meant a plush new locker room for the home team. Big new scoreboards were put up in the north end in 1989 and the south end in 1996.

With adroit leadership from athletic director DeLoss Dodds, the stadium underwent a number of developments in the late 1990s, costing a reported $92 million. Besides badly needed infrastructure work, grass made its return, 14 luxury boxes were built on the west side and 52 on the east side along with an upper deck one-third the size of the other one. Etched in the exterior stonework were the words "Texas, Our Texas." The track was removed and the field lowered, allowing room for more rows east and west.

Prior to the 1998 season (when Ricky Williams won the Heisman

Trophy and broke Tony Dorsett's all-time rushing record), the name of the 81,050-seat facility was changed to the rather daunting Darrell K Royal–Texas Memorial Stadium. And the field was named in honor of Joe Jamail, one of UT's biggest donors in both the academic and athletic realms. Despite what some critics may regard as an edifice complex, long-range plans foresee Royal-Memorial Stadium with a seating capacity of 115,000.

Tiger Stadium (Louisiana State)

Sure, LSU went 10–0 and won a version of the national championship in 1908, but the Tigers had fallen on hard times by the early 1920s. Nevertheless, the university decided it was time to replace old State Field. Not far from the Mississippi River, a set of east and west stands capable of holding 12,000 people was ready in time for the last game of the 1924 season, a loss to Tulane.

Tiger Stadium's first expansion came four years later. More rows were added, and the stands were extended to the end zones, allowing room for 22,000 fans. The space underneath did not go to waste, as 1,500 dormitory rooms were built; the stadium was home to many an LSU student until the dorms were converted into office and storage use. Athletic director T. P. "Skipper" Heard was responsible for the erection of lights in 1931, which helped build the mystique of raucous and rollicking Tiger Stadium. Although the name derived from a later era, it was viewed by the Bayou Bengals' opponents as Death Valley. With LSU in Baton Rouge, the state capital, Governor Huey Long involved himself in the operation of the football program. In 1936, a year after the Kingfish's assassination, Tiger Stadium got a horseshoe in the north end (site of the home locker room), which more than doubled seating capacity. And in 1953, a similar addition in the south end brought it up 67,720.

Such greats as Steve Van Buren, Y. A. Tittle, and Jim Taylor played at LSU during a twenty-two-year gap between Southeastern Conference titles. That ended with a bang in 1958 when Paul Dietzel's purple and gold team went undefeated and won the national championship. But it was the next season when the most

— Courtesy of LSU sports information department

fabled play in LSU history occurred before a packed house at Tiger Stadium: Billy Cannon's 89-yard punt return to beat Mississippi on Halloween night. Cannon, who also intercepted seven passes as a defensive back, won the Heisman Trophy in 1959.

No changes were made to the stadium for a quarter of a century, but the Tigers did finally integrate. Along with Ole Miss and Georgia, they had their first black varsity player in the 1972 season—the last of the last. It is perhaps indicative that LSU did not play a single game outside the South from 1943 to 1970. In 1978, an upper deck was appended to the west side, which increased seating capacity by 10,000. New bleachers and chair-back seats were added in the mid-1980s, and other alterations made Tiger Stadium an 80,000-seat arena. An east-side upper deck (including seventy luxury boxes) in 2000 brought it to 91,664, the fourth-largest stadium in the country.

LSU has been among the leaders in attendance almost every season since the NCAA started keeping such records. This, although the Tigers have had just two top-ten finishes in the past thirty years. Their performance on the road does not approach what they do in Baton Rouge, partly because Tiger Stadium has been voted by five different entities as the most intimidating place in college football.

Memorial Stadium (Oklahoma)

Undefeated teams in 1911 and 1915 were about all Oklahoma fans could brag about during the early days. Being so far removed from the coasts, and thus the attention of the major media, effectively precluded consideration for national honors. In 1923, the Sooners were in the midst of a three-year span of sub-.500 play when they got a new home on the east side of campus in Norman. With encouragement from longtime AD and coach Bennie Owen, OU students started a campaign which led to construction of a $293,000 stadium there. Some 16,000 seats on the west side were ready for the first game of the 1925 season, a 7–0 defeat of Drake. It was called Memorial Stadium, to honor Oklahoma veterans of World War I. In later years, the field was named for Owen.

A matching set of stands was built on the east side in 1929, raising seating capacity to 32,000. Not much happened over the next two decades other than a Big 6 title (and subsequent Orange Bowl win) in 1938, nothing to indicate Oklahoma would soon establish one of the greatest dynasties in college football history. The sea change began with the arrival of Bud Wilkinson as coach in 1947. In his third season at the helm, OU went 11–0. That same year, the track at Memorial Stadium was removed, the field was dropped six feet, and the east and west stands got new rows down near the field. The north end was enclosed, too, allowing the stadium to hold 55,000 fans of the red and white.

OU put some great teams on the field in the 1950s. Wilkinson's Sooners had the first of three Heisman Trophy winners, were crowned as national champs in 1950, 1955, and 1956 and reeled off a staggering 47-game winning streak, a record unlikely ever to be challenged. After south-end bleachers added 6,186 seats in 1957, the stadium remained essentially the same until artificial turf was installed in 1970. It was the site of what people in the Big 8 called the game of the century—Nebraska's narrow defeat of Oklahoma in 1971. The Sooners, masters of the Wishbone offense, featured quarterback Jack Mildren (later lieutenant governor of the state) and running back Greg Pruitt.

With Barry Switzer, a coach who would win 84 percent of his games over a sixteen-year career in Norman, OU won more national titles in 1974 and 1975, although they could not play in a bowl game after the former season due to probation. Amid such success, the athletic department saw fit to expand Memorial Stadium, and a 10,000-seat upper deck and a new press box were built on the west side for $5.7 million. In 1980, a number of renovations improved the look and feel of the stadium, and the south end-zone seating was made permanent, bringing it up to 75,004. That total was later reduced to 72,726 to accommodate wheelchair seating.

The Oklahoma Board of Regents approved a master plan in 1994 in which natural grass returned to Memorial Stadium, and lights and a new scoreboard were erected. The old facility got a major upgrade at the turn of the century, most notably twenty-seven luxury boxes and 2,200 club seats. The cost was $100 million, but that pain was assuaged by another golden age for Sooner football. Coach Bob Stoops' team won it all in 2000, capped by a defeat of Florida State in the Orange Bowl.

Ryan Field (Northwestern)

William Dyche, a Northwestern graduate and former mayor of Evanston, Illinois, joined the university's Board of Trustees in 1893. Also assuming the duties of vice president and business manager, in 1905 Dyche directed the construction of a 10,000-seat wooden athletic facility on campus, a mile west of Lake Michigan. By the early 1920s, though, NU's big games were being held at Soldier Field in adjoining Chicago. His energy undiminished, Dyche organized support for a new stadium on the site of the old one. It had sloping contours with an upper deck on the west side and towers at both ends. The football field was encircled by a running track and 45,000 seats. Dyche Stadium, which cost $1.4 million, was first used on October 2, 1926, when the Wildcats blanked South Dakota 34–0, but dedication day was six weeks later when they beat Chicago 38–7. The 1926 team, with two all-Americans, Ralph Baker and Bob Johnson, shared the Big 10 championship. The Cats won or shared the title three more times in the next decade and beat two-time national champ Minnesota at Dyche Stadium in 1936, ending the Gophers' twenty-seven-game winning streak.

From 1941 to 1943, Northwestern fans were privileged to watch the play of quarterback Otto Graham. An all-American in both basketball and football, he did his part in World War II before moving on to a Hall of Fame career with the Cleveland Browns. In Graham's senior season at NU, temporary lights were first used at the stadium. The U.S. Olympic track and field trials were held there in 1948, the year Bob Voigts' team went 8–2 with a defeat of California in the Rose Bowl. Every home game was sold out, so the south end was enclosed, elevating seating capacity to 49,256, although north-end bleachers would be erected when the need arose, permitting crowds of over 55,000.

Besides the most basic maintenance, changes were few at Dyche Stadium. A new press box was built on the west side prior to a great season for the purple and white. In 1962, coach Ara Parseghian led the way as they won their first six games and spent two weeks ranked No. 1 before coming back to earth. Parseghian, 4-0 against Notre Dame, was soon running the show at South Bend. Northwestern's football fortunes, meanwhile, entered a steep decline. The Wildcats went from bad to worse to downright terrible, with an excruciating six-year span (1976–81) when they won a total of three games. Average attendance fell below 20,000, and some fans showed up at the aging stadium just to mock their own team. Things improved slightly in the 1980s and early 1990s because of a watered-down non-conference schedule.

Gary Barnett's first three years in Evanston were inauspicious with a won-loss ratio of one to three. Then came the magical season of 1995 when running back Darnell Autry, linebacker Pat Fitzgerald, and others brought home the first Big 10 crown since 1936. They lost to USC in the Rose Bowl, but roses had never smelled so sweet. Barnett was national coach of the year. While doubts persisted that perhaps they were one-year wonders, a 9–3 record in 1996 showed that NU's football renaissance was real.

Students and alumni noted a change in spirit; fans who once opposed the whole ethos of winning finally embraced it.

At that time, a fundraising campaign was begun, aided in large part by a gift of $10 million from Patrick Ryan, chairman of the Board of Trustees. Ryan, who had led a similar drive in 1982 to erect new basketball (the arena was named for him) and baseball facilities, saw it add up to $30 million. Northwestern used the money prudently, doing a top-to-bottom renovation of the stadium in 1997. Changes included a high-tech sound system, new locker rooms in the north end, all-new seating, and a new press box with requisite VIP areas. The track was removed, the field was lowered five and a half feet, and grass replaced artificial turf, which had first been installed in 1973. In the process, seating capacity was reduced to 47,130.

In return, the university rechristened the stadium, pitching the Dyche name like an old baloney sandwich. Thenceforth, said president Henry Bienen, it would be called Ryan Field. But that set off a big brouhaha among fans who liked the old name just fine. Furthermore, Dyche's descendants pointed to a 1926 resolution—not legally binding—which said the name was to remain in perpetuity, even if a new stadium were built. All to no avail. It prompted former sports information director George Beres, a man who bled purple, to pull a creative publicity stunt. As the cameras rolled, Beres ceremoniously plucked petals from a long-stemmed rose, uttered a curse, and said the Cats would not return to the Rose Bowl until the Dyche Stadium name was reinstated.

Be that as it may, refurbished Ryan Field was a beautiful facility, deeply rooted on campus. It was the scene of an unforgettable game in 2000 when NU and Michigan ran up 1,189 yards of total offense. The final score was 54–51 in favor of the Wildcats, and the deciding play was a touchdown pass from Zac Kustok to Sam Simmons with 20 seconds left. When it was over, many in the sellout crowd stormed the field in celebration.

Memorial Stadium (Missouri)

Chester Brewer, football coach and athletic director at the University of Missouri, had an idea prior to the 1911 season finale against archrival Kansas. He urged alumni and other fans of the Tigers to "come home" for the game and a celebration. Some 10,000 of them packed Rollins Field in what began a great collegiate tradition—homecoming.

More than a decade later, Brewer was no longer coaching but still served as AD. The team won Missouri Valley Conference titles in 1924 and 1925, and lineman Ed Lindenmeyer was Mizzou's first all-American. Brewer had the vision and drive to build a new stadium to replace Rollins Field. Carved between two bluffs south of the university and costing $350,000, Memorial Stadium was like so many others of that era, dedicated to Americans who had fought in World War I. It had 25,000 seats and a 440-yard track encircling the field. The first game was on October 2, 1926, against Tulane. Heavy rain for the entire month of September made the field a quagmire in which the two teams battled to a scoreless tie.

Memorial Stadium's first change came prior to the 1927 season opener. A block "M," measuring 90' x 95', was built on the incline above the north end zone by 500 freshmen and has been maintained ever since. Missouri football slumped badly during the Great Depression, however. Between 1931 and 1934, the Tigers won just four games and suffered eighteen shutouts, and average attendance was a puny 7,500. The athletic department was insolvent when Don Faurot stepped in as coach and AD. A three-sport star in the 1920s, Faurot had helped lay the sod at Memorial Stadium. Except for three years in the Navy during World War II, he coached until 1956 and was AD through 1966. Employing a split-T offense, the Tigers won the Big 6 crown in 1939 and 1941, appearing in the Orange Bowl and Sugar Bowl, respectively. Faurot left a huge legacy at MU and would be honored in 1972 when the field was named after him.

Before the 1949 season, Memorial Stadium underwent its first expansion as the number of rows on the west side nearly doubled. Thus began a series of piecemeal additions that created a two-tier horseshoe with overflow space in the north end. After Dan Devine's 1960 team briefly reached No. 1, there was further growth of the stadium up to a seating capacity of 62,000. That began a decade of excellence in which the black and gold never lost more than three games in a season. The other high points came in 1965, when two-way star Johnny Roland led them to an 8-

2-1 record with a Sugar Bowl defeat of Florida, and in 1969, when the Tigers were 9–2 and fell to Penn State in the Orange Bowl, finishing No. 6.

But it did not last. While attendance reached a peak in the late 1970s (with four games seen by crowds of over 73,000), Missouri regressed. There were thirteen straight losing seasons, and apathy set in among fans; average attendance at one point reached a nadir of 37,000.

On October 6, 1990, Memorial Stadium was the scene of a weird and memorable game. The visiting Colorado Buffaloes, on their way to the national title, were inadvertently given an extra down in the final minute which allowed them to score and steal a victory that seemed to belong to Mizzou. Even now, people in Columbia believe a crime was committed. The stadium has changed considerably since that day. The wooden seats present since 1926 were replaced by aluminum, a new home locker room was built under the south stands, grass replaced the slippery artificial turf, and lights were installed. More than $12 million in infrastructure and cosmetic changes were done in 1997, resulting in a stadium that was more convenient to fans and more aesthetically pleasing. The small and underequipped west-side press box, the subject of some derision by members of the media, was replaced in 2000 by a four-level edition which included thirty-five luxury boxes, all at a cost of $16 million.

Michigan Stadium (Michigan)

The name of Fielding Yost resonates for those who appreciate college football history, especially regarding the University of Michigan. His "point-a-minute" teams after the turn of the century won four national championships and played in the first Rose Bowl, thrashing Stanford 49–0. Beginning in 1906, Yost's Wolverines played home games at Ferry Field, which grew from a seating capacity of 18,000 to 48,000 during two decades of use.

After winning two more national titles and becoming athletic director, Yost's power increased. He did not believe Ferry Field was suitable for a major football program like Michigan. Sellouts were becoming increasingly common by the mid-1920s, and the maize and blue had recently played dedication games for new facilities at Vanderbilt, Ohio State, Michigan State, and Illinois, and three more Big 10 schools—Minnesota, Northwestern, and Purdue—also had nice new homes.

Some members of UM's administration and faculty were already alarmed about the undue attention paid to football, and they were even more so when Yost proposed construction of a new stadium on the campus in Ann Arbor. To compound matters, he wanted a whopper of a facility, one capable of holding between 100,000 and 150,000 fans. While the academics had their say, they did not prevail. In 1926, the Michigan Board of Regents approved a plan to construct a stadium, big but not quite up to Yost's grandiose proportions, southwest of Ferry Field. The land was the site of an underground spring that caused construction problems, once sinking a crane which remains below ground even today. Michigan Stadium, patterned after the Yale Bowl, cost $950,000 and had 72,000 permanent seats. Yost, who had given up his coaching duties by then, made sure it had room for expansion.

The Wolverines had scored two victories before crowds that filled but a third of the huge bowl. Dedication day, October 22, 1927, was a splendid vindication for Yost, however. More than 10,000 temporary seats were set up on the concourse at the top of the ground-level stadium, which was still not enough for the 84,401 fans who saw Michigan blank Ohio State. The star of that team was Bennie Oosterbaan, a three-time all-American who would coach his alma mater from 1948 to 1958.

Seating at Michigan Stadium was expanded to 85,753 in 1928, and electronic scoreboards were placed in the north and south ends in 1930. In the years to follow, Michigan had some great teams (national champs again in 1932, 1933, 1947, and 1948) and a few weak ones. They had a lot of big crowds and some garden-variety ones, depending on the visitor. The Wolverines, with their distinctive winged helmet, saw the stadium grow to 97,239 seats in 1949. That year, the first in which the NCAA kept attendance records, UM led the nation with an average of nearly 94,000, which was 18,000 more than the second-place school.

The "Big House," as Michigan students liked to call it, got a $700,000 press box on the west side and another 4,000 seats in

1956. Some twenty-two miles of wooden seating were replaced with blue fiberglass, except for the maize block "M" in the eastside stands. Artificial turf was installed in 1969 (and gave way to grass in 1990), when Bo Schembechler's team beat defending national champion Ohio State 24–12 in a titanic game witnessed by over 103,000 fans.

The stadium got a facelift in the mid-1970s, and more rows were added as capacity climbed to 101,701. Further renovations in 1992 and 1998 (which did not, however, include lighting) made it 107,501—still the biggest despite encroachment by Tennessee's Neyland Stadium and Penn State's Beaver Stadium. In 1997, UM went 12-0 including a Rose Bowl win over Washington State to win the national championship, and defensive back/receiver/kick returner Charles Woodson became the school's third Heisman Trophy winner. The Wolverines played seven home games that year before almost three-quarters of a million fans. Michigan Stadium, whose size has long taxed sportswriters' collection of adjectives, has probably not been expanded for the last time. With east and west upper decks, it may yet reach the outlandish 150,000 mark Fielding Yost dreamed of seventy-five years ago.

Kenan Stadium (North Carolina)

Way back in the early days, North Carolina did what was customary for Southern schools in places like Chapel Hill, holding some of its major games in larger towns. Travel, accommodations, and other factors caused the Tar Heels to play in neutral sites like Charlotte, Greensboro, and even across state lines in Virginia and South Carolina. This was partly because Emerson Field had permanent seating for just 2,400 fans, although as many as 16,000 sometimes gathered there.

In May 1926, a group of UNC alumni met to discuss building a new football stadium. With a plan approved by the Board of Trustees, they began raising money. The process was moving along at a moderate pace when William Kenan Jr. got involved. Blueblooded in more ways than one, he had lettered for Carolina in the 1890s, and his great-great-grandfather had helped found the university a century earlier. Kenan was a wealthy chemist and industrialist then living in New York who wanted a way to memorialize his parents. With the grateful blessings of the other alums, the fundraising effort ended when he donated $303,000 to erect a stadium and accompanying fieldhouse. The athletic complex would be located in a wooded valley, a natural amphitheater one-half mile from the center of campus. Kenan Stadium, designed by Atwood and Nash and built by T. C. Thompson and Brothers (with Kenan's close involvement every step of the way) had curving north and south stands and a seating capacity of 24,000. The dedication game was on November 24, 1927, a 14–13 defeat of Virginia witnessed by an overflow crowd of 28,000.

Kenan's family later established a charitable trust that has given more than $100 million to higher education in the state. In addition to the stadium and two other buildings on campus, UNC's business school bears the ubiquitous Kenan name. According to folklore, the university's greatest benefactor stipulated that the stadium should

— Courtesy of North Carolina sports information department

never rise higher than the surrounding pine trees. No changes were made to Kenan Stadium until 1949 when a new press box—paid for by Kenan—was built on the south side. That was during one of the happiest times in Carolina football history, when Charlie "Choo-Choo" Justice played. A World War II vet and all-American in 1948 (when UNC finished No. 3 in the nation), he gained nearly 5,000 yards running and passing, a school record that would stand for forty-five years. With Justice and coach Carl Snavely leading the way, the Tar Heels won two Southern Conference titles and played in three New Year's Day bowls, the Sugar Bowl twice and the Cotton Bowl. They have not played in a major bowl since. In fact, when Justice left, North Carolina endured a twenty-year drought that included just three winning seasons.

In 1963, two years before his death, Kenan made a $1 million donation which helped pay for upper decks on the stadium's north and south sides, raising seating capacity to 48,000, counting bleachers in the west end. A new press box and lighting were added in 1988, and other incremental expansions gave Kenan Stadium 4,000 more seats.

The university began a five-year, $43 million renovation project in 1995 which resulted in a new playing field, the Chancellor's Box on the north side, and 8,000 permanent seats in the west end. Beneath it was a new locker room for the Tar Heels. Kenan Stadium, where John F. Kennedy spoke in 1962 and Bill Clinton in 1993, saw its largest crowd (62,000) in 1997 when No. 5 UNC played No. 2 Florida State to see who was king of the Atlantic Coast Conference. The Seminoles won, but it was Carolina's only loss of the season.

Legion Field (Alabama–Birmingham)

In 1926, the city of Birmingham spent $439,000 erecting a 21,000-seat football stadium on the west side of downtown. Named Legion Field in honor of the American Legion and as a memorial to all who had died in military service, the facility was meant to be used by local high schools and colleges. It was dedicated on November 27, 1927, when Birmingham Southern and Howard (now Samford) met. The two major schools in the state, Alabama and Auburn, began using Legion Field that season, although it was far from both campuses. Due to various disagreements, the Crimson Tide and the Tigers had a forty-year football hiatus that did not end until 1948. Legion Field, by then double its original size, hosted the game, a 55–0 rout by Bama. And while both used it frequently as a home away from home, the Iron Bowl would be the main attraction in Birmingham for half a century before reverting to Bryant-Denny Stadium (Alabama) and Jordan-Hare Stadium (Auburn). Bear Bryant, who coached more games in Birmingham than in Tuscaloosa, is honored with a bust outside the stadium.

The north end was enclosed in 1961, the east-side upper deck was built in 1963, and the south end was enclosed in the late 1970s, raising seating capacity to 78,000. By then it was a lighted stadium with artificial turf, and a new west-side press box with luxury boxes went up in 1991. Legion Field, and all the history it had witnessed, was the reason Birmingham was called the football capital of the South. Repeated efforts to entice the NFL, by expansion or franchise relocation, failed, so there have been several pretenders: the Birmingham Americans of the World Football League, the Birmingham Stallions of the United States Football League, and the Birmingham Barracudas of the Canadian Football League, to name but three.

The University of Alabama at Birmingham, founded in 1969, gained some renown with basketball, coached by Gene Bartow. His 1982 team reached the Elite Eight round of the NCAA tournament. Competing in football, however, was another matter. Some enterprising students began playing it as a club sport in 1989. Two years later (when Bartow had become athletic director), UAB had a Division III team, and home games were held at newly expanded Legion Field. The Blazers, who moved up to Division I-A by 1996, played an increasingly difficult schedule and saw attendance rise from miniscule in the early part of the decade to an average of 20,000, which still left about 60,000 empty seats at Legion Field. The hiring of former Rice and Vanderbilt coach Watson Brown gave the program legitimacy, too. As a member of Conference USA, UAB went 7–4 in 2000, and the players drafted or signed by NFL teams has been another indication of quality.

Birmingham has struggled to keep the stadium viable, though. Grass was installed in 1995, partly to accommodate early-round soccer matches in the 1996 Olympics. Alabama plays there rarely and only because of contractual obligations due to run out in 2008. And the Southeastern Conference title game has been moved to Atlanta's Georgia Dome, which is modern and clean—the antithesis of Legion Field. These days, the biggest crowd is for the annual Magic City Classic between Alabama State and Alabama A&M, a fixture at Legion Field for sixty years. Surprisingly, given Birmingham's former reputation as a bastion of segregation, black schools have been welcome at the stadium since 1927.

But the fact remains that the "Gray Lady" is rusty and well past her prime. A variety of options have been suggested in recent years. The most extreme is that the stadium is unsafe and should be razed, although civil engineers have determined otherwise. Still, the city is not spending nearly enough money to maintain it. Reducing the size of Legion Field is another possibility, although that, too, would cost money. There have been discussions of a tax to soak the out-of-towners (via rental cars and hotel rooms) to finance a domed stadium, rendering Legion Field unnecessary. So would UAB's favored idea of building a cozy 35,000-seat facility on campus. It may be years before these issues are decided, and they will come down to weighing the economic value of the events Legion Field still hosts against its rising maintenance costs. The stadium's historic and sentimental value may not count for much in the end, but if it were set on an SEC campus, funds for maintenence and improvements would be found and its future would be bright.

Bryant-Denny Stadium (Alabama)

Dr. George Denny began service as president of the University of Alabama in 1912 and stayed on for a quarter-century. The students named their football stadium Denny Field when it was erected in 1915. Fourteen years later, however, a new facility went up a few blocks to the west. Also named for UA's leader, Denny Stadium had 12,000 seats and was dedicated on October 5, 1929, with a 22–7 homecoming defeat of Ole Miss.

—Courtesy of Alabama sports information department; photo by Kent Gidley

The Crimson Tide, which had claimed national championships in 1925, 1926, and 1930, won again in 1934. That team was coached by Frank Thomas and had one of the all-time greats, Don Hutson, at end. Such success necessitated expansion of the stadium in two parts, up to a capacity of 24,000. Bleachers were added in the end zones in 1946, and the east and west stands got more rows in 1961 (another national championship year), giving Denny Stadium 43,000 seats.

By that time, of course, Paul "Bear" Bryant was back in Tuscaloosa. A former Tide player, he had coached and won at Maryland, Kentucky, and Texas A&M. But the legend was built at Bama, where he labored for twenty-five seasons. His career encompassed 323 wins and six national crowns, as well as dozens of star players, such as linebacker Lee Roy Jordan, quarterback Joe Namath, offensive lineman John Hannah, and receiver Ozzie Newsome. Bryant was a bit slow to integrate, however, losing five games in both 1969 and 1970 before negating Jim Crow.

The Bear's stadium underwent major changes in 1966, becoming a 60,000-seat bowl with permanent lighting. Denny Stadium was a fine on-campus facility, but it did not get much use. Legion

Field in Birmingham had been the Crimson Tide's other home since 1927, and the bigger games tended to be played there. In some seasons, UA held as many as five games at Legion Field. The Alabama legislature enacted a resolution in September 1975 to add the name of the great coach, who retired in 1982, to the campus stadium.

Bryant-Denny Stadium got an upper deck on the west side in 1988 and ten years later, another on the east side, bringing seating capacity to 83,818. The latter expansion included a new scoreboard in the south end and two levels of luxury boxes. That followed the 1992 national championship team, coached by Gene Stallings (a Bryant protégé from his days at Texas A&M), which went 13–0 with a Sugar Bowl victory over Miami.

In 1999, amid the growing sentiment of students, alumni, and media, athletic director Bob Bockrath announced that UA would no longer play Southeastern Conference games in Birmingham. Legion Field had structural problems, and it no longer dwarfed Bryant-Denny Stadium, anyway. For decades, the Auburn game had been a fixture at Legion Field, and Alabama's home game against Tennessee was always there. Two of the biggest contests of each season, against longtime rivals, and they were away from campus, but no more. It was a sign of maturity for the Tide's football program, Bryant-Denny Stadium, and the city of Tuscaloosa.

Arizona Stadium (Arizona)

The Wildcats' lair began on a very small scale. In December 1928, at a spot in the southeast corner of campus, ground was broken for a football/track facility. It could not have taken long to build Arizona Stadium, a single block of 7,000 seats on the field's west side. Play commenced on October 12, 1929, when UA defeated Cal Tech. Coach J. F. "Pop" McKale (whose name would later grace Arizona's basketball arena) led the team to a 7–1 record.

Daytime football in the heat of the Sonoran Desert was tough, so lights were added before the 1931 season. Almost 80 percent of the games played there in the years since have been at night. In 1938, 3,000 seats were built on the east side between the 25-yard

— Courtesy of Arizona sports information department

lines, and that was extended to the end zones in 1947, providing UA with a 14,000-seat stadium that had matching stands. A connecting horseshoe in the south end was added in 1950, bringing it up to 22,671. In the mid-1950s, Art Luppino, the "Cactus Comet" who toiled away in obscurity for the Wildcats of the Border Conference, twice led the nation in rushing.

Every home game of the 1964 season was sold out, so Arizona Stadium grew again. Thirty-five rows with room for 10,000 fans were added to the west side, and a new press box was built. In 1976, UA, then a member of the Western Athletic Conference but soon to join the Pac-10, built a two-tier upper deck on the east side, which raised seating capacity to over 49,000. The track was taken out in the early 1980s, and permanent seating in the north end then gave the stadium its present level of 57,803 seats. In 1989, a four-level press box (with one level set aside for luxury boxes) was erected at a cost of $6.3 million. With lush turf and surrounded by the Santa Catalina Mountains and the Tucson skyline, it was a nice place to hold a football game. Perhaps for that reason, the Copper

Bowl (later called the Insight.com Bowl) chose to use Arizona Stadium. The inaugural contest in 1989 featured the home team in a 17–10 defeat of North Carolina State. The red and blue also played in the game in 1997, beating New Mexico.

Arizona Stadium, which contains several academic offices and dormitory rooms underneath the stands, got a multimedia scoreboard in the north end in 1993. The biggest crowd in its history, 59,920, saw the Cats lose 56–14 to their in-state rival, Arizona State, in 1996. Two years later, however, coach Dick Tomey's team went 12–1 and finished No. 4 in the nation.

Wade Stadium (Duke)

Citing "professionalism," physical danger, and detraction from academics, the Duke Board of Trustees banned football from campus, and their edict lasted for twenty-five years. The sport was not revived until 1920. The Blue Devils then played at Hanes Field on the school's east campus. A new Gothic-oriented campus was being built a mile to the west, and that included a stadium for football and track and field. Set in a ravine, Duke Stadium was designed and constructed by the W. S. Lee Engineering Corporation. It was three-quarters of a bowl, with the open end to the south, and had room for 35,000 fans. The inaugural game was a disaster, however. A small crowd gathered on October 5, 1929, when the Blue Devils took on Pittsburgh, and the visitors from the north gave them a 52–7 spanking.

But things would soon change. Wallace Wade, who had won three national titles at Alabama, became coach in 1931 and produced some teams that scaled the heights or got close. Led by all-Americans Frank Ribar, Dan Hill, and George McAfee, the 1938 team, No. 3 in the nation, became known as the "Iron Dukes." They shut out all of their regular-season opponents (including a sweet payback win over Pitt) but lost a squeaker to Southern Cal in the Rose Bowl. Wade's 1941 team also went undefeated and was ranked second before losing in the Rose Bowl, but the game was not played in Pasadena. Because of the recent Japanese bombing at Pearl Harbor and the desire to avoid crowds on the West Coast, that year's game was held in Durham. Semi-permanent bleachers erected on the rim of Duke Stadium allowed 56,000 people to see Duke lose to Oregon State. Never again would the Blue Devils come within shouting distance of the national championship. The biggest crowd ever (57,500) at the stadium was when Duke and neighboring North Carolina met in 1949, toward the end of Wade's tenure.

One piece at a time, the stands surrounding the original stadium were removed, eventually bringing seating capacity down to 33,941. As the Duke basketball program (housed in nearby Cameron Indoor Stadium) rose in prominence, the football program receded. Occasional ACC titles were won, but this fact remains: Following the 1960 season, when Duke beat Arkansas in the Cotton Bowl, the blue and white have not been back to a major bowl and have not finished any season ranked in the top twenty. Things looked promising with Steve Spurrier as coach, but after three years he returned to Florida, his alma mater. Still, Duke has a storied football tradition. In 1967, after hearing from alumni and former players, the university administration approved renaming the stadium in honor of Wade, the coldly efficient strategist who had put Duke on the map three decades earlier.

Prior to the 1980s, the proud old facility was looking a bit down at the heels, so aluminum seats and lights were installed, as was a new press box on the west side. New locker rooms were part of the Murray Building, located off the north concourse of Wade Stadium. The track was rubberized in 1990 and has since played a bigger role at the stadium, hosting a number of international track meets and the NCAA championships twice. An $18 million project began in 2000, with the changes taking place immediately outside the stadium. In the face of nine losing seasons in the 1990s, AD Tom Alleva called the five-level, 62,000-square-foot, multipurpose facility an indication that the rebirth of Duke football was more than just a dream.

Sanford Stadium (Georgia)

Dr. Charles Herty had learned about football as a graduate student at Johns Hopkins, and he introduced it as a faculty member at the University of Georgia. In a quadrangle bordered by dorms and academic buildings, he laid out Herty Field, where the Bulldogs played from 1892 to 1910. It was replaced by a new athletic home, Sanford Field, located beside Tanyard Creek. Like Herty before him, Dr. Steadman Sanford was a professor and a booster of the football team. Sanford Field, where baseball was also played, was just some wooden grandstands that held a few thousand spectators. Sanford, later dean, president, and chancellor of the UGa system, fancied a tangled hollow downstream that might be just the place for a big stadium. Many schools then refused to make the trip to Athens, and the game against Georgia Tech was held each year at spacious Grant Field in Atlanta.

Something had to be done, and Sanford was the man to do it. He convinced Georgia alumni to sign promissory notes worth $360,000 to build a 30,000-seat (18,000 on the north side and 12,000 on the south) facility in the spot he had chosen. In eighteen

—Courtesy of Georgia sports information department

months, mules and convict labor transformed the wooded valley into Sanford Stadium. Sanford was initially opposed to the idea of planting privet hedges between the stands and the field, but he relented and thus made possible one of the most endearing traditions in college football. The term "between the hedges" is said to have originated with sportswriter Grantland Rice. The inaugural game played amid that esteemed shrubbery was on October 12, 1929. Sanford had convinced mighty Yale to make its first foray below the Mason-Dixon line. But to the chagrin of the Elis, Georgia won 15–0 with Vernon "Catfish" Smith accounting for all the points—he caught a touchdown pass, returned a blocked punt for a score, kicked an extra point, and tackled a Yale player in the end zone for a safety. A crowd of 33,000 was there, and much of the overflow sat on a hill and railroad tracks to the east, another festive tradition at Georgia in the decades to come.

Although the stock market crashed a week later, bringing on the Great Depression, attendance at Sanford Stadium was strong enough that the debt was paid off a year early. Field-level lights were installed at the stadium in 1940, the second year of Wally Butts' long coaching reign. His 1942 team featured a couple of Pennsylvania running backs, Heisman Trophy winner Frank Sinkwich and Charley Trippi. They went 11–1 with a Rose Bowl defeat of UCLA to win the national crown. The 1940s were glory days for the Bulldogs, who compiled a seventeen-game winning streak right after World War II.

Sanford Stadium expanded to 36,000 seats in 1949 and 43,621 in 1964 with bleachers in the end zones. The field-level lights were removed at that time. Major work was done in 1967, when both sets of stands were double-decked (adding nearly 20,000 seats) and a new press box was built on the south side. The architectural firm Heery & Heery did the design and would be involved in four subsequent alterations to the stadium. In the early 1970s, when many other schools were installing articifial turf, Georgia refrained.

Perhaps the most significant thing to ever happen in UGa football history was when coach Vince Dooley convinced running back Herschel Walker to pursue higher education in Athens. Walker's achievements have been well chronicled: thrice an all-American, he led the red and black to the 1980 national championship (capped by a Sugar Bowl win over Notre Dame), scored 52 touchdowns, gained more than 5,000 yards, and won the 1982 Heisman Trophy. During Walker's sophomore season, both levels of the east end of Sanford Stadium were enclosed (at a cost of $11.5 million), raising seating capacity to 82,122. A modern lighting system was installed prior to Walker's junior season, after which he went on to the pros.

The lower level of the stadium's west end was enclosed in 1991, and two later construction projects added a number of luxury boxes, elevating total seating to 86,520. UGa has blueprints for a west-end upper deck, which would top the 100,000 mark, but there is no immediate plan to enact that. Billy Payne, who had been an all-SEC defensive end in 1968, led the drive to make Atlanta (sixty-seven miles west of Athens) the host city for the 1996 summer Olympics. As a result, several of the Georgia athletic facilities were used, including Sanford Stadium for the medal round in soccer, aka "world football." To make room for a soccer field, the sixty-six-year-old hedges were removed, provoking dismay and outrage among the Bulldog faithful. But new hedges, propagated from the originals, were back in time for the 1996 season. Sanford Stadium is a large and handsome facility, a masterpiece of college football. Surely history can be found between the hedges.

Kinnick Stadium (Iowa)

With much help from all-Americans Aubrey Devine and Duke Slater, the Iowa Hawkeyes won twenty straight games and a pair of Big 10 titles in the early 1920s, but they would not finish atop the conference standings again until 1956. Although their wooden stadium on the east side of the Iowa River could hold 28,000 fans, it was in disrepair. So in 1929, the university invested $497,000 in a new facility on the west side of the river. It took six months to build, and both stands had seventy-nine rows, the lowest of which were quite close to the field. Iowa Stadium, with a seating capacity of 53,000, was an ambitious project. Perhaps too ambitious, because the Great Depression began just a week after the dedication game (a 7–7 tie with Illinois), and thus the debt was not paid off for ten years.

—Courtesy of Iowa sports information department

The black and gold had an undistinguished run after the stadium was built, at least until 1939, when coach Eddie Anderson's team went 6–1–1 and running back Nile Kinnick won the Heisman Trophy. His numbers (374 yards and five touchdowns) look puny to modern eyes, but he excelled in his time. Kinnick was a scholar, too, a Phi Beta Kappa who went on to earn a law degree. His Heisman Trophy acceptance speech contained a World War II reference which came to seem like a premonition after his death in a U.S. Navy training flight in 1943.

Portable bleachers were needed in 1955, when Iowa averaged over 60,000 in home attendance. For that reason, 7,000 permanent seats were installed in the south end, and a five-level press box was built on the west side. In 1972, a layer of artificial turf was put down, and Iowa Stadium was renamed in honor of Nile Kinnick. There had been a move to do that earlier, but Kinnick's father resisted, saying it was unfair to others who had lost their lives in the war effort. Almost thirty years after UI's hero died, a sportswriter for the *Cedar Rapids Gazette* campaigned for the change, and the administration concurred.

Iowa was a coaching graveyard until Hayden Fry arrived in 1979. The drawling Texan turned the Hawkeyes into contenders by his third year, when they went to the Rose Bowl. The fans responded, and Kinnick Stadium got matching stands in the north end, increasing seating capacity to 66,000. Fry's 1985 team, led by quarterback Chuck Long, spent five weeks at No. 1 in the national polls.

The stadium continued to evolve. Grass made its return in 1989, and fill-in sections between the end zones and east and west stands made room for 70,397 fans. Yet somehow the Hawkeyes exceeded capacity by nearly 5,000 per game in 1990. A $3 million renovation of the press box was done in 1995, along with the construction of eighteen "private viewing suites." A big new scoreboard went up in 1997, a year before Fry's retirement. To show its appreciation for all he had done over two decades (such as getting to 14 bowls and winning 143 games), the athletic department named all the football offices and facilities, excluding the stadium, the Hayden Fry Complex.

Peden Stadium (Ohio)

Chartered in 1804 as the first institution of higher learning in the state, Ohio University began playing organized football ninety years later. In 1929, as coach Don Peden was leading the Bobcats to a 9–0 record and the Buckeye Athletic Association title, the university opened its new stadium on the north shore of the Hocking River. Ohio Stadium had east and west stands with room for 12,000 fans and cost $185,000. The dedication game was a 14–0 defeat of Miami University.

Peden coached and served as AD at Ohio for twenty-seven years and helped found the Mid-American Conference in 1946. For these reasons, the campus landmark would later be renamed Peden Stadium. And the eight-lane track (rubberized in 1977) encircling the football field was named in honor of longtime athletic physician Blaine Goldsberry. At the bucolic campus in southeastern Ohio, where else would President Dwight Eisenhower's helicopter land in the 1950s and Lyndon Johnson's in the following decade but on the 50-yard line of Peden Stadium.

The green and white, paced by linebacker Dick Grecni and running backs Robert Brooks and Robert Harrison, won the 1960 small-college national championship. And the 1962 team, although not undefeated, played in the school's first bowl game, bowing to West Texas State in the Sun Bowl. In the mid-1980s, the Cats were trudging through a lonesome football valley when OU embarked on a three-phase renovation of the stadium. Two curving sections were added in the north end, bringing seating capacity to 19,000. The Peden Tower, built above the west stands, provided athletic department offices, club seating, locker rooms, and a press box on the fifth level. Lights and a south-end scoreboard completed the project, which cost $9 million. An overflow crowd of 22,233 was there in 1996 to see running back Kareem Wilson set a school record with 282 yards rushing as Ohio blanked Bowling Green 38–0.

Peden Stadium is among the smallest of the 115 NCAA Division I-A schools, which ostensibly must have facilities with at

—Courtesy of Ohio sports information department; photo by Scott Gardner

least 30,000 seats. Like several other Mid-American Conference schools, Ohio is fighting to retain that treasured status. Discussions are currently going on in Athens about how to raise money for expansion of the stadium.

Carter Stadium (Texas Christian)

In 1929, the TCU Horned Frogs were barreling toward their first Southwest Conference championship. Simultaneously and propitiously, a fundraising drive to build a new stadium pulled in $350,000. A key figure in that endeavor was Amon Carter, publisher of the *Fort Worth Star-Telegram* and a civic leader. Just as the city's airport, its primary art museum, and a lake would later bear his name, so did TCU's stadium on the western fringe of campus. With a seating capacity of 22,000, Carter Stadium was dedicated on October 11, 1930, when the Frogs ripped Arkansas 40–0.

The 1930s were a proud time for fans of the purple and white. Francis Schmidt had some strong teams, and when he left to coach at Ohio State, things got even better under Dutch Meyer. In 1935, two 10–0 teams, TCU and SMU (a bitter rival from nearby Dallas) met at Carter Stadium in what Texas sportswriters subsequently called the "game of the first half-century." A throng of 40,000 gathered to see a close win by the Mustangs, although both teams ended up in the two major bowls of the time, TCU in the Sugar and SMU in the Rose. Sammy Baugh, one of the greatest quarterbacks in the history of the game, had gone on to the NFL by 1938, but Meyer had another dandy team. Heisman Trophy winner Davey O'Brien, linebacker Ki Aldrich, and lineman I. B. Hale carried the Frogs to the national championship.

No significant changes were made to Carter Stadium during its first two decades. From 1948 to 1953, however, a three-phase expansion was done in which more rows were added to the east side, and both end zones were filled in, raising seating capacity to 37,000. After all-America running back Jim Swink paced TCU to the 1955 SWC title, the stadium received a steep 9,000-seat upper deck on the west side with a new press box at the top. This was in the days of one-platoon football and small budgets, minimal tele-

78 HOME FIELD

—Courtesy of TCU sports information department

vision impact, and no pro football presence in Texas, when a private school like TCU could go toe-to-toe with the heavyweights. In the mid- to late 1950s, the Horned Frogs scored victories in intersectional games with such teams as Alabama, Pittsburgh, Southern California, Ohio State, Penn State, and Syracuse.

Like so many schools, in the early 1970s TCU installed artificial turf and then took it out twenty years later. There were a number of lean seasons in Fort Worth, but coach Jim Wacker had it going in 1984. The stadium was newly lighted, he had an outstanding runner in Kenneth Davis, and the team went 8–4 and played in a bowl game for the first time since 1965. A record crowd of 47,280 saw the TCU-Texas game. But the momentum was halted with revelations of a slush fund which paid top players like Davis.

Aluminum benches replaced weathered wooden seating in the east and west stands of Carter Stadium in 1985 and in the upper deck in 1991, which reduced seating capacity to 44,008. A new scoreboard graced the north end the next year. After the dissolution of the SWC in 1995, TCU was not invited (along with Texas, Texas A&M, Texas Tech, and Baylor) to join the Big 8 and form the Big 12. So the Frogs participated in the Western Athletic Conference for six seasons prior to joining Conference USA. LaDainian Tomlinson led the nation in rushing in 1999 and 2000, including an NCAA-record 406 yards against UT-El Paso at Carter Stadium during the former season.

Kyle Field (Texas A&M)

In the earliest years of football at Texas A&M University, games were held on the main grounds for military drilling. Fortunately for the Aggies, agriculture professor Edwin Kyle took it upon himself to provide a stadium of sorts just south of there. In 1905, he spent $313 of his own money to buy lumber with which to erect bleachers capable of holding 500 fans. The Corps of Cadets showed their gratitude by informally naming it Kyle Field. The all-purpose athletic area, which would serve for the next quarter-century, underwent almost constant change and eventually came to have grandstands and a seating capacity of 8,500. That was not nearly big enough for the crowds who wanted to see the Ags, especially in their biennial Thanksgiving tilt with the University of Texas.

The athletic department was $17,000 in debt, and business manager James Sullivan knew that a larger, not to mention permanent, stadium was in order. It took Sullivan almost ten years to achieve his dream, but he was successful. Campus enthusiasm was aided by the A&M football team, Southwest Conference champs in 1925 and 1927, led by coach Dana Bible and offensive star Joel Hunt. Architecture professors Ernest Langford and Carl Sandstedt served as construction superintendents of the new stadium, which was also known as Kyle Field. Begun in 1927 and completed two years later at a cost of $365,000, the U-shaped facility had a running track and 32,890 seats. Students, alumni, and dignitaries from all over the state gathered in College Station for the final game of the 1929 season. The Aggies defeated Texas 13–0.

Building a new stadium did not turn the maroon and white into world-beaters. They were at .500 or below four of their first six seasons at Kyle Field. Attendance at most games in the 1930s was poor, and the athletic department was sinking in debt. But coach and AD Homer Norton persuaded some wealthy alums to help out and at least stop the bleeding. Money and morale both picked up in 1939 when the Aggies won every game, including the Sugar Bowl, to take the national championship. Their top player was bruising running back John Kimbrough.

Texas A&M won two more SWC crowns before World War II took its toll, and it had some woeful years until the mid-1950s. Paul "Bear" Bryant whipped the Aggies into shape by 1956, when they had a 9–0–1 record but could not play in a post-season bowl because they had been caught cheating. Prior to Bryant's departure for Alabama, Kyle Field was modified for the first time. About twenty rows were added to the middle of the west-side stands, lending limited but good seating to the stadium. A new press box and lighting were also welcome additions.

— Courtesy of Texas A&M sports information department

More changes came in 1967. Even though Texas A&M won just 34 percent of its games in the 1960s, it was time to expand Kyle Field. Twin upper decks, each with 9,000 seats, were built. The track remained in place, but it was no longer used for track meets after the university constructed a new facility one-half mile to the west.

Artificial turf, laid down in 1970, would be replaced by grass twenty-six years later. Kyle Field underwent another major expansion in 1980 when two third decks were built above the first pair, bringing seating capacity to 70,210. Coach Jackie Sherrill, lured from Pittsburgh in 1982, took his lumps for a while but got the Ags in the Cotton Bowl three straight seasons. It was more of the same for Sherrill's successor, R. C. Slocum. He recruited linebacker Dat Nguyen, surely the most decorated Vietnamese-American football player ever. Nguyen, who started all fifty-one games of his college career, was gone when the biggest change in the stadium's long history began. The north-end horseshoe was removed, and a massive three-level block of seats, sixty-five feet closer to the field, was built at a cost of $35 million. When the Aggies and Notre Dame met at Kyle Field in 2001, the game was seen by more than 87,000 fans, the largest crowd ever at a football game in the Lone Star State.

Florida Field (Florida)

They had shared quarters with the baseball team for years, so the Florida Gators were quite pleased when the university began work on a football-only facility south of the old place. Excavation and construction took six months, and Florida Field, with a seating capacity of 21,269, was ready to go on November 8, 1930, when UF and Alabama faced off. Red Barber, a Florida student who later went on to fame as a baseball announcer, did the play-by-play. Alas, the Crimson Tide threw a 20–0 shutout.

In 1934, although the war had been over for fifteen years, Florida Field was dedicated to Americans who had died in World War I. After the Great Depression and another global conflict, the west stands were expanded, and with bleachers in the north and

— Courtesy of Florida sports information department

south ends, stadium capacity rose to 40,116. Lights were added at the same time. UF was not a major player on the national scene; in fact, the Gators usually could not compete with the big boys of the Southeastern Conference—Bama, Tennessee, Georgia, and LSU. They achieved a modicum of success under coach Bob Woodruff, playing in their first bowl game in 1952, yet they did not get into a major bowl until the mid-1960s. That was when Florida Field grew again. An addition to the east side made it a 62,800-seat facility. The quarterback, kicker, and punter of the orange and blue in 1966 was Heisman Trophy winner Steve Spurrier, who would later return to Gainesville and bring more football glory than since the program began in 1906.

Artificial turf made its debut there in 1971 and would be removed in favor of grass nineteen years later. A more significant change occurred when the coaches and athletic administration, responding to the age-old desire to win games, made Florida the first SEC school to thoroughly integrate its football team with players like Nat Moore, Wes Chandler, and Sammy Green. No further changes were made to the stadium until 1982, when a 10,000-seat, three-level section was erected in the south end. UF also built a new press box (with forty-six luxury boxes) on the west side. A longtime Gator benefactor was honored prior to the 1989 season when the building was named after him: Ben Hill Griffin Stadium. That was the year coach Galen Hall was forced out in a messy situation that depressed Florida fans. Nevertheless, Hall's 1984 and 1985 teams, both 9–1–1, were an indication that UF was moving up.

In 1991, Spurrier's second year as coach, a steep north-end section costing $17 million made Florida Field essentially complete with a seating capacity of 83,000, although the Gators regularly play before crowds of 85,000-plus. The stadium, seen from the outside or inside, is not seamless but has a rather jerry-rigged look. Spurrier dubbed it "the swamp," alleging that only Gators could get out alive. Somewhat more objectively, the *Sporting News* agreed, twice calling Florida Field crowds the loudest and most demonstrative of all. And those fans had plenty to cheer about. Spurrier, taking advantage of the hotbed of high school football that was the Sunshine State, brought in a bunch of big-time athletes who started winning the SEC title with regularity. Quarterback Danny Wuerffel (a Heisman Trophy winner like his coach) guided the team as they administered a 52–20 beating to Florida State in the Sugar Bowl, securing the 1996 national championship.

Notre Dame Stadium (Notre Dame)

Notre Dame football did not begin with Knute Rockne, although it may seem that way. He and Gus Dorais helped popularize the forward pass for the 1913 Ramblers (soon to become the Fighting Irish), and Rockne was head coach five years later. Under his guidance, Notre Dame reached national prominence. Rockne boldly took his teams all over the country, forming rivalries with Southern California, Army, and several Big 10 schools. During a career that spanned thirteen seasons, this great coach won six national titles, had the Four Horsemen, and made the famous "win one for the Gipper" speech in the locker room of Yankee Stadium

—Courtesy of Notre Dame sports information department

before a crucial game. The Irish were enormously popular in the big cities, especially Chicago; three times in the late 1920s they played in games at Soldier Field seen by more than 110,000 people.

At home in South Bend, the gold and blue played in the southeast corner of campus at Cartier Field, which could hold just 30,000 fans. Rockne, also the athletic director and business manager, realized a bigger stadium was needed, and the university's administration agreed. Cartier Field was razed prior to the 1929 season, forcing the Irish to play all their games on the road. Adjacent to the former stadium, excavation and construction began on a new one. Rockne consulted with the Osborne Engineering Company, which had designed more than fifty pro and college stadiums from coast to coast. Patterned after Michigan Stadium (which had been patterned after the Yale Bowl), though on a smaller scale, Notre Dame Stadium cost $750,000 and contained 400 tons of steel, 15,000 cubic yards of concrete, and two million bricks. The first rows were remarkably close to the field.

It was ready at the start of the 1930 season. The Irish beat Southern Methodist and did the same to Navy a week later in the dedication game witnessed by 40,593 fans. The team went 10–0 and won another national championship before Rockne, traveling to California for a much-needed vacation, died in a plane crash. As if that tragedy were not enough, the next decade was rather unkind to Notre Dame fans, whose team was coached by a pair of Rockne protégés who could not sustain his penchant for winning. The stadium was sold out just three times before Frank Leahy, who also had played for Rockne, took over. He had three Heisman Trophy winners and claimed four national championships in the 1940s.

Although Notre Dame Stadium was never actually expanded, its capacity slowly increased during this time to over 59,000. The Irish floundered again before Ara Parseghian arrived, taking them back to the pinnacle twice. He was the coach when Notre Dame ended a high-minded but fairly unrealistic forty-five-year bowl ban, encountering Texas in the Cotton Bowl after the 1969 season. The Longhorns won it, however.

For a guy whose college career began as a sub on the junior varsity squad, quarterback Joe Montana turned out all right. He rose through the ranks, led the Irish to the 1977 national crown, and cemented his status as one of the school's all-time greats by winning four Super Bowls with the San Francisco 49ers. He was a bigger pro success than any of Notre Dame's seven Heisman Trophy winners, although Paul Hornung (1956) did quite well with the Green Bay Packers.

The lush bluegrass field at Notre Dame Stadium never gave way to artificial turf, and with the help of portable lights, night football began in 1982. As just the forty-fourth-largest college football stadium, it created one of the toughest tickets in all of sports—a Notre Dame home game. A sellout streak that began in 1966 continues unabated. Thus, the alumni urged expansion of the stadium in 1991. The institutional decision was made in 1994, and the $50 million project was completed in time for the 1997 season. Twenty-six rows were added all the way around, lights were erected at each corner, and a new three-level press box was built on the west side. New scoreboards were installed in the north and south ends, and considerable infrastructure work was performed. All that money and labor resulted in an 80,225-seat, aesthetically pleasing facility, one suited for perhaps the most storied program in the game's history.

Skelly Stadium (Tulsa)

Little is known about McNulty Park, where the University of Tulsa played home football games in the 1920s. But coach Elmer Henderson must not have liked it, because he began cajoling wealthy Tulsa oilmen about the need for a new stadium. The Board of Trustees was amenable, especially after William Skelly, a longtime friend of TU, gave $125,000. Another $150,000 was raised between groundbreaking on May 11, 1930, and dedication day on October 4. Skelly Field, which had 14,500 seats, was almost full when the Golden Hurricane met Arkansas and took a 26–6 win. The stadium was such a pleasant home that in its first five seasons there, Tulsa played just eight games out of town.

Nothing changed at Skelly Field for a while, except in 1938 the university gave it to the Tulsa school system in a real estate swap, leasing the stadium for the next thirty years before another deal returned it to TU's ownership. The Golden Hurricane was master

—Courtesy of Tulsa sports information department

of the Missouri Valley Conference in the early 1940s and played in the Sugar Bowl twice and the Orange Bowl once. Glenn Dobbs, an all-American in 1942 (when the team finished No. 4 in the nation), was an outstanding passer and punter who would later return to coach his alma mater.

Following the addition of 5,000 seats in the north end in 1947, Tulsa's football facility was renamed Skelly Stadium. The next expansion coincided with another golden era for the Golden Hurricane. With Dobbs running the show, quarterbacks Jerry Rhome and Billy Anderson made wide receiver Howard Twilley their favorite target. He caught a total of 239 passes in 1964 and 1965. Both Rhome and Twilley were all-Americans and Heisman Trophy runners-up. Amid such success, the track at Skelly Stadium was removed, the field was lowered, and box seats were installed. Stands were built in the south end, and more rows were added to the west side, which was topped off with a new press box. Seating capacity grew to 40,385, and the price tag for the whole job was $1.25 million.

Artificial turf made its debut at Skelly Stadium in 1972, and later that decade, a local oil company donated $350,000 for refurbishing and infrastructure work. In the 1980s, new scoreboards were erected in the north and south ends, and the stadium got a lighting system. Top-ranked Oklahoma paid a visit to Tulsa in 1987, and the largest crowd in stadium history, 47,350, saw a 65–0 Sooner mauling.

Apart from serving as home to TU (now a member of the Western Athletic Conference), Skelly Stadium has hosted a National Football League exhibition game, an American Football League exhibition game, a Billy Graham rally, and a minor league baseball exhibition game, and has had two pro tenants: the Oklahoma Outlaws of the United States Football League and the Tulsa Roughnecks of the North American Soccer League.

Scott Stadium (Virginia)

Founded by Thomas Jefferson as an "academical village," the University of Virginia has an interesting but tortured football history. Faculty and administrators protested creeping professionalism and enforced a strict athletic code. So they were none too pleased when, in 1913, UVa built 8,000-seat Lambeth Stadium, which served as home to the football, baseball, track, and lacrosse teams. Like much of the architecture on the Virginia campus, it was a stately building with colonnades on both sides. But volatility in the athletic department and student indifference (such as fraternity brothers betting openly against their own team) made it hard to compete. Earle "Greasy" Neale had moderate success coaching the Cavaliers from 1923 to 1928 and quit; he later won two NFL titles with the Philadelphia Eagles.

Nevertheless, the university found land on which to build a new stadium, and rector Frederic W. Scott financed it as a way to honor his parents. With gently sloping east and west stands, Scott Stadium had a seating capacity of 22,000. It was first used on October 18, 1931, when the Cavs lost to Virginia Military Institute. The tug-of-war between academics and athletics was fierce in Charlottesville, much like what happened to the schools that eventually formed the Ivy League. Indicative was a statement by AD Norton Pritchett: "Virginia is not going in for 'big league' football and never will, so long as I can prevent it."

Likewise, Scott Stadium remained virtually unchanged for more than four decades. There was no need to expand, and the Wahoos, as they are known in the shadows of the Blue Ridge Mountains, dared not try. Occasionally, UVa fans took pride in individual stars such as Bill Dudley, Johnny Papit, Henry Jordan, Gary Cuozzo, and Frank Quayle who could do little to change the losing culture. Compounding matters was the Gooch Report, issued in 1951 by a faculty committee headed by a former Cav letterman, which urged the abolition of athletic scholarships and the football program itself. Although that rather drastic possibility did not happen, president Colgate Darden affirmed that the Cavs would not play in bowl games, regardless of regular-season success.

Coincidentally or not, when Virginia joined the newly formed Atlantic Coast Conference in 1953, it began a dismal era, even by the orange and blue's own low standards. The nadir was a twenty-eight-game losing streak from 1958 to 1960. Games at Scott Stadium were little more than social events for many years. The stadium finally got a new look in 1974 when artificial turf, aluminum seats, and other modernizing touches were done.

When the Cavs hosted VMI in 1975 (their only win of the season), it was Virginia's first television appearance. Construction problems caused a two-year delay in the stadium's first expansion, but it was ready in 1980—additional rows to both lower stands, plus two upper decks, which pushed seating capacity to 40,000. A new press box was built, too.

George Welsh, formerly the coach at Navy, was hired in 1982. Despite a 2–9 record in his inaugural season, the wheel had begun to turn. With Welsh in charge, Virginia slowly became competitive in the ACC and then nationally. In 1984, the Cavs broke into the Associated Press' top-twenty-five rankings for the first time since 1952 and played in their first-ever bowl game, defeating Purdue in the Peach Bowl. Quarterback Shawn Moore and receiver Herman Moore finished fourth and sixth, respectively, in Heisman Trophy voting in 1990, when UVa briefly reached No. 1 in the nation. A record crowd of 49,700 filled Scott Stadium for the Georgia Tech game, which the visiting Yellow Jackets won. Virginia went on to play in the Sugar Bowl, however. Another milestone came in 1995 when UVa hosted and defeated No. 2 Florida State, ending the Seminoles' twenty-nine-game ACC winning streak.

During Welsh's tenure, many things changed at Scott Stadium. Lights were installed in 1983, and new locker rooms were built two years later in the south end. Grass replaced artificial turf in 1995, thanks largely to a $5 million donation by alumnus David A. Harrison III, prompting the university to name the field after him. A three-year fundraising and construction project commenced in 1998, transforming the place. A 100-foot-high videoboard was installed behind 4,000 new seats in the north end, previously a grassy hillside. The biggest change of all came in the south end, where the lower and upper levels were wrapped around, bringing seating capacity to 60,017. These and other alterations inside and outside the stadium cost $86 million, of which $23 million came from former player Carl Smith, who had gone on to success as an investment banker. In appreciation, UVa took renaming to new heights. The Cavaliers now play at Carl Smith Center, home of David A. Harrison III Field at Scott Stadium.

Floyd Stadium (Middle Tennessee)

Horace Jones, who headed the math department at Middle Tennessee, was also a one-man athletic committee. He was most responsible for the university setting up an athletic field with portable bleachers in the northwest corner of campus. For his volunteer efforts, MTSU named the humble facility Jones Field, and it was dedicated in the 1933 season opener when the Blue Raiders and Jacksonville State fought to a scoreless tie.

A concrete grandstand was built in the late 1940s, making room for 6,200 fans. Charles Murphy was just beginning his twenty-two-year reign as coach at Middle Tennessee, and he would have four undefeated teams—1947, 1957, 1959, and 1965. One of Murphy's top players was quarterback Teddy Morris, who led the Blue Raiders to three Ohio Valley Conference titles. Due in part to Morris' fine play, the stadium was twice expanded in the 1960s to a seating capacity of 15,000 with a new west-side press box. In 1973, to help accommodate Murfreesboro-area high school football teams, MTSU installed artificial turf and lights at the sta-

— Courtesy of Middle Tennessee sports information department

dium. Six years later, the university decided to honor its ancient past. Johnny "Red" Floyd coached the team in 1917 and again from 1935 to 1938, winning 78 percent of his games. Those achievements were recognized by naming the stadium after Floyd, although the field still bears the Jones name.

Quarterback Marvin Collier and defensive back Don Griffin powered the 1985 Middle Tennessee team to an 11–0 regular-season record, which put them at No. 1 in NCAA I-AA ranks, although they lost in the first round of the playoffs. With an eye on moving up to I-A competition, MTSU embarked on a $25 million expansion and renovation of Floyd Stadium in January 1997. The result was a new press box with one level set aside for sixteen luxury boxes, a weight room in the north end, a new scoreboard in the south end, and more than double the previous number of seats. Construction went slower than expected, and the project was not completed until the summer of 1998. The first game at the revamped Floyd Stadium, witnessed by 27,568 fans, was a 28–27 win over Tennessee State that was sealed in the final seconds.

Spartan Stadium (San Jose State)

The Great Depression was in full swing by 1933, and the federal government's Work Projects Administration had a variety of ways to keep people employed. They built schools, post offices, municipal swimming pools, and even a few football stadiums. San Jose State got one, a cozy facility seating just over 15,000 fans. Spartan Stadium was inaugurated on October 7, 1933, with a 44–6 defeat of San Francisco State.

The stadium, a mile from the SJSU campus, was fairly new when the Spartans had perhaps their greatest era. From 1937 to 1940, under coach Dudley DeGroot, they won 46 games. The 1939 team, with small-college all-Americans Lloyd Thomas and Leroy Zimmerman, went 13–0 and gave up just 29 points. In subsequent decades, the blue and gold featured Bob Pifferini, Bill Walsh, Dick Vermeil, Steve DeBerg, and Louie Wright, all of whom went on to pro football success.

—Courtesy of San Jose State sports information department

Spartan Stadium remained unchanged until 1980 when an open-air press box and upper deck were built on the west side, raising seating capacity to 22,000. Five years later, the stadium was expanded again, up to 30,456. That came from more seats on the west side, private boxes for well-heeled Spartan fans, and bleachers in the north and south ends. San Jose State's record crowd there was in 1990 when a 42–7 defeat of rival Fresno State was seen by 31,218 people, although 37,000 later attended a ZZ Top concert. Pro and college soccer, religious convocations, commencements, and other events have been held at the stadium as well.

In 1994, the Simpkins Stadium Center and Administration Building was erected adjacent to the Spartans' home. The $3 million facility contained, among other things, locker rooms, a weight room, and the office of athletic director Chuck Bell. He was the driving force behind the Silicon Valley Football Classic, which began at Spartan Stadium following the 2000 season.

Williams-Brice Stadium (South Carolina)

Melton Field, a 7,000-seat campus facility, was home to South Carolina football, although a 15,000-seat wooden bowl at the state fairgrounds was used for big games, especially when the Gamecocks met Clemson, their main rival. A group of USC alumni, the mayor of Columbia, the Chamber of Commerce, and others met in early 1932 to discuss building a stadium that could be used by the university and local high schools. After overcoming some financial difficulties, land south of the fairgrounds was purchased and construction began. The Virginia Bridge and Iron Company and W. A. Cray and Sons built 17,600-seat Municipal Stadium at a cost of $82,000. It had a quarter-mile track and thirty-seven rows, east and west, with room to grow. On October 6, 1934, there were flags on Main Street, a band concert, a parade to the stadium, and an airplane which flew low and dropped the game ball. USC, coached by Billy Laval, beat Virginia Military Institute 22–6.

The stadium was deeded to the university in 1941 and got a new name—Carolina Stadium. Bleachers in the north and south ends were built, later replaced by steel stands, as the facility expanded to a seating capacity of 34,000 and then 43,000 in 1957. The Gamecocks had some good players over the years, such as lineman Lou Sossamon, running backs Steve Wadiak and Alex Hawkins, and defensive back/kick returner Bobby Bryant. But they did not win very often. The garnet and white somehow made it into the inaugural Gator Bowl (following the 1945 season) with a 2–3–3 record and lost to Wake Forest. They would wait twenty-four years to play in another bowl and did not win one until 1995. A charter member of the Atlantic Coast Conference beginning in 1953, South Carolina won just one championship, in 1969, and had minimal impact on the national football scene.

USC fans thought it would all be different when Paul Dietzel was hired away from Army in 1966. Prior to that, he had earned a national championship at LSU, but he would find out how hard it was to win in Columbia, leaving after nine years with a losing record. Dietzel, also the AD, began clamoring for a new stadium, but that went nowhere when campus academics (particularly in law and nursing) pointed out that their building needs were at the top of the university's list of priorities. So Dietzel compromised by going after another goal—expansion and renovation of Carolina Stadium. The process got a boost from the estate of Mrs. Martha Williams Brice, whose husband had played for the Gamecocks in the 1920s before becoming a furniture tycoon. A bequest of $2.75 million, combined with $5 million of athletic department money, allowed big changes. The track was removed, and artificial turf was installed, as was aluminum seating throughout the stadium. A new cantilevered lighting system went in, and an upper deck on the west side brought seating capacity to 53,865. The lady's generosity was repaid in a familiar way by renaming it Williams-Brice Stadium. The first game at the revamped facility was on September 9, 1972, a loss to Virginia.

Eight years later, George Rogers finally provided some excitement. He led the nation in rushing and claimed the Heisman Trophy. Not only was his number retired, but a nearby street became George Rogers Boulevard. After Rogers left and before the arrival of Sterling Sharpe (another of USC's all-time greats), Williams-Brice Stadium got a matching east-side upper deck, making room for 72,400 fans. Attendance was good, although teams

—Courtesy of South Carolina sports information department; photo by Jim Covington

generally were not. In 1992, after twenty-one years as an independent, South Carolina joined the SEC, a hypercompetitive conference.

The stadium grew again in 1995 and 1996 with a new press box on the west side, VIP amenities, and a restoration of grass to the field. New stands in the south end brought it up to a seating capacity of 80,250, among the biggest college football stadiums. A record crowd of 83,700 witnessed the 1997 Clemson game, a 47–21 mauling by the Tigers. More than 4,000 people gathered at Williams-Brice Stadium on December 4, 1998, to welcome Lou Holtz as the new coach of the Gamecocks. Holtz had been a head coach for twenty-seven seasons, and like Paul Dietzel many years before, he had won a national championship (at Notre Dame), but his first USC team went 0–11 before turning it around the next season with a win over Ohio State in the Outback Bowl.

Citrus Bowl (Central Florida)

Long before Orlando became a city with a theme park for every taste, it was in the throes of the Great Depression. President Franklin Roosevelt put people to work, authorizing the WPA to erect a 10,000-seat stadium just south of downtown, costing $115,000. Orlando Stadium, which opened in 1936, served a variety of purposes, but primarily high school football. Jacksonville, its neighbor up the road, started the Gator Bowl in 1946, so Orlando followed suit. The stadium's name was changed to the Tangerine Bowl, and Catawba and Maryville were invited to play in the first college football game ever held there, on January 1, 1947. Long known as the "little bowl with the big heart" because it benefited a local children's hospital, the Tangerine Bowl was soon the unofficial small-college national championship game.

The stadium's seating capacity expanded to 17,000 and a press box was finally built in 1968, although the bowl game was on shaky ground. The University of Florida was the first major school to participate, in 1973, but with the embarrassing stipulation that the game be played in the Gators' stadium in Gainesville. With television coverage and the addition of 33,000 more seats in the mid-1970s, however, the Tangerine Bowl—both the game and the stadium—were moving up. The Florida Department of Citrus got involved in 1983, becoming the first title sponsor of a college bowl game, and thus it became the Citrus Bowl. In 1989, a $30 million project resulted in upper decks on the east and west sides, thirty luxury boxes, and a pair of 9,000-square-foot locker rooms. The 1990 national championship, or at least one version of it, was decided there when Georgia Tech defeated Nebraska 45–21. With tie-ins to major conferences and a series of new corporate sponsors, the Citrus Bowl's payouts grew to more than $4 million per team. Nearly 73,000 fans gathered on January 1, 1998, to see Florida defeat Penn State, one of many epic battles to have been played in the erstwhile WPA-era high school stadium. It has also hosted motocross races, rock concerts, World Cup and Olympic soccer, and pro football in the form of the Florida Blazers of the World Football League and the Orlando Rage of the XFL.

In 1963, the year Western Kentucky beat Coast Guard in the Tangerine Bowl, Florida Tech was founded on the outskirts of Orlando. It became the University of Central Florida fifteen years later, and a rudimentary football program was started in 1979. The Golden Knights played in the NCAA's Division III with non-scholarship athletes. Their home was the big old facility downtown, even if average attendance was on the south side of 10,000. It was not easy, what with a 0–10 record in 1982 and a mid-season firing of coach Lou Saban in 1984. The athletic department was more than $1 million in debt when Gene McDowell became coach and AD. On the way up to Division I-A competition in 1996, UCF won more games, drew more fans, and played better teams. The most prominent moral victory came when they met Nebraska in Lincoln in 1997 and led at the half before losing to the national champs. And another breakthrough came in 2000 when Central Florida beat Alabama on the road.

By far the most prominent player to have come out of UCF has been quarterback Daunte Culpepper, who started every game from 1995 to 1998, the year the Golden Knights went 9–2. Culpepper finished sixth in Heisman Trophy voting, was chosen in the first round of the NFL draft, and now plays for the Minnesota Vikings. Although student enrollment tops 32,000, Central Florida remains a school with little history and little clout and thus continues to search for a conference affiliation. By any measure, the program is on the rise, and AD Steve Sloan can only anticipate the Knights playing on New Year's Day at their home stadium.

Martin Stadium (Washington State)

Ever since Washington State University opened its doors in 1892, there has been a football stadium in the middle of campus. The original Soldier Field was renamed Rogers Field ten years later to honor the governor, John Rogers. An overflow crowd of 22,000 was there in 1930 when the Cougars, led by all-America linemen Mel Hein and Turk Edwards, beat Southern California 7–6 and went on to play in the Rose Bowl. Not even the clearest clairvoyant, however, knew that it would take sixty-seven years for WSU to get back to Pasadena.

—Courtesy of Washington State sports information department

That stadium was razed and a new one, with a seating capacity of 23,500, was erected on the same spot in 1936. Also known as Rogers Field, it was an all-wood structure set on concrete pilings with a press box on the south side and an electronic scoreboard in the west end. Although Rogers Field was entirely adequate for Washington State, home games were sometimes held in Spokane and Seattle. Located in a region of rolling wheat fields known as the Palouse, Pullman was eight miles from the Idaho border and was thus an isolated—not to mention cold—place for staging football games.

The Cougars had suffered through a 1–9 season in 1969 when fire destroyed the south stands. As a result, every home game in 1970 and 1971 was played at Joe Albi Stadium in Spokane. In the meantime, Los Angeles businessman Dan Martin donated a quarter of the $1 million needed to rebuild. That generous act was done with the stipulation that the stadium would be renamed for his father, Clarence Martin, another ex-governor. Martin Stadium, with lights and artificial turf, reopened on September 30, 1972, with a 44–25 loss to Utah. New seating on the north side three years later made room for 27,600 fans. Those fans got to witness the career of Jack Thompson, the "throwin' Samoan." Responsible for 7,698 yards in total offense, he was thrice all-Pac-10. Following on Thompson's heels were three other excellent quarterbacks, Timm Rosenbach, Drew Bledsoe, and Ryan Leaf.

Martin Stadium got another 12,400 seats in 1979 when the track was removed and the field dropped sixteen feet, creating a more intimate feel for spectators. The Martin family again gave $250,000. When Mike Price lifted WSU to a 10–2 record in 1997 (with a Rose Bowl loss to Michigan), he received several coach-of-the-year awards. The athletic department floated plans to expand Martin Stadium by 13,000 seats, which would, in theory, encourage big-name opponents to visit Pullman, which would help draw blue-chip recruits, which would help the Cougars keep winning. But a string of losing seasons, with sagging attendance figures, caused those plans to be shelved. In fact, 2,600 end-zone seats have been removed, so it got smaller and not larger. Since 1999, Martin Stadium has been the main home to the Idaho Vandals, whose 16,000-seat Kibbie Dome is too small according to NCAA Division I-A standards.

Glass Bowl (Toledo)

In 1930, the University of Toledo was in the process of building a new campus and moving in when Jim Nicholson was hired to coach the football team. Besides upgrading the schedule and recruiting, he designed a stadium. Nicholson's plans remained on the shelf for four years before work began. It was another WPA job, financed by $272,000 from the federal government and $42,000 from the city of Toledo and the university. A 300-man crew took a year to complete the work because bulldozers and other heavy equipment were not available. They built a 7,500-seat facility with two towers on the north end and a stone wall surrounding the field. The inaugural game (a 26–0 defeat of Bluffton on September 27, 1937) had to be postponed three days due to foul weather, while the dedication game on October 16 was a 21–7 loss to Akron.

Big changes came in 1946. The Rockets had not fielded a team

—Courtesy of Toledo sports information department

the previous three years due to World War II. Not only were 3,300 new seats in place, but the stadium got a name—the Glass Bowl. Toledo, headquarters of three major glass companies, had long been called the Glass City. Flat glass was donated for the press box and locker rooms, and a lighted glass sign was erected outside the enlarged stadium. Furthermore, in a burst of post-war optimism, the city fathers founded the Glass Bowl game, joining the Rose, Sugar, Orange, Cotton, Sun, Tangerine, and Gator bowls. It lasted just four years, from 1946 to 1949, and UT played in each game with the opponents being Bates, New Hampshire, Oklahoma City, and Cincinnati. The Glass Bowl game was discontinued, purportedly due to the advent of the Korean War.

Some fine athletes had suited up for the blue and gold, such as lineman Dan Bukovich, defensive back Emlen Tunnell, and running back Mel Triplett, and others would follow, such as lineman Mel Long, quarterback Gene Swick, lineman Dan Williams, and running back Wasean Tait. But quarterback Chuck Ealey stands above them all as one of the most intriguing players in the history of college football. After leading his Portsmouth, Ohio, team to thirty straight wins, it was more of the same at Toledo. Ealey guided the Rockets to a 35–0 record from 1969 to 1971 (with a No. 12 ranking in 1970) and was three-time player of the year in the Mid-American Conference. Ealey's exploits brought national attention to the program and nearly 20,000 fans per game to the stadium during his senior season. As a result, it got artificial turf and grew to a seating capacity of 18,500 in 1972.

Longtime sports information director Max Gerber did much of the planning for the Glass Bowl's latest renovation from 1988 to 1990 as another 8,000 seats were added, a new three-level press box (with forty-one "executive suites") was built on the west side, and the Larimer Athletic Complex went up in the north end. The $18.5 million project was done to save a proud but aging facility in dire need of attention. A record crowd of 33,040 was on hand for the opening game of the 1994 season, a three-point loss to Indiana State. The next year, coach Gary Pinkel's team went 11–0–1 with an overtime defeat of Nevada in the Las Vegas Bowl, bringing back memories of Chuck Ealey. Another record crowd, 34,950, piled into the Glass Bowl in 2001 to see the Rockets put a 38–7 whupping on Minnesota of the Big 10.

Orange Bowl (Miami)

The University of Miami was struggling in the early 1930s, once even declaring bankruptcy. The downtown campus was no campus at all, known to derisive students as "Cardboard College." The Hurricane football team played in Moore Park, a 9,000-seat facility. It served as home to the Orange Bowl Classic, second of the major bowl games. Local businessmen, led by Roddy Burdine, started the annual New Year's Day game and then believed a better stadium should be built to hold it, as well as UM's home games. They convinced the city to invest $340,000 in a 22,000-seat arena running east and west. Roddy Burdine Municipal Stadium (later renamed the Orange Bowl in a tribute to Florida's citrus industry) was dedicated on December 10, 1937, when Miami lost to Georgia. The first Orange Bowl game there, Auburn versus Michigan State, took place three weeks hence.

During World War II, stands erected in the east and west ends brought seating capacity to 35,030. An overflow crowd saw an unforgettable ending to the 1946 Orange Bowl game. The Canes and Holy Cross were tied in the waning seconds when a desperate Crusader pass was intercepted by UM's Al Hudson, who returned it 89 yards for the winning touchdown as time expired. In 1947, shortly after Winston Churchill received an honorary degree before a large convocation, the stadium was expanded by nearly 25,000 seats with north and south upper decks.

In the late 1940s, the university left its woeful downtown quarters for 160 acres set aside in Coral Gables, a few miles southwest of the Orange Bowl. Due mostly to the popularity of the January 1 game and not the Hurricanes, the stadium underwent three expansions in the early 1950s, making it a 75,000-seat facility. UM was on three-year NCAA probation in 1956 when the largest crowd in minor league baseball history (57,000) saw Satchel Paige, Miami's fifty-one-year-old pitcher, beat Columbus in an International League game.

The stadium was desegregated in 1961, the same year Miami started enrolling black students. After the west end was filled in, on both lower and upper decks, seating capacity peaked at 80,101. The Orange Bowl became the first bowl game played at night in

1965 when Texas and Alabama tangled. The following season marked the debut of defensive end Ted "the Mad Stork" Hendricks, a two-time all-American who was later a star with the Baltimore Colts, Green Bay Packers, and Oakland Raiders. He is still regarded by some as the greatest player in Miami history. Also in 1966, the Orange Bowl got another tenant—the Miami Dolphins. In 1971, after the first of five Super Bowls played in the Orange Bowl, UM's basketball program was suspended due to lack of funds and fan support. Football was not doing much better at the time; while Don Shula's Dolphins won consecutive NFL titles, the collegiate Hurricanes saw average home attendance drop to 17,000. But better times were ahead.

Artificial turf had a brief stay at the Orange Bowl, being replaced by grass in 1977, the same year 5,000 seats in the east end were removed. Later changes brought seating capacity to below 73,000. In his fifth season as coach, Howard Schnellenberger did the improbable: Miami won the 1983 national championship with a dramatic Orange Bowl win over Nebraska. His successor, Jimmy Johnson, brought in more thoroughbred athletes who kept UM at or near the top, starting a fifty-eight-game home winning streak. Miami won the 1987 crown, and coach Dennis Erickson led the team to another in 1989 and shared one more with Washington in 1991, Miami's first season as a member of the Big East Conference. Two Hurricanes have won the Heisman Trophy, quarterbacks Vinny Testaverde and Gino Torretta.

A $15 million renovation of the Orange Bowl in the aftermath of Hurricane Andrew could not stop the construction of Joe Robbie (now Pro Player) Stadium, and it suffered a double whammy in 1996 when the Dolphins and the fabled bowl game moved to the new stadium. Nevertheless, the Orange Bowl remains a historic football venue, a place where the game is played to a calypso beat, where the beams of the stadium rattle to the rhythm.

Reynolds Razorback Stadium (Arkansas)

The University of Arkansas first played home football games at a venue that was far from majestic—a roped-off field which

— Courtesy of Arkansas sports information department

later got enough wooden bleachers to hold 2,500 fans. Then FDR's Work Projects Administration came to the rescue and built a modest steel stadium on the west side of campus. A capacity crowd of 13,500 gathered in Fayetteville on October 8, 1938, for the dedication game, a narrow loss to Baylor. Originally named for Governor Carl E. Bailey, it soon became Razorback Stadium.

The scintillating play of running back Clyde Scott (a medalist in the 1948 Olympics) brought in more fans, which caused coach and athletic director John Barnhill to press for expansion of the stadium. In 1947, it got a pair of northern extensions, and soon more rows and a press box were erected on the west side for a total of 23,700 seats. At the same time, War Memorial Stadium was built in Little Rock. The Hogs had played occasional games in the state capital as early as 1907, and the construction of a 31,000-seat (and thrice-expanded to 53,727) facility that was, by most accounts, nicer than Razorback Stadium, was a welcome development. A half-century later, however, it would be a problem.

Another 5,200 seats were appended to the east side of Razorback Stadium in 1957, one season before Frank Broyles arrived. As coach and athletic director, he went on to have a huge impact on UA athletics. The Razorbacks had won a few Southwest Conference titles and played in some bowl games, but it was a fairly undistinguished record until Broyles put Arkansas on the map. His 1964 team won the national championship, and that was nearly repeated in 1965 except for a Cotton Bowl loss to LSU. Thus ended a twenty-two-game winning streak.

Artificial turf was in, and further expansion brought seating capacity to 42,678 in 1969, the year of the "big shootout" in Fayetteville. On a cold, cloudy day, No. 1 Texas and No. 2 Arkansas battled in front of a crowd that included President Richard Nixon. Quarterback Bill Montgomery had the Hogs up by two touchdowns before they lost a 15–14 heartbreaker. Following the 1976 season, Broyles turned over the coaching reins to Lou Holtz, who spent seven years in Fayetteville, which he once described as "not the end of the world, but you can see it from there." In 1985, the stadium got a fairly steep west-side upper deck with luxury boxes and expanded press box. Still, an all-steel 50,000-seat stadium in the Ozarks was not so impressive to recruits who expected only the best.

Lights were added in 1990, although the first actual night game at Razorback Stadium did not happen until seven years later. A lot had changed by then, including a return to natural grass on the field and a switch from the SWC (where Arkansas had been the only non-Texas member) to the Southeastern Conference. That launched a number of other such changes in the college football landscape. The Hogs lost a lot in the early SEC years until Houston Nutt got the head coaching job in 1998.

Just as Arkansas had to struggle to compete with the big boys of the SEC, the campus football facility had to keep up, as well. Broyles led the charge to raise money (the original figure was $66 million, later escalated to $85 million and finally to $103 million) to bring Razorback Stadium up to par. Besides a rather dramatic exterior makeover and the ubiquitous VIP amenities (132 luxury boxes), an upper deck was built on the east side, and the south end got lower and upper decks, raising seating capacity in 2001 to 72,000. Broyles, the Boss Hog, also looks to the future, when the north end will have two decks, adding another 25,000 or so seats.

The biggest donor in the process has been the foundation of late media magnate Donald Reynolds, which brought a new name—Reynolds Razorback Stadium.

One reason the stadium grew was that Arkansas was trying to pull away from the old policy of playing half, and sometimes more than half, of its home games in Little Rock. A variety of financial and political factors entered into such a decision, which set off a civil war of sorts, since Razorback football had long been the most unifying force in the state. There were threats and counterthreats, and even the governor got involved. Some Little Rock financiers proposed expanding War Memorial Stadium, but Broyles did not encourage it, as the Hogs were virtually the stadium's sole reason for existing. Fayetteville's advocates took the high road by saying that college football is for the students and rightfully belongs on campus. A compromise was reached in which the Hogs will play two games in Little Rock for the next ten years.

Waldo Stadium (Western Michigan)

President Dwight Waldo was a proponent of intercollegiate athletics for nearly three decades and helped keep the Western Michigan football program alive in the Great Depression. So when the university built a $250,000 stadium in 1939, it was named in his honor. Waldo Stadium had 15,000 seats on the north and south sides, an eight-lane running track, Kentucky bluegrass, and a press box that was considered modern for its time. The Broncos had beaten Miami and Akron at home before the dedication game on November 4, 1939, a 20–14 loss to Western Kentucky.

Mike Gray concluded his thirteen-year coaching career in 1941 with a memorable team. WMU went 8–0–0 (the last undefeated and untied team in school history), led by lineman Jack Matheson and offensive star Horace "Hap" Coleman. The Broncos were able to compete with other teachers colleges by recruiting regional talent. Soon after World War II, they joined the Mid-American Conference and found it fairly tough going, not winning a championship until 1988.

The stadium underwent occasional facelifts and got some end-

—Courtesy of Western Michigan sports information department

zone seating in 1973, making room for 25,000 fans. In that year, artificial turf was added and the track was removed, ending a nice tradition in which Bronco cross-country teams would conclude home meets by finishing inside Waldo Stadium at halftime. Following the aforementioned MAC title, more rows were added in the east and west ends, bringing seating capacity over 30,000, although crowds as large as 36,000 have gathered at the stadium in Kalamazoo.

Artificial turf was out and grass was back in 1992, and lights were installed the next year. The press box was expanded and club seating was unveiled as part of a $2.6 million upgrade. And in 1998, Waldo Stadium got a much-needed annex. Bill Brown, a letterman in the early 1950s who had gone on to success in the real estate business, helped raise $8.2 million to pay for the facility that now sits on the north side of the stadium. Named for Brown, it includes locker rooms, administrative offices and a weight room, among other things. It is an investment designed to help Gary Darnell's teams keep up with their MAC brethren.

Jordan-Hare Stadium (Auburn)

Auburn, located on the plains of eastern Alabama, was a remote and somewhat poor agricultural school, and perhaps that is why the Tigers did not play a home football game until 1896, their fifth season. The difficulty in getting other teams to venture there continued for several more decades, and Birmingham and Montgomery frequently served as home. Coach Jack Meagher's team played no games on campus in 1937 or 1938, an odd streak that lasted until November 30, 1939, when Auburn Stadium was unveiled. It consisted of 7,500 seats on the west side, although a total of 15,000 fans showed up to see a 7–7 tie between AU and Florida.

While capacity or above-capacity crowds were the norm, the stadium got little use initially. Just twelve games were played there in its first decade. Even in 1949, when the stadium received a 14,000-seat east-side addition, the Tigers hosted but a single game, defeating Mississippi State. That year, the university honored professor Cliff Hare by naming the stadium after him; Hare had been a member of Auburn's first football team and president of the Southern Conference, predecessor of the SEC.

—Courtesy of Auburn sports information department

Tiger football was in bad shape—three wins in three years—when AD Jeff Beard hired Ralph "Shug" Jordan in 1951. His teams got progressively better. By 1955, when another 13,000 west-side seats were created, Auburn had eight victories. And in 1957, with stars like linemen Zeke Smith and Jackie Burkett and receiver Jimmy Phillips, the Tigers won the national championship, although for some reason they did not play in a bowl game. They went 9–0–1 the next season and again did not go bowling.

Expansions of the north and south ends in 1960 and 1970 brought seating capacity of Hare Stadium to 61,261. With 1971 Heisman Trophy winner Pat Sullivan throwing to Terry Beasley, the orange and blue challenged for SEC supremacy, and only a loss to LSU kept them from going undefeated in 1972. In gratitude for all the coach had done, AU's home was renamed Jordan-Hare Stadium. He retired after the 1975 season with 176 victories.

The stadium had two more growth spurts in the 1980s as west- and east-side upper decks (with sixty-seven luxury boxes) were built, adding room for another 24,000 fans. Heisman Trophy winner Bo Jackson, who combined size and speed like few other running backs in the game's history, packed them in at one of college football's classic stadiums.

The annual game with Alabama was a fixture at Birmingham's Legion Field, but off-campus football was becoming a rarity. A bitter fight involving politicians and administrators was needed to make the change in this case. Finally, Auburn hosted the game on campus in 1989, and a crowd of 85,319 saw the Tigers settle the score and win. Jordan-Hare Stadium got a nice touch in 1998 when ten murals, each 11' x 29', depicting Auburn football history, were set on the east side's exterior. The Tigers have subverted the old pattern, now playing as many as eight home games per season.

Rubber Bowl (Akron)

In 1933, B. E. "Shorty" Fulton, the manager of Akron's airport, convinced the Depression-era WPA to excavate 180,000 cubic yards of dirt to build an amusement park which became Derby Downs, home of the Soap Box Derby. A few years later, a group

An Illustrated History of 120 College Football Stadiums   109

of citizens raised $30,000 and received a $516,000 federal grant to erect a football stadium adjacent to the airport and Derby Downs but seven miles from the University of Akron. The Zips had been playing on campus at Buchtel Field for nearly a half-

—Courtesy of Akron sports information department

century, and they were happy to have a new if distant home. With a west-side press box and lights on the field due to the airport, Akron Municipal Stadium was built on a surprisingly large scale; the horseshoe, open on the north end, had room for 35,202 fans. Since Akron was home to four tire and rubber companies, the stadium has almost always been known as the Rubber Bowl. The first game played there was on October 5, 1940, when Akron lost to Western Reserve.

Like many other schools, Akron dropped football during World War II. The Zips, playing in the Ohio Athletic Conference, won just nine games from 1947 to 1951, and attendance slipped as low as 3,400 per game. Survival of the football program hung in the balance when athletic director Kenneth Cochrane took over. He coached the team for two years and started a winning tradition. Cochrane instituted an exhibition game each August in which Akron played the Cleveland Browns (a series that lasted until 1974), and he also started the annual Acme-Zip game. The Acme food chain, the local newspaper, and the university administration forged a plan to sell discount tickets to fill the Rubber Bowl once a year. That was the start of one of the most successful ongoing promotions in college football. An all-time record crowd of 43,171 saw a victory over Butler in the 1971 Acme-Zip game.

Coach Gordon Larson's 1969 team went 9–1 and finished third in the AP's college-division poll. Two years later, the city sold the Rubber Bowl for $1 to the university, which soon began renovating what some regarded as a "white elephant." The initial objectives were to improve the lighting and install artificial turf, since the stadium had always been heavily used by high schools in northeastern Ohio. A new scoreboard in the north end, a drainage system, and other basic changes followed.

The blue and gold had a pair of fine linebackers in the late 1970s and early 1980s, as both Steve Cockerham and Brad Reese were two-time all-Americans in Division I-AA. Akron joined the Mid-American Conference in 1978, and when Gerry Faust arrived from Notre Dame in 1986, Zip fans hoped it was their time to shine. Moving into Division I-A was another big step, and Faust gave it his best for nine seasons but won just 45 percent of his games as attendance fell below the 10,000 mark.

The Rubber Bowl, which has not been expanded in six decades

of existence, has also hosted many concerts—classical, as well as the more rambunctious sort. The Rolling Stones, the Grateful Dead, the Allman Brothers, and Ozzy Osbourne are just a few of the acts to have graced its stage. After a melee that brought twenty-seven arrests, vandalism, and the explosion of a small bomb, rock concerts were banned for nine years before being reinstated, with more security, in 1998.

Robertson Stadium (Houston)

The Houston Independent School District and the WPA joined forces in 1941 to build Public School Stadium at a cost of $650,000. With room for 20,500 fans, it was one of the biggest and best high school stadiums in the country. It sat on the western edge of the University of Houston campus, and when the Cougars began playing football, they held games there. The first was a loss to Southwestern Louisiana on September 21, 1946.

—Courtesy of Houston sports information department

Although average attendance was a paltry 10,000 per game, the Cougars did not stay long. When 70,000-seat Rice Stadium opened across town in 1950, UH shared quarters with the Owls. That, according to coach Bill Yeoman, was "like trying to sell Plymouths out of a Ford dealership." Houston continued to use Public School Stadium as a practice facility and to hold track meets there, sharing it with local schoolboys. Renamed Jeppesen Stadium to honor Holger Jeppesen, a longtime member of the school board, it served as home to the Houston Oilers of the American Football League starting in 1960. The Oilers, who built 14,000 end-zone seats (since removed), won the first two AFL titles there and lost the third before fading into mediocrity.

With the opening of the Houston Astrodome in 1965, the Oilers left Jeppesen Stadium and UH left Rice Stadium to play indoors and on artificial turf, the first pro and college teams to have that distinction. Sparked by running back Warren McVea, the Cougars had attendance figures that have never since been approached, and a 37–7 upset of No. 1 Michigan State in 1967 gave the program some national visibility. UH won the Southwest Conference championship in 1976, its first year as a member, and beat Maryland in the Cotton Bowl, finishing No. 4. And quarterback Andre Ware used the run-and-shoot offense to put up some big numbers in winning the 1989 Heisman Trophy.

Meanwhile, the university had purchased Jeppesen Stadium for $6.7 million and renamed it for Corbin Robertson, a former member of the Board of Regents and chairman of the Athletic Committee for twenty-one years. It got a $2 million facelift in 1983 prior to hosting the NCAA championship track meet and was the home track for Carl Lewis, one of the greatest track and field performers of all time. Lewis donated money to have the track and runways rebuilt. By that time, Robertson Stadium had become a track mecca of sorts as Lewis, Leroy Burrell, Mike Marsh, and others trained and competed there regularly.

But UH football was struggling. As the SWC dissolved, the Cougars won just four games in a three-year span, and the Astrodome had all the collegiate atmosphere of a mausoleum. The athletic department was a financial mess, too. Somewhat as an experiment, the Cougars played one game at Robertson Stadium in 1995, two in 1996 (when they shared the Conference USA title), three in 1997, and every home game starting in 1998. The stadium had to be upgraded to meet NCAA Division I-A specifications, and it was do-or-die time for Houston. AD Chet Gladchuk had plans, but he needed money to enact them. He got it in 1999 from lawyer and regent John O'Quinn, who donated $6 million. In the familiar quid pro quo, the field was named for O'Quinn. Pocket change compared to what other schools have invested to redo their stadiums, the money was still well spent. The field was lowered nine feet, the track was removed, the west-side press box was modernized, and new stands in the north and south ends raised seating capacity to 32,000. Twenty luxury boxes were built, as was a south-end scoreboard. The second phase of the expansion of Robertson Stadium depends on finding another $18 million to build more luxury boxes and upper decks with room for 18,000 fans. The stadium gets plenty of use, as the Cougars share it with Texas Southern's football team, a major league soccer team, and a spring pro football team.

Vaught-Hemingway Stadium (Mississippi)

In 1915, Ole Miss students constructed some wooden stands beside an athletic field in the southeast quadrant of campus. Adjacent to that spot, twenty-six years later, the university (with WPA assistance) built a new home for the Rebel football team. Seating 24,000, it was named to honor Judge William Hemingway, a professor and longtime chairman of Mississippi's athletic committee. The dedication game at Hemingway Stadium took place on October 4, 1941, and the Rebs beat Southwestern 27–0.

But there were problems in Oxford. The team had four straight losing seasons, and money was so tight in 1946 that Ole Miss had to borrow football jerseys from Southeastern Conference rival Alabama. When Johnny Vaught was hired as coach, things improved quickly. With Vaught on the sidelines and Charlie Connerly at quarterback, Mississippi went 9–2 and won the 1947 SEC crown. While changes were few at Hemingway Stadium, an eighty-yard-long press box was built on the west side in 1950. The Rebels seldom crossed the Mason-Dixon line and did not play a

—Courtesy of Mississippi sports information department

single non-southern opponent over a twenty-year span, but they were on a roll. They played in fifteen straight bowl games, won five conference titles from 1954 to 1963, and won some version of the national championship in 1959, 1960, and 1962.

In the latter year, Ole Miss went undefeated and Vaught's name was added to that of Judge Hemingway atop the stadium. Winning football was a pleasant diversion from more weighty matters afflicting Ole Miss: James Meredith, the school's first black student, was enrolled only after the National Guard quelled a riot in which 2 people were killed, 188 injured, and dozens arrested. Other southern schools resisted integration, but none so fiercely as Mississippi, which had chosen the Rebel mascot with all its Confederate baggage. A decade passed before any black player would suit up for the red and blue, and fairly or not, Ole Miss continued to be viewed as a symbol of Deep South segregation.

Vaught was still coaching when quarterback Archie Manning arrived. Generally considered the school's greatest player, he was a two-time all-American and was third in 1970 Heisman Trophy voting. Perhaps ominously, Mississippi has not finished in the AP's top ten since Manning left, nor have the Rebels been in a major bowl. They have gone almost forty years without winning the SEC championship.

Artificial turf was installed at Vaught-Hemingway Stadium in 1970, but a reversion to grass happened fourteen years later. Blue fiberglass seating in the early 1970s gave fans more comfort and improved the look of the place. The students at Ole Miss and Mississippi State could not have been pleased when, in 1973, that big rivalry was shifted to Jackson, where it stayed for eighteen years. And how could recruits have been impressed, as late as 1979, with a 24,000-seat bandbox of a stadium? After that season, UM erected semi-permanent aluminum benches in the north and south ends, elevating seating capacity to 41,000.

Further changes were made, including an $8 million facelift in 1988, lights in 1990, a new scoreboard in 1997, and a $10.5 million covered east-side upper deck (with twenty-nine luxury boxes) in 1998 which added 9,000 new seats. Also, the field was named in honor of Dr. Jerry Hollingsworth, a donor to the Ole Miss athletic department. The expanded stadium held a record 50,577 fans when running back Deuce McAllister led the Rebs to a 37–31 overtime defeat of LSU.

Since Johnny Vaught retired, every new coach has had the fervent hope that he would be the next Vaught, but none have come close. To be fair to those men, however, they have worked in a vastly different era from that of the glory days of the late 1950s and early 1960s. The current coach, David Cutcliffe, may achieve great things. His chances were not hurt in 2001 when the south end of Vaught-Hemingway Stadium was turned into a horseshoe with another thirty-three luxury boxes, which brought seating capacity to 60,000.

Memorial Stadium (Clemson)

Banks McFadden, an all-American in both football and basketball, was Clemson's greatest athlete of the pre-integration era. He led the Tigers to a 9–1 record and a Cotton Bowl win in the 1939 season. McFadden's coach, Jess Neely, had been there ten

— Courtesy of Clemson sports information department

years and was leaving for Rice when he told Clemson officials, "Don't ever let them talk you into building a big stadium. Put about 10,000 seats behind the YMCA and that's all you'll ever need." Neely's advice was ignored, and the university soon began planning a 20,000-seat stadium on the west side of campus by the shore of Lake Hartwell. The new coach and AD, Frank Howard, would head the program for the next thirty years. He actually supervised clearing and grading prior to construction of Memorial Stadium, and many of his players aided in the cause. The $125,000 expense was covered by IPTAY (acronym for "I Pay Ten A Year"), Clemson's athletic fundraising arm, which had begun in 1934. The facility had an analog clock, a hand-operated scoreboard, and no locker rooms, so the players had to trek over from a nearby gym. The inaugural game was on September 19, 1942, when the Tigers beat Presbyterian College. The coach of that school called it Death Valley, a name later adopted by LSU's Tiger Stadium.

Due to the paucity of lodging in Clemson, a little town in the foothills of the Blue Ridge Mountains, fans could hardly stay overnight. The first game under the lights was in 1948, but that is still a rarity. In 1958, more rows on the north and south sides jacked up seating capacity to 38,000. Another 5,638 seats were built in the west end in 1960, and there was room for another 10,000 fans on a grassy slope in the east end. With an enlarged stadium, Clemson brought an end to the "Big Thursday" classic in which the Tigers always played their in-state rival, the University of South Carolina, in Columbia. The 1966 season was the first for Howard's Rock, set on an obelisk in the east end of Memorial Stadium. Clemson players rub it before each game, a mystical act which is alleged to give them game-winning powers.

Howard had retired in 1974, when the field was named after him, and four years later, the stadium received a south-side upper deck, a new press box, and the first of 108 luxury boxes. The Tigers had won a bunch of ACC titles and could boast of two top-ten finishes (1950 and 1978), but 1981 was the greatest year in Clemson football history. With quarterback Homer Jordan, receiver Perry Tuttle, and defensive back Terry Kinard leading the way, they beat defending national champ Georgia at Memorial Stadium and kept on winning, edging Nebraska in the Orange Bowl for the national crown. Such success merited a matching upper deck on the north side of the stadium, making room for 81,473 fans, although crowds as large as 85,000 have seen games there.

When the Carolina Panthers were admitted to the NFL in 1995, they had to build a stadium in Charlotte. So for that first season, they called Memorial Stadium home, an arrangement financially beneficial to the university. The stadium, which had been expanded several times over a six-decade span but never truly renovated, needed attention. In 2000, Clemson began a $30 million modernizing project which also brought further seating in the west end. Tentative plans to fill in the east end would raise seating capacity to the 100,000 level.

Jones SBC Stadium (Texas Tech)

If not for the success of coach Pete Cawthon, Texas Tech might not have needed a new stadium. For eleven years, he equipped his teams in colorful uniforms, employed coast-to-coast scheduling, and beat some big-name schools. Tech Stadium, built in the northeast corner of campus in 1926 and expanded ten years later, could hold 14,000 fans. But the Red Raiders desperately wanted to join the Southwest Conference, and a better facility was paramount in that effort. The fundraising drive got off to a great start with a $100,000 check from former president Clifford Jones. The Lubbock business community gave another $150,000, and the university put up an equal amount. Adjacent to the old facility, construction commenced in March 1947, but a fire swept through the site in June, causing $200,000 in damage. For that reason, 18,000-seat Jones Stadium could not be unveiled until the final game of the 1947 season, when a crowd of 20,000 witnessed a 14–6 defeat of Hardin-Simmons.

Since lighting was an original feature of the stadium, night games were fairly common in the hub city of the South Plains. The 1953 Red Raiders went 11–1 with a Gator Bowl win over Auburn, finishing No. 12 in the nation. After twenty years of asking, Texas Tech was admitted to the SWC in 1960. But Jones Stadium had to be expanded first. In a difficult engineering feat, the east stands—

—Courtesy of Texas Tech sports information department; photo by Norvelle Kennedy

six tons of steel and concrete—were pulled back 226 feet on railroad tracks over a three-month span. The field was lowered 28 feet to allow additional seating on both sides. The $2 million project made room for 41,500 fans of the red and black.

Two names dominated Texas Tech football in the 1960s, E. J. Holub, a linebacker and center, and Donny Anderson, the "Golden Palomino," a running back and punter. Both were two-time all-Americans and both played on Super Bowl winners in the pros—Holub with the Kansas City Chiefs and Anderson with the Green Bay Packers.

Further expansion of the stadium occurred in 1969 and 1972 when new stands in the north and south ends raised seating capacity to 50,500. The summer of 1970 was an interesting time. Repairs had to be made to the lighting system, which had been twisted like a pretzel during a tornado. And artificial turf was installed; a new carpet appears every few years as Texas Tech resists the trend back to grass.

The revolving door of coaches ended in 1987 with the hiring of Spike Dykes, a quotable native son. During Dykes' thirteen seasons at the helm, one of the most thrilling games was in 1988 when a near-capacity crowd at Jones Stadium saw the Red Raiders, trailing Texas by 17 points at the start of the fourth quarter, mount a rousing comeback led by quarterback Billy Joe Tolliver to beat the Longhorns.

The stadium, which featured a south-end scoreboard and a neon double-T on its east exterior, was among the smallest in the SWC and the Big 12, which was formed in 1996. Finally, the athletic department and administration bit the bullet, embarking on a $90 million, three-year renovation and expansion project. Jones Stadium was made compliant with the Americans with Disabilities Act, new concourses were built, and the small and inefficient press box was replaced. The new one had three levels, the first two of which were given over to luxury boxes and club seating. The exterior was redone in Spanish Renaissance style, and 10,000 seats were added. Texas Tech, whose new basketball arena was named for a donating supermarket chain in 1999, did the same with its football stadium. When the parent company of Southwestern Bell gave $20 million, the name was changed to Jones SBC Stadium. And AD Gerald Myers has acknowledged other "naming opportunities" such as the field, press box, and stadium entrances.

War Memorial Stadium (Wyoming)

The Wyoming Cowboys had not enjoyed a winning season since 1931, but Bowden Wyatt got that turned around in his third year in Laramie. His 1949 team went 9–1, which helped convince the university administration to build a suitable stadium. Despite some skepticism, they went forward. At a cost of $1.5 million, Porter & Bradley designed and Spiegelberg Lumber and Building Company erected a stadium and adjoining fieldhouse. War Memorial Stadium, named in honor of Wyoming's World War II veterans, had 20,000 seats and a well-manicured field. At an elevation of 7,220 feet, it was the highest football stadium in the U.S. Dedication day was September 23, 1950, when the Cowboys avenged their only loss of the previous year by beating Baylor 7–0 despite an injury to star running back Eddie Talboom. That was one of the greatest seasons in school history; UW went 10–0 with a Gator Bowl victory and finished No. 12 in the nation. "The War," as Wyoming students like to call it, set the standard for later stadiums built in the Rocky Mountain region at places such as Colorado State, Air Force, Utah, Utah State, and Brigham Young.

A charter member of the Western Athletic Conference, Wyoming spent $1.1 million in 1970 to build a west-side upper deck, boosting seating capacity to 25,500. They also replaced the old press box, which was made of corrugated steel and resembled a walk-in freezer during many a frigid football game. Another upper deck on the east side seven years later and a north-end "knothole" section made room for 33,500 fans. Average attendance peaked at 24,800 in 1977, but the single-game record came in 1997 when 34,745 packed War Memorial Stadium to witness a 14–7 loss to Colorado State.

The Cowboys have had some fine players, especially receivers Jerry Hill, Jay Novacek, Ryan Yarborough, and Marcus Harris. And the stadium has hosted notable visitors like Barry Sanders of Oklahoma State, Andre Ware of Houston, and Ty Detmer of BYU,

—Courtesy of Wyoming sports information department

all Heisman Trophy winners. Games played amid blizzards are not uncommon, and wind whipping down off the mountains only adds to the ambience. The first night game in War Memorial Stadium history, done with temporary lights for the sake of a television audience, came in 1988. Wyoming's biggest problems have been recruiting in a state with few blue-chip athletes and keeping coaches; Wyatt went on to greater fame at Arkansas and Tennessee, and the same could be said for Bob Devaney (Nebraska), Fred Akers (Texas), Pat Dye (Auburn), Dennis Erickson (Miami), and Joe Tiller (Purdue).

Casey Stadium (Baylor)

In the first fifty years of Baylor's football history, three facilities served as home: Carroll Field, the Cotton Palace, and Waco Municipal Stadium. The high points were a Southwest Conference championship in 1924 and the play, a few seasons later, of Barton

"Botchey" Koch. In the era of one-platoon football, Koch was a force both ways. Such authorities as Grantland Rice and Knute Rockne called him the best guard they had ever seen.

Following World War II, some dedicated alumni formed a corporation which would raise money to build a new stadium for the Bears. Their efforts were successful, bringing in $1.5 million to erect 50,000-seat Baylor Stadium three miles southwest of campus. It was first used on September 30, 1950, when Baylor defeated Houston 34–7. BU had some good teams in the 1950s. They finished No. 9 in 1951 with an Orange Bowl loss to Georgia Tech and No. 11 in 1956 with a Sugar Bowl win over Tennessee. During the latter season, the Bears fell to Texas A&M in Waco before an overflow crowd in what the Aggies' Bear Bryant called "the meanest, dirtiest, toughest, bloodiest game I ever coached."

Although never expanded, Baylor Stadium has seen some changes. Artificial turf was installed in 1972 before a reversion to grass in 1997. The wooden bleachers were replaced with aluminum over an eight-year span, the original lights were renovated, administrative offices were built in the north end, and the stadium

—Courtesy of Baylor sports information department; photo by Joe Griffin

has been sandblasted and painted. In 1999, the west-side press box was expanded and modernized with the addition of thirty-six luxury boxes at a cost of $9 million. The biggest change, however, came during halftime of the homecoming game against Arkansas (a 33–3 loss to the Razorbacks) when AD Bill Menefee announced that longtime trustee and benefactor Carl Casey had given $5 million and, in gratitude, the stadium's name had been changed to honor his father, Floyd.

It was still Baylor Stadium in 1972 when Grant Teaff was hired. The Bruins had won just three games in three seasons, and some people wondered aloud whether BU should get out of big-time football. But Teaff took them from laughingstock to respectability by 1974, winning the SWC title before falling to Penn State in the Cotton Bowl, and he was named coach of the year. Baylor won the conference championship again in 1980—thanks in large part to the inspired performance of three-time all-America linebacker Mike Singletary—but lost to Alabama in the Cotton Bowl. In both instances, the green and gold finished No. 14.

Teaff, surely the greatest coach the school ever had, retired after the 1992 season. Since then, it has been hard to tell whether Casey Stadium is half-empty or half-full, but since the founding of the Big 12 in 1996, Baylor has usually brought up the rear in attendance as well as in the standings. The Bears lost all but one game in 1999, and it would have been two except for a heartbreaking denouement in the home opener against UNLV. Baylor was ahead by three points with four seconds remaining when coach Kevin Steele sent a running back up the middle in an attempt to score another touchdown, but he fumbled. The ball was picked up by defensive back Kevin Thomas, who sprinted 99 yards to give the Rebels a victory that left 32,272 fans in shock.

Byrd Stadium (Maryland)

H. C. "Curley" Byrd showed enduring dedication to the University of Maryland, lettering on the football team from 1905 to 1907 and coaching it from 1911 to 1934. As if that were not enough, he served as president from 1935 to 1954. The students first honored him in 1923 by naming the Terrapins' modest new facility Byrd Field. While UM made nary a peep on the national football scene, it was one of the best in the East after the formation of the Ivy League. That was especially so during the Jim Tatum era. Tatum's 1949 team used a split-T offense to go 9–1 with a Gator Bowl win over Missouri and finished No. 14. As a result, Byrd forged a plan to build a 34,680-seat stadium for the bargain-basement price of $1 million. A horseshoe with the open end facing east, Byrd Stadium was inaugurated on September 30, 1950, with a 35–21 defeat of Navy. Temporary seating allowed more than 43,000 people to witness the game.

The Tatum years were truly the heyday for Terp football. A nineteen-game winning streak ran from 1950 to 1952, and the 1953 team, led by all-America lineman Stan Jones, allowed just 31 points in the regular season and won every game before falling to Oklahoma in the Orange Bowl. Still, Maryland was chosen the national champion. In 1955, Tatum's last season before moving on, it was the same story—rolling over every opponent but losing to OU in the Orange Bowl and ending up No. 3.

In 1955, Cole Field House was built nearby. That classic col-

—Courtesy of Maryland sports information department

lege basketball arena would be the last new athletic facility on campus for thirty-five years, and virtually nothing changed at Byrd Stadium, either. While the Terps disappeared from the top-twenty polls for nearly two decades (and attendance dipped as low as 14,000 per game), some fine players passed through and memorable games were held. In 1957, Queen Elizabeth was there to see UM beat North Carolina, and in 1963, Darryl Hill, the first black player in the ACC, caught 43 passes and a lot of jeers, catcalls, and cheap shots from opponents. And in 1974, defensive star Randy White helped the Terrapins to their first conference title since Tatum had left. In the season opener, played at home before a then-record crowd of 54,412, Maryland lost to Alabama, whose coach, Paul "Bear" Bryant, had spent one tantalizing season at College Park in the mid-1940s.

The Baltimore Stars of the now-defunct USFL rented out the stadium for their spring games from 1983 to 1985. Those were good years for the Terrapins. Coached by Bobby Ross, they won three ACC crowns and were thought to have a chance to win it all in 1985, but a home loss to Penn State in the first game of the season ended any such notions. In the last fifteen years of the twentieth century, only once did they have a winning record, going 6–5–1 in 1990. The university then began five years of renovation and construction at Byrd Stadium, investing $50 million. The five-level Tyser Tower—a press box and luxury seating—was built on the south side. The Gossett Football Team House then went up in the east end, and a two-level upper deck was erected on the north side, expanding seating capacity to 48,055. The stadium became a football-only facility in 1995. The track where UM's Renaldo Nehemiah became the greatest 110-meter high hurdler in the world in the late 1970s was removed. Track and field, as well as soccer and lacrosse, which sometimes drew crowds of over 25,000, got their own campus homes.

Rice Stadium (Rice)

Horseshoe-shaped Rice Field had 40,000 seats, but that was not nearly enough for the Owls in the late 1940s. Jess Neely's

—Courtesy of Rice sports information department

teams won SWC titles in 1946 and 1949 and scored victories in the Orange Bowl and Cotton Bowl, respectively. The latter team, with quarterback Tobin Rote and all-America end Froggy Williams, finished No. 5 in the nation. University officials and civic leaders agreed on the need for a new stadium. Houston was gradually becoming the fourth-largest city in the U.S., and Rice was the darling of the local media. Brown & Root worked twenty-four-hour shifts over nine months to build the $3.3 million stadium. It was spectacular at the time—a wraparound stadium with two upper decks and room for 70,000 fans. It had lights, a three-level press box, and an intimate feel for such a huge stadium. Rice Field was turned into the Owls' track facility, even today retaining a portion of the grandstand. Houston Stadium (soon renamed Rice Stadium) was dedicated on September 30, 1950, when the blue and gray beat Santa Clara 27–7.

For the first fifteen years of its existence, the stadium was shared by Rice and the University of Houston, which had to tailor its schedule to conform with that of the Owls; the two teams did not meet until 1971. Although Rice just had a 5–5 record in 1958, that was a remarkable season at the second-biggest stadium in the Lone Star State, trailing just the Cotton Bowl in Dallas. In consecutive home games, the Owls crushed Texas and nearly upset No. 2 Army. Average attendance of more than 57,000 put Rice right behind Ohio State, Michigan, and LSU.

Rice Stadium became home to the Bluebonnet Bowl in 1959, and the Owls played in the game following the 1961 season, losing to Kansas 33–7. Who knew that would be Rice's last bowl game for four decades? The Owls were in decline, and with the arrival of the Houston Oilers and Houston Colt .45s/Astros, the city turned its head away from the team representing the small school ranked in the highest echelons of American academe. Fair-weather fans were part of the problem, especially since Rice cut its prospective student-athletes no slack. After Neely retired in 1966, Rice went through nine coaches in twenty-eight years, and they all lost more games than they won. Three winless seasons (1968, 1982, and 1988) were as foul and noxious as the sputum of a camel.

Artificial turf first appeared at Rice Stadium in 1970. And there were other interesting moments, such as in 1973 when, following a surprise defeat of Texas A&M, the Rice band, which had a penchant for cleverness and irony, was chased by a group of perturbed Aggies. In January 1974, the stadium hosted the Super Bowl, in which the Miami Dolphins beat the Minnesota Vikings. However, the coaches groused about poor training facilities and locker rooms, and the media found fault with the press box.

The Oilers spent two seasons, 1965 and 1966, at Rice Stadium before moving to the Astrodome (and later to Tennessee), which also became home to the Bluebonnet Bowl. The paradigm shift seemed complete. By the late 1980s, Rice football was at a crossroads with rising costs, losing teams, and a dwindling fan base. Only a nucleus of ardent supporters allowed Rice to average 15,000 per game. Bobby May, a track star for the Owls in the 1960s, became AD in 1989, and he started crafting an athletic renaissance of sorts. Under his direction, the stadium has gotten new scoreboards, refurbished locker rooms, and a top-to-bottom steam cleaning, although the splintered wooden benches remain. The two coaches May has hired, Fred Goldsmith and Ken Hatfield, topped the .500 mark more than once, and attendance has climbed as high as 35,000 per game, which still leaves a gulf of empty seats at Rice Stadium. The Houston Texans, an NFL expansion team which began play in 2002, considered modernizing Rice Stadium and making it their home on Sundays, an arrangement that would have benefited the Rice athletic department immeasurably. But they chose instead to build (with considerable help from the taxpayers of Harris County) Reliant Stadium next to the vacated Astrodome for more than a half-billion dollars.

Campbell Stadium (Florida State)

After forty years as a women-only school, Florida State admitted men in 1946. And the football program began on a very small scale the next year. The Seminoles played at Centennial Field their first three seasons. During that time, fans could pay $50 for a five-year pass to games at the new stadium being built in the southwest quadrant of the FSU campus. The lighted 15,000-seat

—Courtesy of Florida State sports information department

stadium, surrounded on all sides by parking lots that would eventually give way to expansion, was named in honor of Dr. Doak Campbell, the president and a staunch supporter of Seminole athletics. It was dedicated on October 7, 1950, with a 40–7 romp of Randolph-Macon.

That opponent was indicative of Florida State football, which was taking baby steps in establishing itself. First as a member of the Dixie Conference and then as an independent, Florida State rather often served as homecoming fodder for other schools. Campbell Stadium had grown to 40,500 seats by 1964, when coach Bill Peterson used the pitch-and-catch combination of Steve Tensi and Fred Biletnikoff to go 9–1–1 with a Gator Bowl win over Oklahoma. The stadium remained unchanged for fourteen years while FSU's pigskin proclivities plummeted. In 1973 and 1974, "the tribe," as they are known in Tallahassee, won just one game and got beaten more than a rented mule.

But athletic director John Bridgers found the right man to fix things, hiring Bobby Bowden away from West Virginia. Within a year, the Seminoles had the first ten-win season in school history, played in a bowl game, and got attention in the Associated Press poll. By 1980, they were legitimate national championship contenders, and the stadium had to be expanded to meet demand; it could hold 51,094 fans then and grew to 55,246 in 1982 and over 60,000 in 1985. Bowden's teams gained a reputation for fearlessly taking on all comers. In a four-week span in 1981, they went on the road to face Ohio State, Notre Dame, Pittsburgh, and LSU, winning three times.

Like their downstate rivals, Florida and Miami, they have exploited the mother lode of high school football in Florida. Bowden has had five two-time consensus all-Americans—lineman Ron Simmons, defensive back Deion Sanders, linebacker Marvin Jones, kicker Sebastian Janikowski, and receiver Peter Warrick—and all but one played Friday-night football in Florida. Florida State joined the Atlantic Coast Conference in 1992, but it was something of a cakewalk, with just four losses in the first eight years. The Seminoles have not limited themselves to such mundane matters as conference titles. No, they have reached for the brass ring with amazing consistency, finishing no lower than fourth every year from 1987 through 1999.

FSU fans do the war chant with accompanying chop (both of which have been adopted by the Atlanta Braves), but Campbell Stadium is rather placid compared to Florida's famous "swamp," where a veritable tsunami of sound leaves people with ringing ears. It is a formidable place, however. The old erector-set look has given way to a beautiful brick facade containing offices and classrooms. Luxury boxes run from goal line to goal line on the east and west sides, and construction in the north and south ends has raised seating capacity to 80,000. A record crowd of 81,614 at the 1998 Florida State–Florida game saw a wild melee of players pushing, shoving, and mouthing prior to kickoff that embarrassed the alumni and administrations of both schools.

Bowden has managed to change with the times in so many ways, and he has gotten in some trouble with the NCAA for failing to keep agents off campus. Indeed, he has put together teams that might be competitive in the NFL. The 1993 Seminoles (with Heisman Trophy–winning quarterback Charlie Ward) went 11–1 and beat Nebraska in the Orange Bowl to win the national crown, and they were even more impressive in 1999. FSU led from wire to wire, blasted Virginia Tech in the Sugar Bowl, and won it again. Bowden has built an empire perhaps unmatched in the history of college football. In 2000, as he approached Bear Bryant's career victory mark, the Florida legislature passed a bill that would name Campbell Stadium's field for Bowden the day following his retirement.

Fouts Field (North Texas)

However much money J. Theron Fouts made, it was not enough. Beginning in 1920, he coached football, track and field, basketball, and golf at North Texas. And after giving up coaching, Fouts served as athletic director until 1954. The Eagles had gained regional renown under Jack Sisco and Odus Mitchell when Fouts convinced the university to build a new stadium on the western fringe of campus in Denton. In November 1950, a bonfire was lit to commemorate grading and construction of a 20,000-seat football and track facility. Facing northwest, parallel to what would soon be Interstate 35, Fouts Field had lights and a press box on the southwest side. It opened on September 27, 1952, when the green and white routed North Dakota 55–0 before 12,000 fans.

The Eagles won Missouri Valley Conference titles in 1958 and 1959 (when they played in the Sun Bowl) with help from Abner Haynes, the first black player at a major Texas college. He led UNT in rushing, receiving, punt returns, kickoff returns, and scoring in all three of his varsity seasons, even grabbing five interceptions as a defensive back in 1958, and made a big splash with the Dallas Texans, winners of the 1962 AFL championship. North Texas' willingness to integrate with Haynes and other luminaries like Carl "Spider" Lockhart and Joe Greene forced the more prominent Southwest Conference schools to follow suit.

In the early 1970s, UNT installed artificial turf and a rubber track and wooden bleachers in both end zones, although sellouts at Fouts Field were infrequent. In fact, spotty attendance figures caused the athletic department to play some "home" games at the Cotton Bowl, thirty-five miles south in Dallas, and at Texas Stadium, the Dallas Cowboys' palatial new facility. But renting such places cost money, and that was in short supply in 1972, when a total of 30,000 people attended five home games, four of them off campus.

Such a depressing situation improved when Hayden Fry was hired to coach the team. Victories and attendance both picked up as Fry cultivated the media and sought UNT's admission to the SWC. But that was not to be, and Fry moved on to Iowa after the 1978 season. While he was in the big time, the Eagles dropped down to Division I-AA status for thirteen years, playing in a variety of conferences or enduring life as an independent.

Athletic director Craig Helwig, with support from the administration, decided to roll the dice in 1994. In order to regain I-A status, North Texas added 10,500 end-zone seats, refurbished the Eagles' locker room, put in new scoreboards, and replaced the old wooden benches with aluminum. They also went back to having one home game per season against a well-known opponent at Texas Stadium. Nearly 46,000 fans were there in 1997 to see North Texas lose to Texas A&M 36–10. Helwig even hired a marketing firm that promised to put "a butt in every seat" when Nevada–Las Vegas came to Denton in 1999. John Robinson, former Southern

Cal and Los Angeles Ram coach, was starting a new job, and that created quite a stir, but Fouts Field still had a few butt-less seats.

Reser Stadium (Oregon State)

A charter member of the Pacific Coast Conference, predecessor of today's Pac-10, Oregon State held its home games at Bell Field, which was built on the eve of World War I. But Portland, a much bigger city than Corvallis, was just a few miles up the road, so the Beavers played there frequently (as late as 1986). Just one game was on campus in 1952, the year fundraising and construction of a new stadium began. OSU alum Charles Parker ponied up $125,000, nearly half the $280,000 it cost, so the 28,000-seat facility was named in his honor. Scoreless in their first five games of the season, the Beavers managed a 7–0 defeat of Washington State on November 14, 1953, as 13,500 people looked on.

Tommy Prothro was coaching the orange and black in 1962 when left-handed quarterback Terry Baker guided them to a 9–2 record, winning the Heisman Trophy and drawing much-needed attention to the football program. Two years later, Prothro had Oregon State in its first Rose Bowl since the 1941 season, only to get whacked by Michigan 34-7. There would be no more bowls for the next three and a half decades, but athletic director Slats Gill decided it was time to expand Parker Stadium. End-zone seating made room for 5,000 more fans. And in 1967, it grew to a seating capacity of 40,593 when an extra forty-two rows were added to the west side. One of the major donors for that project was Parker, and the architect was Dan Zarosinski, a letterman from 1949 to 1951. A crowd of 41,494 was there on a soggy day in 1967 when OSU, led by fullback Bill "Earthquake" Enyart, took a 3–0 win over Southern Cal, the only blemish for the national champion Trojans.

The Beavers had winning records every year from 1966 to 1970, and then they essentially vanished. What followed were twenty-eight straight losing seasons with one 0–11 record, six 1–10 records, and others that were almost as bad. With attendance dipping as low as 20,000 per game, Oregon State regularly brought up the rear in the Pac-10.

—Courtesy of Oregon State sports information department

Several changes were made to the stadium during those long, lonely years. A $4 million renovation in 1987 included aluminum benches and a 1,500-seat VIP area. In 1990, 5,000 seats were removed from the north end to allow construction of the Valley Football Center, a complex containing the home locker room, a weight room, and offices and which was expanded in 1996. The stadium also got a fancy scoreboard in the south end, a new press box, and a cantilevered roof over much of the west stands.

But with all that losing, the OSU athletic department was $9 million in debt. Artificial turf (first installed in 1969) was too seldom replaced, with one rug lasting fifteen years. Finally some good things happened in Corvallis. The school's forty-year-old AD, Mitch Barnhart, hired Dennis Erickson. Fired after four lackluster seasons as coach of the Seattle Seahawks, he nevertheless had solid credentials—two national championships at the University of Miami. His first Beaver team went 7–4 with record home attendance and got into a minor bowl.

Before Erickson's first game at OSU, Barnhart announced that the stadium's name was being changed. Al Reser, an alumnus and food magnate, gave $5 million for ten-year naming rights, with an option to extend it to 2024 for another $7.5 million. The Parker family did not protest, partly because an entrance plaza was named in honor of Charles Parker. But the matter tweaked the sensibilities of many alumni and other traditionalists. Sarcastic newspaper columns were written asking what else was for sale, but Barnhart was unfazed. "We're a small-market school in debt," he said. "We have to be creative."

Alumni Stadium (Boston College)

In 1913, Boston College moved from its original campus in Boston's south end to Chestnut Hill, a western suburb. Alumni Stadium was built there two years later, but the Eagles seldom used it, preferring Fenway Park (home of the Boston Red Sox) and Braves Field (home of the Boston Braves). They played in those two baseball venues a lot. Perhaps the Jesuit fathers who ran the college did not want the team to travel much, because for twenty-eight straight seasons BC never had more than two games outside of Boston, and in five of those seasons, there were none.

The Boston College football program picked up steam in the late 1930s. Quarterback Charlie O'Rourke and fullback Mike Holovak were the stars of those teams. The 1939 Eagles were 9–2 with a Cotton Bowl loss to Clemson, becoming the first New England school in twenty years to play in a major bowl. The 1940 team won all eleven games, including a Sugar Bowl defeat of Tennessee, and ended up No. 5. The 1942 team also made a serious bid for the national championship but dropped its last two games, a 55–12 Thanksgiving Day upset by Holy Cross at Fenway Park and a loss to Alabama in the Orange Bowl, finishing No. 8. It would be four decades before the maroon and gold played in another bowl game or finished in the top ten.

In 1951, Holovak, who had enjoyed a successful playing career with the Los Angeles Rams and Chicago Bears (and would later coach the Boston Patriots of the American Football League and serve as general manager of the Houston Oilers), returned to run the show at his alma mater. Five years later, Fenway Park was declared off-limits to college football, and BC briefly considered

— Courtesy of Boston College sports information department

dropping the sport. But president Joseph Maxwell chose otherwise. Some $250,000 was raised to build a new facility on campus. The second Alumni Stadium was set adjacent to a filled-in reservoir with a nice view of the Boston skyline to the east. Massachusetts Senator John F. Kennedy helped arrange the dedication game against Navy on September 26, 1957. A standing-room only crowd of 26,000 saw the Midshipmen clobber Boston College 46–6.

The stadium, also home to the Boston Patriots for two seasons, got lights, artificial turf, and an extra 6,000 seats in 1971. Probably the biggest moment from that decade came in 1976 when the Eagles edged No. 1 Texas at home. They were at rock bottom two years later, losing all eleven games. Just as suddenly, however, the picture changed due to Doug Flutie, a lightly recruited, diminutive quarterback. He guided BC to wins over big-time opponents like Texas A&M, 1981 national champion Clemson, Penn State, Alabama, and 1983 national champion Miami. Flutie won the 1984 Heisman Trophy, and his Eagles whipped Houston in the Cotton Bowl, ending a storied season at No. 5.

Further renovations of Alumni Stadium in 1988 and 1994 brought seating capacity to 44,500 with upper decks on both sides and in the end zones, a new west-side press box, thirty luxury boxes, new scoreboards and lighting, and a brick-and-glass outer facade that blended with other campus buildings. The running track, a feature since 1957, was taken out. Boston College, a member of the Big East Conference since 1991, has regressed from the glory days of Flutie but still manages to get into minor bowls with some frequency.

Sun Devil Stadium (Arizona State)

Originally, they were the Bulldogs of Arizona Normal College. Their home games were held at Normal Field (which had no stands at all) from 1897 to 1926, then Irish Field from 1927 to 1935, and Goodwin Stadium (twice expanded to a seating capacity of 15,000) for the next twenty-two seasons. The athletic department proposed a new campus stadium as early as 1949, but nothing was done, as dorms, a library, classrooms, and a student union had higher priority for the fast-growing university. In the midst of Dan Devine's three-year stint in which the Sun Devils went 27–3–1 and dominated the Border Conference, a $1 million fundraising drive commenced. Architect Ed Varney designed a lighted 42,000-seat stadium, and contractor Frank Antrim built it between a pair of cactus-covered mountain buttes. Sun Devil Stadium was first used on October 4, 1958, when ASU beat West Texas 16–13 before a crowd of 27,000.

Devine and his successor, Frank Kush, had a number of splendid players—like running back John Henry Johnson, receiver Charley Taylor, quarterback Danny White, running back Woody Green, and defensive back Mike Haynes, all of whom would make their mark in the NFL. The Sun Devils went undefeated in 1970

— Courtesy of Arizona State sports information department

and 1975, and the latter team finished just behind Oklahoma in the national championship race. Sun Devil Stadium, with new south-end locker rooms and another 7,800 seats in the north end, began hosting the Fiesta Bowl in 1971. It only made sense that Arizona State would play in the game five of its first seven years. In time, the Fiesta Bowl became one of the majors, with national championship-deciding games in 1986, 1988, 1995, 1999, and 2002.

After a decade and a half in the Western Athletic Conference, ASU was preparing to join the Pac-10. The stadium grew as a result. In 1976 and 1977, an upper deck wrapping from west to north to east was built at a cost of $11 million, which raised seating capacity to 70,491. Kush was a high-strung martinet of a coach, comparable to Vince Lombardi or Woody Hayes, and his downfall came in the middle of the 1979 season. Enraged over a poor punt in a home game against Washington, Kush hit the offending player (although a subsequent trial resulted in his acquittal) and was ousted. To make matters worse, the NCAA found thirty rules violations, put the school on probation, and turned five victories into forfeits. Kush went on to an itinerant existence in three pro leagues before he got back in the good graces of ASU. The field at Sun Devil Stadium was named in his honor in 1996, and he became a special assistant to AD Gene Smith four years later.

In the meantime, the maroon and gold's stadium underwent substantial change. A 90,000-square-foot complex in the south end provided a new home locker room and offices for coaches and administrators. It was flanked by a pair of video scoreboards. Elsewhere, two new locker rooms were constructed, and a new three-level press box (towering 150 feet above the field) with sixty luxury boxes was installed on the west side. Sun Devil Stadium, then accommodating 73,379 fans, also became home to the Arizona Cardinals of the NFL. In 1988, they had been enticed to leave St. Louis for the location and weather of a booming sunbelt city like Phoenix, but it was an uneasy alliance for ASU, the pro fans and a perpetually losing team. After years of complaints from the players, the field was redone for $2 million. It was lowered four feet, and a high-tech drainage and irrigation system provided a lush green surface, one of the best anywhere.

After eight consecutive mediocre-to-bad seasons in which average attendance dropped to 46,000, the Sun Devils went 11–1 in 1996 as quarterback Jake "the Snake" Plummer (soon to man the same position with the Cards) took them to the Rose Bowl. Earlier that year, the stadium got a facelift in preparation for the Super Bowl, in which the Dallas Cowboys beat the Pittsburgh Steelers. But NFL commissioner Paul Tagliabue was not impressed, contrasting Sun Devil Stadium with dazzling new facilities in Miami and Atlanta. Parking, concessions, and restrooms were woeful, and even the luxury boxes were not very luxurious. Alumni who had long considered their stadium a jewel in the desert and the most visible symbol of the university heard it characterized in less flattering terms. A work in progress since 1958, it did in fact lack the cutting-edge amenities by then considered mandatory in the NFL.

Bill Bidwell, owner of the Cardinals, had whined about Sun Devil Stadium since arriving in Tempe. He asked for and then insisted on a new place of his own. And when the Arizona Diamondbacks got a $238 million baseball park, financed mostly by the taxpayers, Bidwell had a point. The Fiesta Bowl was in firm agreement, as the pro team and bowl game made noise about leaving town. While a referendum was voted down in 1999, a different one passed two years later. It provided for a $355 million (and counting) facility with a retractable field and dome, seating 73,000 fans, due to open in 2005 in Glendale. And what of the Sun Devils? Some people thought ASU might have missed the boat by not casting its lot with the new stadium, which will be fairly close to campus. Were Sun Devil Stadium abandoned and razed, however, it would break a lot of hearts.

Navy–Marine Corps Memorial Stadium (Navy)

Robert Thompson, an 1868 graduate of the U.S. Naval Academy, later founded the Navy Athletic Association and helped prepare a plan to rebuild facilities all over campus, known to Midshipmen as "the yard." In 1923, steel from the recently scrapped USS *Washington* was used to erect a 12,000-seat football stadium in Annapolis, and it was named after Thompson. The Middies made it to the Rose Bowl that season, tying Washington. And they might have won the national championship in 1926 except for the finale, a tie with archrival Army before 110,000 fans at Chicago's newly dedicated Soldier Field. Then, as now, few of Navy's big games have been played at home. Other than two instances caused by World War II travel restrictions, Army-Navy and games against popular schools like Notre Dame, Michigan, and Southern California have been played at these venues: the Polo Grounds, Yankee Stadium, and Giants Stadium in New York; Municipal Stadium, Memorial Stadium, and Ravens Stadium in Baltimore; Franklin Field, JFK Stadium, and Veterans Stadium in Philadelphia; the Oyster Bowl in Norfolk; RFK Stadium in Washington, D.C.; Municipal Stadium in Cleveland; and the Citrus Bowl in Orlando.

Over more than three decades at Thompson Stadium, Navy had some fine teams. All-Americans George Brown, Don Whitmire, and Dick Scott brought glory to the academy with top-five finishes in 1943, 1944, and 1945, and it happened two more times in the 1950s with victories over Mississippi in the Sugar Bowl and Rice in the Cotton Bowl. The old place had served well, but it was time for a change, so $3 million in private donations was collected to build 30,000-seat Navy–Marine Corps Memorial Stadium two miles west of the yard. It was a lighted, double-decked horseshoe with the open end to the southeast,

— Courtesy of Navy sports information department; photo by David Wallace

facing the Severn River and Chesapeake Bay. The stadium walls bore such exotic names as Midway, Iwo Jima, Normandy, Guadalcanal, Inchon, and (later) Mekong Delta—places where Navy and Marine Corps grads had fought and died. On September 26, 1959, it was dedicated with all the pomp and circumstance a military school can muster. With cries of "Anchors aweigh" and "Semper fidelis," the Midshipmen defeated William & Mary 29–2.

The first few years at Navy–Marine Corps Memorial Stadium were happy ones for fans of the blue and gold. In 1960, they went 9–2, falling to Missouri in the Orange Bowl, and running back Joe Bellino won the Heisman Trophy. And in 1963, quarterback Roger Staubach won the Heisman (and would later lead the Dallas Cowboys to two NFL titles), too, as Wayne Hardin's team was ranked No. 2 before losing to Texas in the Cotton Bowl. Then Navy virtually disappeared from the college football scene. They fielded a team every year but became less and less competitive, never again ending a season in the top twenty-five, even in 1978, 1980, and 1981, when they appeared in the Holiday, Garden State, and Liberty bowls, respectively. Running back Napoleon McCallum was named an all-American in 1985, but none have come from Navy since. The rigorous academics, honor codes, and five years of post-graduation military service are enough to deter most high school football stars. Perhaps that is balanced by the one-hour march into the stadium by a white-clad brigade of 4,000, the emphasis on courage and commitment, and 150 years of customs and traditions.

President Jimmy Carter was at the stadium in 1977 when Navy and Georgia Tech met; he had attended the latter school and graduated from the former. A record crowd of 36,172 attended the 1997 game with Air Force, which had by then become the most dominant of the three service academies. The stadium, which has never been expanded (other than new locker rooms in 1992), is in need of renovation such as infrastructure work, a new press box, and better seating. In 1999, superintendent John Ryan included a refurbished and possibly expanded Navy–Marine Corps Memorial Stadium in the academy's strategic plan, but people in the quiet neighborhoods surrounding it are wary, since non-football events are being held there with greater frequency.

University Stadium (New Mexico)

Almost thirty years transpired before the University of New Mexico could fully develop its football program. Knowledge of the game was spotty at best, and student and faculty interest was rather low. UNM played against high schools, Indian schools, military teams, and an occasional college. In 1917, a 110–3 loss to New Mexico State was so humiliating that the players refused the award of their football letters. Roy Johnson, the coach from 1920 to 1930 and athletic director from 1920 to 1949, finally put things on a sound basis.

The Lobos moved into Zimmerman Field in 1938, the year they went 8–2 before losing to Utah in the Sun Bowl. They played in desert obscurity in the Border Conference and the Skyline Conference, facing another challenge in 1952 when the university president unilaterally de-emphasized athletics. That led to a five-year swoon which only ended when running back Don Perkins and coach Marv Levy lifted the team to winning records in 1958 and

—Courtesy of New Mexico sports information department

1959. Both moved on to pro success—Perkins as a player with the Dallas Cowboys and Levy as coach of the Buffalo Bills.

New Mexico capitalized on that success, building 30,646-seat University Stadium at a cost of $750,000. The gates opened on September 17, 1960, when the Lobos put a brutal 77–6 whipping on a team representing the National University of Mexico. With Route 66 running through Albuquerque and the Sandia Mountains to the east, UNM had a pleasantly situated if modest home.

The Lobos won three straight Western Athletic Conference crowns in the early 1960s but went 0–10 in 1968 when average attendance fell below 12,000. A new three-level press box (which contained nine luxury boxes) was built on the west side in 1976, and a soccer/track complex went up in 1985, adjoining the east side of University Stadium. Rudy Davalos became New Mexico's AD in 1993, and he instigated an $8 million renovation. The primary change was a building at the south end named for longtime trainer L. F. "Tow" Diehm. It consisted of a locker room four times the size of the old one, as well as a training area, coaches' offices, and three pavilions from which 572 more fans could view games.

Ticket sales had languished for years, but a record crowd of 37,156 was there to see the Lobos take on Rice in 1997. They lost that game, but, with much help from two-time all-America safety/linebacker Brian Urlacher, they won the WAC's Mountain Division and played in their first bowl game in more than three decades. North end-zone seating with room for another 5,700 fans was completed in 2001 at a cost of $3.5 million.

Beaver Stadium (Penn State)

James Beaver led an interesting life and one that has been well memorialized. He was a Civil War hero, a judge, the governor of Pennsylvania, and president of Penn State's Board of Trustees. Beaver Field, with seating for 500 fans, opened in the middle of campus in 1893. It lasted until 1909 when New Beaver Field was built. Providing a home for the Nittany Lions' football, baseball, track, soccer, and lacrosse teams, its wooden structure was replaced by steel in 1936. Penn State's gridiron fortunes were fairly undistinguished due to a ten-year "purity campaign" that prohibited athletic scholarships. But in 1947, Bob Higgins' team won every regular-season game and tied SMU in the Cotton Bowl (integrating that facility with Wally Tripplett and Dennis Hoggard) and finished No. 4 in the nation.

In 1950, Charles "Rip" Engle was hired, bringing in a young assistant named Joe Paterno. The stadium, which was expanded to 30,000 seats after World War II, had a horseshoe configuration. Bunkered in the Allegheny Mountains in the very center of the state, it was a nice place to watch football on autumn Saturday afternoons. Even today, fifteen miles from the nearest major highway, Penn State retains an air of sheltered seclusion, which is why they call it Happy Valley. After the 1959 season, when quarterback Richie Lucas earned all-America honors, the stadium underwent drastic changes. It was dismantled, moved a mile east, and given an additional 16,000 seats. Renamed Beaver Stadium, it was dedicated on September 17, 1960, with a 20–0 defeat of Boston University.

The Lambert Trophy, awarded since 1936 to the top team in the East, was more or less a tacit admission that the best football was played elsewhere. PSU won it eleven times from 1961 to 1975, but their regional schedule did not impress pollsters. Paterno, who had replaced Engle, bemoaned this lack of respect when his 1968 and 1969 teams went undefeated but ended up No. 2 behind Ohio State and Texas, respectively. The Nittany Lions' climb to prominence was a long and gradual one.

Beaver Stadium had been expanded to 57,538 seats when running back John Cappelletti won the 1973 Heisman Trophy. Five years later, seating capacity had grown to 76,039, and to allow for further expansion, the all-steel stadium was cut into sections and raised eight feet by hydraulic jacks. The track, a feature since 1909, was taken out and new seats installed around the field. With 110 rows on the east side and 100 on the west (site of the press box), Beaver Stadium had become one of the biggest, and it would get bigger still. By 1980, average attendance topped 83,000.

Paterno was lifted onto his players' shoulders after a Sugar Bowl defeat of Georgia and a Fiesta Bowl defeat of Miami as Penn State won national titles in 1982 and 1986. Students, alums, and other fans simply could not get enough of the Nittany Lions; some-

—Courtesy of Penn State sports information department

times as many as 60,000 attended the blue-white spring football game. The stadium, lighted since 1984, got an upper deck in the north end in 1991, making room for 93,000. This was in preparation for Penn State joining the Big 10. When Paterno's 1994 team went 12–0 and beat Oregon in the Rose Bowl, he became the only coach to win in the Orange, Cotton, Sugar, Fiesta, and Rose bowls.

Following the 1999 season (when defensive lineman Courtney Brown and linebacker LaVar Arrington were the top two picks in the NFL draft—another first), more changes were made at Beaver Stadium, and they cost $94 million. A new home locker room was built, and an upper deck in the south end obscured the treasured view of Mt. Nittany but added 12,000 more seats. Sixty luxury boxes on the east side and a six-story videoboard in the north end replete with corporate advertising made it a gargantuan football facility, one of the three biggest, along with Michigan Stadium and Tennessee's Neyland Stadium.

Memorial Stadium (Indiana)

Even before the formation of the Western Conference (the Big 10) in the 1890s, Jordan Field had been home to the Indiana Hoosiers. A fundraising drive began in 1922 in which 14,000 people gave $250,000 to finance Memorial Stadium, recognizing IU students and alumni who had served in World War I. The 22,000-seat horseshoe was built on the grounds of the campus golf course adjoining Tenth Street. The first game held there was against Purdue on November 21, 1925; the two teams battled to a scoreless tie.

That stadium, later expanded to a seating capacity of 30,000, was the site of football games for just twenty-five years. The high-water mark for Indiana there came in 1945 when coach Bo McMillin's team went 9–0–1, won the conference title, and finished No. 4 in the nation. They did not, however, play in a bowl game. Proof that Indiana is one of the Big 10's weak sisters is seen

—Courtesy of Indiana sports information department; photo by Nick Judy

in the fact that McMillin, who left Bloomington after the 1947 season, is the school's last coach with a winning record. Whether that may be attributed to the dominating presence of Notre Dame upstate, the lack of a deep-rooted football culture, or some other factor is anyone's guess.

In the late 1950s, the university began moving its athletic facilities to a 160-acre site on the northern edge of campus. What was initially called Indiana University Stadium was designed by Eggers & Higgins of New York and built on 17th Street (thus its informal name of 17th Street Stadium) by Hunt & Nichols of Indianapolis. Costing $6 million, it had a concave shape with 109 rows on the west side and 72 on the east, providing 48,500 seats. The first game held at the new stadium was on October 8, 1960, when the Hoosiers fell to Oregon State.

IU's years of futility and losing continued. The 1966 team had an odious 1–8–1 record, but coach John Pont engineered a dramatic turnaround the next year. Quarterback Harry Gonso, running back John Isenbarger, and receiver Jade Butcher led them to a 9–1 regular-season mark and, rather incredibly, Indiana's first-ever bowl game; the Hoosiers lost to national champ Southern Cal in the Rose Bowl.

Three significant things happened in 1971. Artificial turf was installed, north and south bleachers added nearly 4,000 new seats, and the facility was renamed Memorial Stadium, honoring IU's sons and daughters who had served in World War II and subsequent wars. The old facility, which was not razed until 1982, became 10th Street Stadium. It was perhaps best known as home to the Little 500 bike race, which began as something of a lark in 1951 and has evolved into the premier intramural collegiate cycling event in the nation.

Memorial Stadium got a facelift in the late 1980s as lights and computerized scoreboards were installed, aluminum benches replaced the old wooden ones, and a 50,000-square-foot athletic facility was built below the east-side stands. It cost $2 million and had a locker room, weight room, offices, and an auditorium. Coach Bill Mallory and AD Ralph Floyd called it evidence that Indiana was serious about football. Fortunes improved somewhat as running back Anthony Thompson gained more than 5,000 yards in his career and finished second in Heisman Trophy voting in 1989. The

Hoosiers played in five minor bowls during Mallory's stint as coach and broke a thirty-six-year losing streak to Ohio State and a twenty-year losing streak to Michigan.

Indiana joined the back-to-nature movement in 1989, replacing artificial turf with Kentucky bluegrass. The athletic department is now in the research and discussion stage regarding possible expansion of the press box and construction of club seating and/or luxury boxes.

Falcon Stadium (Air Force)

The U.S. Army and Navy have existed from the earliest days of the republic, and their academies have long and rich football his-

—Courtesy of Air Force sports information department

tories, as well. The Air Force Academy, on the other hand, did not come into being until 1954 when an 18,000-acre site in Colorado Springs was chosen. The Falcons played a freshman schedule in 1955 and began varsity competition the next year, holding games at Washburn Field and Penrose Stadium and occasionally in nearby Denver, Boulder, and Pueblo. In 1958 (the first of coach Ben Martin's twenty seasons), the blue and silver went 9–0–1 and battled TCU to a scoreless tie in the Cotton Bowl.

Soon afterward, a fundraising drive was begun to build a campus stadium. Air Force personnel and civilians gave $3.5 million for Falcon Stadium, sitting 6,749 feet above sea level in the Rampart Range of the Rocky Mountains. Its original seating capacity was 40,828, and an overflow crowd was there on September 22, 1962, for the inaugural game as the Falcons blanked Colorado State 34–0. But the dedication game later that month was a 35–20 loss to Oregon. Visitors to the stadium were treated to free parking, jet planes providing an aerial salute to the national anthem, and, sometimes, the "Wings of Blue" parachuting team. Artificial turf was installed at Falcon Stadium in the early 1970s, and bleachers on the east side made room for another 3,500 fans. Bleachers in the north and south ends raised seating capacity to 47,352, and by the mid-1990s, those had been replaced with permanent stands, making it 52,480. Grass returned to Falcon Stadium in 1997, and lighting was installed prior to the 2002 season.

Air Force has always had undersized teams composed of young men with military obligations, but they manage to compete at a high level. In 1970, all-America receiver Ernie Jennings paced them to a 9–2 regular-season record and a Sugar Bowl loss to Tennessee. Members of the WAC from 1980 to 1998, they have had two more really exceptional teams. The 1985 Falcons went 12–1, beat Texas in the Bluebonnet Bowl, and finished No. 8; sophomore lineman Chad Hennings would later win the Outland Trophy and three Super Bowl rings with the Dallas Cowboys. And a one-point loss to TCU was all that prevented the 1998 team from going 13–0. With quarterback Blane Morgan and defensive back Tim Curry leading the way, Air Force ended up No. 13. In games with their fellow service academies, the Falcons prevailed easily, beating Navy 49–7 and Army 35–7.

Dowdy-Ficklen Stadium (East Carolina)

Since 1949, the East Carolina Pirates had played at College Stadium, a wooden 5,000-seat structure that cost just $26,000 to build. Fans did not exactly revel in palatial splendor there, so a dozen years later, chancellor Leo Jenkins began raising funds for a new one. It would be named for the late James Ficklen, whose foundation had helped many students attend ECU. And because he had been one of America's leading tobacconists, it was only proper that Ficklen Stadium be erected on the site of a former tobacco field. The $300,000 facility had fifty-eight rows and 10,000 seats, all on the south side of the field. Temporary stands were needed on the north side on opening day, September 21, 1963, as 17,000 fans saw the Pirates beat Wake Forest 20–10. It was the first time an ACC team had ever deigned to play the unpretentious teachers college, and in Greenville no less.

Each of the first three years of the stadium's existence, the Pirates went 9–1 under coach and AD Clarence Stasavich. In 1968, matching north-side stands were built, and in 1975, the lights were moved from field level to the top of the stands. Amid eight consecutive winning seasons (1972 to 1979), ECU invested $2.5 million to expand Ficklen Stadium at all four corners, raising seating capacity to 35,000. A three-level press box and east-end scoreboard were added, too.

Probably the best team in school history came in 1991. Quarterback Jeff Blake and linebacker Robert Jones, both of whom would go on to productive NFL careers, carried the Pirates to an 11–1 record capped by a Peach Bowl defeat of North Carolina State. They ended up No. 9, and Bill Lewis was named national coach of the year before heading off to Georgia Tech.

In the 1990s, the stadium got bigger and so did its name. Ron Dowdy, an East Carolina grad and member of the Board of Trustees, gave $1 million to spur a renovation project, and thus it became Dowdy-Ficklen Stadium. Then Al Bagwell, another alumnus and donor, was honored as the field got his name. In 1998, Dowdy-Ficklen Stadium grew to a seating capacity of 43,000 with the addition of a $13 million north-side upper deck.

Cosmetic changes on the inside and outside, luxury boxes and

AN ILLUSTRATED HISTORY OF 120 COLLEGE FOOTBALL STADIUMS   151

— Courtesy of East Carolina sports information department

club seating, and a $10.5 million strength and conditioning facility in the west end have brought the stadium to a level few could have imagined forty years ago. The purple and gold play in Conference USA, and their boosters insist ECU has achieved parity with four in-state rivals—North Carolina, North Carolina State, Duke, and Wake Forest. Due to flooding of the Tar River after Hurricane Floyd in September 1999, N.C. State graciously allowed ECU to use Carter-Finley Stadium for a home game. But in November, when the Wolfpack visited Greenville, they lost 23–6 before a record crowd of 50,092.

Sun Bowl (Texas–El Paso)

Set in the foothills of the Rocky Mountains, El Paso is a city with 400 years of history. Its primary institution of higher learning is the University of Texas at El Paso, known previously as Texas

—Courtesy of UTEP sports information department

College of Mines and Metallurgy (until 1949) and Texas Western (until 1967). The Miners held their home football games at 15,000-seat Kidd Field, named after faculty member John "Cap" Kidd, who had sustained the program in its infancy. Even before Kidd Field was built in 1937, local officials founded the Sun Bowl, now among the oldest of bowl games. Under coach Jack Curtice and then Mike Brumbelow, UTEP played in the Sun Bowl following the 1948, 1949, 1953, 1954, and 1956 seasons. One of the stars of that 1956 team was speedy running back/receiver/kick returner Don Maynard, destined for a Hall of Fame career with the New York Jets.

Although Kidd Field was adequate for all but the biggest of the Miners' home games, Sun Bowl officials wanted a new and more spacious stadium. So El Paso County and the university joined forces to erect the Sun Bowl stadium half a mile to the southwest. It was a lighted oval in which the open north end had large block letters spelling out "El Paso, Texas." The 30,000-seat stadium was inaugurated on September 21, 1963, when UTEP faced North Texas. On the first play from scrimmage, running back Larry Durham bolted 54 yards for a touchdown, and the Miners went on to win, 34–7. Kidd Field continued in service as the school's track facility.

The mid-1960s were good times in El Paso. Coach Bobby Dobbs guided UTEP to victories over TCU and Mississippi in the

1965 and 1967 Sun Bowls, quarterback Billy Stevens put up some impressive numbers, and linebacker Fred Carr was a big part of that success. Even more fame accrued to the school when the Miners won the NCAA basketball championship. Just as suddenly, though, things went sour. As the newest member of the Western Athletic Conference, UTEP endured fifteen consecutive losing seasons, and eight of them entailed but a single victory or worse. In 1985, for example, the Miners won just once, but it was a biggie—a 23–16 defeat of defending national champion Brigham Young at the Sun Bowl.

The west-side press box got a second deck in 1969, artificial turf was installed in 1974, and 22,000 more seats were added in 1982. Most of these changes were driven by the post-season bowl game (whose naming rights were variously sold to John Hancock, Norwest, and Wells Fargo) and not the Miners, since sellouts were a rarity. Average attendance peaked at 42,000 in 1987 when Bob Stull's team went 7–4 and broke that string of losing seasons. The next year, the Miners won ten games and played in the Independence Bowl, but Stull went on to greener pastures and another desultory decade ensued.

The university and the county maintained a cooperative relationship until 2000 when a fierce legal tussle occurred over possession of the Sun Bowl. Although the taxpayers of El Paso County had gone into debt to build the stadium and gave the university a generous ninety-nine-year lease, the UT System Board of Regents moved to take it by power of eminent domain. The county had agreed to perform $11 million in improvements, but it was felt that the stadium, an integral part of the campus, was best managed and owned by UTEP. Among the changes due at the Sun Bowl are a new scoreboard and a facility to house sports medicine, a training area, and a locker room. The primary donor is Larry Durham, who scored the stadium's first touchdown back in 1963.

Edwards Stadium (Brigham Young)

In 1847, Brigham Young led the Mormons on their famous westward trek to Utah and later founded an academy which bore his name. It was in Provo, forty miles south of Salt Lake City. Toward the end of the century, football players representing BYU met their cousins at the University of Utah in a series of games that ended in brawls. As a result, football was abolished and not reinstated until after World War I. Beginning in 1928, the Cougars' home was a facility which, with hillside seating, could accommodate 5,000 spectators. They played a regional schedule, sometimes venturing as far away as California and Texas. The closest thing to a star player was running back Eldon Fortie, an honorable-mention all-American in the early 1960s.

Groundbreaking ceremonies were held in October 1963 in the northwest corner of the Brigham Young campus. Cougar Stadium, with a seating capacity of 28,812, was ready for the first home game of the 1964 season, a 26–14 loss to New Mexico. Bleachers in the north and south ends soon added another 6,000 seats. A unique feature of Cougar Stadium from its earliest years was one of the largest collections of dinosaur bones in North America. James Jensen, a BYU employee, although not on the faculty, amassed the collection, which helped generate much-needed positive publicity for the school.

For many years, Mormon culture, history, and theology had involved two controversial issues—polygamy and racism. The former supposedly ended when Utah became a state, but the latter endured and was defended by the church's leaders, who, citing specious Biblical interpretations, insisted that people of African lineage could not ascend to the priesthood. Such views were anathema by the 1960s, and protests against BYU were loud and frequent; games were interrupted and violence sometimes broke out among spectators. A number of schools refused to play the Cougars in football games, basketball games, or any other kind of contest. Those were perilous times for the athletic department, the university, and the Mormon hierarchy, which finally abjured its odious stance. The football team, meanwhile, was not integrated until well after such foot-draggers as LSU, Georgia, and Mississippi.

Life in Provo got better with that change and when LaVell Edwards was hired as coach. His 1976 team was the first of nine straight to either win or share the WAC title. The blue and white won thirty-four games from 1979 to 1981, prior to further development of Cougar Stadium. The field was lowered eight feet and the track was removed, allowing construction of ten rows at the base of the east and west stands. A new three-level press box, with one level devoted to luxury boxes, went up on the west side, and sweeping stands in the north and south ends brought seating capacity to 65,000, easily the biggest in the conference. The price tag for these enhancements was $15 million.

The Cougars started the 1984 season unranked but kept winning and moving up in the polls, finally reaching the top. They were voted the national champs amid furious debate over the strength of their schedule, which included just two remotely tough games, Pittsburgh on the road and Michigan in the Holiday Bowl. Critics—some of whom had neither forgotten nor forgiven BYU's racist legacy—were many, but it was Edwards (1984 coach of the year) and his players who got to meet President Ronald Reagan at the White House.

There had been several great quarterbacks at Brigham Young, such as Virgil Carter, Gifford Nielsen, Marc Wilson, Jim McMahon, Steve Young, and Robbie Bosco, but none had won the premier prize in college football, the Heisman Trophy. That ended when Ty Detmer took it in 1990 as a junior when he threw for over 5,000 yards. Cougar Stadium, which saw a record crowd of 66,247 at the 1993 Notre Dame game, got a big new scoreboard in the south end three years later. When Edwards, who had won more than 250 games over a twenty-nine-season career, retired in 2000, the facility was renamed in his honor.

Liberty Bowl (Memphis)

What is now the University of Memphis was West Tennessee State Normal School when the football program began in 1912. Civil War memories were still vivid, so the students chose blue and gray as the school colors. While some games were played on campus, downtown Crump Stadium, which originally had one set of wooden bleachers but was twice expanded by the WPA, was the primary home field for forty years. UM's apogee came in 1938 when the team team went 10–0, but the Tigers again made their

—Courtesy of Memphis sports information department

mark under Billy Murphy. His 1962 and 1963 teams, led by running back Dave Cassinelli and offensive lineman Harry Schuh (later a star with the Oakland Raiders) won seventeen games and finished in the top twenty both times.

Following upon that success, the city of Memphis embarked on an athletic facility building boom. Mid-South Coliseum and Memphis Memorial Stadium went up side by side in the fairgrounds a few miles west of the UM campus. The latter, which cost $3.7 million and had 50,000 seats and a four-level press box on the west side, was dedicated to American vets of World War I, World War II, and the Korean War. It was inaugurated on September 18, 1965, when the Tigers fell to Mississippi. The Rebels liked the stadium so much, they began using it as a home away from home. But Memphis had two other reasons for erecting the facility. First, the Liberty Bowl, which had been played in Philadelphia for four years and once in Atlantic City, moved in. And second, it was the beginning of a futile three-decade courtship of the NFL.

The Tigers, who suffered a seventeen-game losing streak in 1981 and 1982, were surrounded by more popular SEC teams like Vanderbilt, Tennessee, Kentucky, Ole Miss, Mississippi State, and Arkansas of the SWC. They took another hit in 1983 when coach Rex Dockery was killed in a plane crash. So the stadium, which had become the Liberty Bowl in 1976, also took on the name of Rex Dockery Field. Again trying to entice the NFL, Memphis spent $19.5 million on the Liberty Bowl in 1987. Another 12,000 seats were built on the east side, along with forty-four luxury boxes. But the Memphis Southmen of the World Football League, the Memphis Showboats of the United States Football League, the Memphis Mad Dogs of the Canadian Football League, and the Memphis Maniax of the XFL (all Liberty Bowl tenants at one time or another) were not even reasonable facsimiles of big-time pro football.

As for UM, they have never been invited to the post-season bowl game played at their home stadium. However, they shocked the college football world on a sunny afternoon in 1996. A record crowd of 65,885 filled the Liberty Bowl to see the Tigers and No. 6 Tennessee. When quarterback Qadry Anderson hit tight end Chris Powell with a touchdown pass in the last minute, it was a victory Memphis fans had lusted for, and the goal posts came tumbling down.

Melancholy permeated the air when the Houston Oilers agreed to move to Tennessee. Memphis, which had built and then expanded the Liberty Bowl in an effort to draw an NFL team, saw Nashville get one instead. While $292 million Adelphia Coliseum was being built, the Oilers spent the 1997 season in Memphis. Attendance was miserable, as were relations between the university and the city vis-à-vis the Oilers (now the Tennessee Titans), so they rented out Vanderbilt's stadium the following season.

The Tigers, now part of Conference USA, keep plugging along. The Liberty Bowl remains an attractive, distinctively designed stadium, and the bowl game and the annual Southern Heritage Classic, featuring teams from two top black schools, have succeeded without much fanfare. The stadium has also hosted such events as Billy Graham revivals, rock concerts, and tractor and truck competitions.

Lane Stadium (Virginia Tech)

In days gone by, Virginia Tech was an all-male engineering, agricultural, and military institution. Since 1926, the Hokies had played home games at Miles Stadium, named after Clarence Miles, one-time captain, coach, athletic director, and dean. The stadium had grown to 8,500 seats by World War II and 17,000 before its demolition in 1964. Blacksburg, situated between the Blue Ridge Mountains and the Alleghenies, was a college football backwater. The 1954 team went 8–0–1 and finished No. 16, and receiver Carroll Dale, who played in the late 1950s, would have a nice career with the Green Bay Packers, but there were few other real highlights.

Some Virginia Tech officials felt uneasy about a proposal to construct a new stadium on the west side of campus. But Edward Lane, an alumnus and former member of the Board of Visitors, headed a foundation that provided most of the $3.5 million needed

—Courtesy of Virginia Tech sports information department

to design and build Lane Stadium. AD and former coach Frank Moseley oversaw a four-year construction project. Work began in April 1964 and was not truly complete (with matching 20,000-seat east and west grandstands) until 1968. On October 2, 1965, Jerry Claiborne's Hokies beat William & Mary 9–7, with dedication day three weeks later when they edged in-state rival Virginia 22–14 before an overflow crowd of 30,000. Surely the top player in the first three years of Lane Stadium's existence was safety and kick returner Frank Loria, who won all-America honors in 1966 and 1967.

On the heels of three straight losing seasons, Virginia Tech expanded the stadium in 1980. At a cost of $3.2 million, 12,500 new seats were added to the east side. And with the installation of lights two years later, Tech had a suitable facility in which Bruce Smith could cavort. The defensive end had a fine career in maroon and orange, winning the Outland Trophy. Smith thus had the honor of being the top pick in the 1985 NFL draft, after which he established himself as one of the all-time greats with the Buffalo Bills and Washington Redskins.

After twenty-six years as an independent, Virginia Tech joined the Big East in 1991, the same year a south-end scoreboard went up at Lane Stadium. The following season, the field was named in honor of Wes Wortham, an alumnus and benefactor. Frank Beamer, a Hokie player in the late 1960s, had mixed results his first few seasons as coach, but things got rolling in time. Beginning with Smith, more players were having an impact in the pros, and Beamer's 1995 team came of age with a 10–2 record which included a 28–10 defeat of Texas in the Sugar Bowl. Amazingly enough, the Hokies had become a top-ten team and were challenging for the national championship. They nearly won it in 1999 when frosh quarterback Michael Vick led them to an undefeated regular season before they fell to Florida State in the Sugar Bowl. Beamer won coach-of-the-year awards bearing the names of such luminaries as Walter Camp, Bobby Dodd, Woody Hayes, Bear Bryant, and Eddie Robinson.

With season-ticket demand rising yearly, Virginia Tech started a four-year project to renovate and expand Lane Stadium. The key components are an 11,000-seat double-deck grandstand in the south end, 3,000 more seats and a scoreboard in the north end, a new visitors' locker room, club seating, fifty-two luxury boxes, and an enhanced press box. This is all due to be completed in time for the 2003 season with a price tag of $65 million. Seating capacity will be between 66,000 and 68,000.

Huskie Stadium (Northern Illinois)

Northern Illinois' first home was cozy Glidden Field which, with expansions in the 1920s and 1940s, came to hold 5,500 fans. The patriarch of the red and black was George "Chick" Evans, coach of the football team for twenty-six years and AD for thirty-nine. He had a couple of undefeated teams, but the program may have peaked in 1963 under Howard Fletcher. With quarterback George Bork passing for over 3,000 yards (the first player to do so), the Huskies went 10–0 and won the NCAA's college-division national championship.

The team was doing well and enrollment was growing, so NIU had to get out of Glidden Field. Groundbreaking for a new facility on the west side of campus took place in January 1964. Huskie Stadium, costing $2.3 million, consisted of a 15,000-seat concrete west grandstand and 5,257 temporary bleachers on the east side. It was dedicated on November 6, 1965, homecoming day, and the Huskies put the wood to Illinois State 48–6.

Artificial turf was installed in 1969, the year NIU moved up to Division I-A status. The "Doghouse" got an extra 5,000 seats in 1982 with bleachers in the north and south ends. That preceded another outstanding team as the 1983 Huskies went 10–2, won the Mid-American Conference, and edged Cal State–Fullerton in the California Bowl. A huge upset occurred in 1990 when No. 24 Fresno State came to DeKalb and fell 73–18.

The stadium was finally lighted in 1993, the senior season for LeShon Johnson, who (like Mark Kellar twenty years before) led the nation in rushing. Johnson, a consensus all-American and sixth in Heisman Trophy voting, is widely considered the finest player in Northern Illinois history.

After three decades of recruits hearing promises that the east side of the stadium would be completed before graduation, it finally happened in 1995. A steel and aluminum grandstand, cost-

—Courtesy of Northern Illinois sports information department

ing $4.7 million, replaced the old bleachers and raised seating capacity to 31,000. NIU, which embodied futility for much of the 1990s, suffered through a twenty-three-game losing streak, but that ended on a rainy day in 1998 at Huskie Stadium when Joe Novak's team beat Central Florida.

Mackay Stadium (Nevada)

The gold and silver ore extracted from Nevada's Comstock Lode in the middle of the nineteenth century produced staggering wealth for several people. One of them was Irish immigrant John Mackay, whose son Clarence inherited quite a fortune. Due to his munificence and desire to perpetuate his father's name, Mackay transformed the University of Nevada, previously just a

162 HOME FIELD

—Courtesy of Nevada sports information department

windswept bit of desert dirt. Beginning in 1906, he funded the design and construction of many academic buildings as well as an athletic field named after his mining-tycoon dad. The original Mackay Stadium lasted for over fifty years before a second one, of the same name, was built on the campus four blocks north of downtown Reno.

Few schools can say with certainty that their greatest athlete played as long ago as the early 1940s, but that is unequivocally so for the Nevada Wolf Pack. Marion Motley, a transfer from all-black South Carolina State, was a 6'1", 240-pound package of muscle and speed who ran like a bull gone mad. As a blocker, running back, and linebacker, he was a devastating force who helped integrate modern pro football. He and quarterback Otto Graham carried the Cleveland Browns to four All-American Football Conference titles and one after the merger with the NFL. Motley was a pioneer and one of the finest players of all time.

By the mid-1960s, it was clear that the old stadium was outmoded and in the way of UNR's progress. In early 1966, construction began on a new facility which would cost $800,000 and seat 7,500 fans. The first game at half-finished Mackay Stadium was on

October 1, 1966, when Nevada beat California–Santa Barbara 33–17. The Wolf Pack's junior quarterback was Chris Ault, who would later spend many successful years as coach and AD.

A rubber track was installed at the stadium in 1988, and as Ault prepared to bring Nevada into NCAA Division I-A, a horseshoe was built in the north end, bleachers in the south end, a second deck on the east side, and a new press box and sixty luxury boxes on the west side. Costing $15 million, these various projects raised seating capacity to 31,545. Artificial turf made a belated appearance in 2000, but the stadium still lacks lighting.

UNR, now averaging 23,000 fans per game, has had other stars, such as defensive lineman Charles Mann, defensive back Brock Marion, and quarterback John Dutton. The silver and blue made an impressive comeback in the 1991 game against Weber State; down by 35 points, they nevertheless managed to win by six. The biggest crowd ever at Mackay Stadium, 33,391, gathered in 1995 to see the Wolf Pack devour its downstate neighbor, Nevada–Las Vegas, 55–32.

Perry Stadium (Bowling Green)

In 1936, the WPA and Bowling Green combined to build University Stadium in the middle of campus. It was first put to use on October 23, 1937 (a 9–7 loss to Ohio Northern) and was the Falcons' home for three decades. Some good players passed through Bowling Green, including Bob Schnelker, Bernie Casey, Bob Reynolds, and Mike Weger, all of whom went on to pro success.

Doyt Perry, a three-sport athlete at the school in the early 1930s, was hired as coach in 1955. Under Perry's direction for the next ten years, the Falcons won 85 percent of their games, five Mid-American Conference titles, and the 1959 college-division national championship. He had given up coaching and was athletic director when Bowling Green decided to build a new facility in the wide-open spaces east of campus. Also known as University Stadium, it cost $3 million and had 23,272 seats evenly divided between east and west stands. The dedication game on October 1, 1966, was a 13–0 defeat of Dayton.

—Courtesy of Bowling Green sports information department

There have been few significant changes to the stadium. North and south bleachers in 1982 raised seating capacity to 30,599, and a 1988 facelift included a new weight room on the west side. Temporary lighting was first used in 1989, and the stadium was named for Perry following his death in 1992. The Falcons, part of the NCAA's Division I-A since 1983, have had some lean years, with average attendance falling below the 10,000 mark. But they have had some good ones, too. A stadium-record crowd of 33,527 was there for the 1983 Toledo game, and the team went 11–1 in 1985 and again in 1991, both times playing in the California Bowl. Brian McClure, who passed for more than 10,000 yards in the mid-1980s, was one of the first quarterbacks to do so.

Carter-Finley Stadium (North Carolina State)

In the earliest days of North Carolina State football, games were held at the local fairgrounds. Then in 1907, a field laid out on campus was named for Wallace Riddick, a faculty member who had coached the team for two seasons with an unprepossessing

1–3–2 record. Football and baseball would be played there for almost sixty years. West stands (with dormitories underneath) were built in 1916, and east stands were built in 1935, shortly after the installation of lights. With a seating capacity of just 14,000, Riddick Stadium was among the smallest in the Southern Conference and later the ACC.

As a result, the Wolfpack sometimes played home games in such locales as Charlotte, Greensboro, Winston-Salem, and Norfolk. In 1960 and 1961, when Roman Gabriel was the quarterback, NCSU had ten straight road games, basically because few major schools would come to Raleigh. Earle Edwards, who coached the team for seventeen years, pushed and prodded the university to build a new facility. When the North Carolina Department of Agriculture gave some land adjacent to the fairgrounds in 1964, the $3.7 million project was on its way. A pond had to be drained and excavation done before building commenced. Brothers Wilbert and Harry Carter, North Carolina State

— Courtesy of North Carolina State sports information department

grads who had done well in the textile industry, were the biggest donors, and thus the name was Carter Stadium. It had two decks on each side, a three-level press box, and 41,000 permanent seats. The stadium was first put to use on October 8, 1966, but the visiting South Carolina Gamecocks spoiled the fun, taking a 31–21 victory. The west stands of Riddick Stadium were preserved, now housing the university's police force, while the former field has become a parking lot.

The 1967 Wolfpack was one of the best teams in school history, reaching No. 3 at one point, and had a 9–2 record with a defeat of Georgia in the Liberty Bowl. The weakness of the ACC at that time, on the cusp of the big change—integration—was evident because it broke a twenty-three-game losing streak by ACC teams to Southeastern Conference foes. North Carolina State, in particular, has never finished in the top ten nor played in a major bowl game.

Sellouts at the stadium were rare, so there was no need for expansion, although bleachers and general-admission seating on the grassy south hillside made room for as many as 58,000 fans on occasion. The main change came in the mid-1970s when Albert Finley, another longtime athletic supporter, was recognized in the familiar way as NCSU's home became Carter-Finley Stadium. Center Jim Ritcher, running back Ted Brown, and receiver Torry Holt are just three of the stars who have worn the red and white before moving on to the NFL. Holt was a senior when North Carolina State pulled a huge upset, beating No. 2 Florida State 24–7 in Raleigh. The Aggie-Eagle Classic, featuring the teams from North Carolina Central and North Carolina A&T, has been played at Carter-Finley Stadium since 1994, and attendance has been surprisingly good.

Expansion and renovation had been discussed for years, and the athletic department got some valuable experience with the construction of the Entertainment and Sports Arena just to the north of the stadium in 1999. The funding of that facility was a joint venture among the university, the city of Raleigh, Wake County, and the Carolina Hurricanes of the National Hockey League. The price tag was $154 million, with considerable wrangling among those four entities. NCSU, determined to avoid a repeat of that fiasco, has embarked on a fundraising drive expected to last five years, with work due to be complete by 2003. Estimated costs to fix up Carter-Finley Stadium have risen from $40 million to over $100 million for a three-phase project that will add 12,000 seats, forty luxury boxes, a new scoreboard and press box, and a nearby building with offices and an indoor practice field. "It's all about facilities," said one North Carolina State observer. "You can't have a championship-caliber program without top players, and you can't attract top players without quality facilities."

Qualcomm Stadium (San Diego State)

Until the mid-1930s, San Diego State played home games downtown at Balboa Stadium and then spent three decades on campus at the Aztec Bowl, which held 13,000 seats. The Aztecs' schedule gradually changed from junior colleges and military teams (San Diego is one of the nation's largest navy outposts) to

— Courtesy of San Diego State sports information department

mid-sized schools and a few Pac-10 big boys. For most of SDSU's football history, 70 percent of its home games have been played at night.

A couple of key events took place in 1961. Don Coryell began a twelve-year run as head coach, using a downfield passing attack that brought 104 victories and three small-college national championships. And *San Diego Union* sports editor Jack Murphy convinced the Los Angeles Chargers of the American Football League to move down the coast. They played in Balboa Stadium, but that ancient edifice would not do for long. Murphy used his bully pulpit to good advantage; with editorials, speeches, and behind-the-scenes cajoling, he got the city to invest $27.5 million to build San Diego Stadium, five miles west of the university. Not only would the Chargers and Aztecs play football there, but Murphy's efforts helped the San Diego Padres go from a minor league baseball franchise to the majors in 1969, so it was a dual-purpose facility. The Chargers were the first to use 52,675-seat San Diego Stadium, losing to the Detroit Lions in an exhibition game on August 20, 1967. A month later, SDSU beat Tennessee State 16–8 before 45,822 fans. The red and black, in the midst of a twenty-five-game winning streak, saw average attendance jump from 15,972 in the last year at the Aztec Bowl to 40,157 in the first year at the new place. With assistants like John Madden, Joe Gibbs, and Ernie Zampese and players like Haven Moses, Dennis Shaw, Fred Dryer, Brian Sipe, and Isaac Curtis, Coryell created a lot of sweet memories for San Diego State football fans. He went on to coach the St. Louis Cardinals for five seasons and was back in San Diego with the Chargers for nine more.

The Holiday Bowl began at San Diego Stadium following the 1978 season, but the Aztecs did not play in it until 1986, a 39–38 loss to Iowa. The stadium hosted major league baseball's all-star games in 1978 and 1992, and some World Series games in 1984 and 1998 when the Padres faced—and lost to—the Detroit Tigers and New York Yankees, respectively. In January 1981, shortly after Murphy's death, the facility he had done so much to build and where he had covered so many events was renamed Jack Murphy Stadium. Banking on the promise of a Super Bowl from the NFL, the city did a $9 million expansion of the stadium in 1985, enclosing what had been the right-field area in its baseball layout. With fifty luxury boxes in place, there was room for 60,409 spectators who saw the Washington Redskins beat the Denver Broncos for the NFL title.

The Aztecs were barely above .500 from 1991 to 1993, but attendance was strong thanks largely to the fine play of Marshall Faulk. A two-time all-America running back, he gained 4,589 yards, merited the second pick in the 1994 pro draft, and went on to more big things with the Indianapolis Colts and St. Louis Rams. As another Super Bowl loomed (in which the Denver Broncos would beat the Green Bay Packers in January 1998), the stadium underwent a $66 million expansion, bringing seating capacity up to 71,400, on five levels, with a total of 113 luxury boxes. Part of the deal was that Qualcomm, a giant but locally based communications company, would pay $18 million for naming rights over the next twenty years, and thus it became Qualcomm Stadium.

There have been baseball/football compromises at the stadium since the beginning, but that finally ended. Voters passed a referendum allowing construction of a new $411 million downtown park for the Padres, which will open in 2004. The Chargers, whose lease at Qualcomm Stadium runs through 2020, are seeking further modifications, both financial and structural. San Diego hosted a third Super Bowl in January 2003.

Autzen Stadium (Oregon)

With two Rose Bowl appearances in the previous five seasons, Oregon felt safe in building a new stadium in 1921. But since the Ducks would not play in another bowl game until 1948, Hayward Field became as well known for track meets as for football games. Great players like Norm Van Brocklin and Mel Renfro were all too rare in Eugene, and the teams seldom achieved national prominence.

By the mid-1960s, the university realized it was time to get football out of Hayward Field. Ninety acres just north of the Willamette River were available at a bargain-basement price, so athletic director Leo Harris spearheaded a fundraising drive that brought in $2.5 million. After Portland lumberman Thomas Autzen gave a tenth of that sum, the stadium was named in his honor. An amphitheater cut into the ground, it had 35,362 seats (some of which, on the south side, were covered by a cantilevered roof), and the first rows stood a mere thirty feet from the sidelines. Autzen Stadium was inaugurated on September 23, 1967, when Colorado beat UO 17–13.

Artificial turf was installed prior to the 1969 season, but the distinctive alternating light green/dark green layout came much later. Average attendance hovered around 30,000 for the first two decades, partly because the Ducks were dead in the water; they went another twenty-six years without a bowl, not counting the so-called "Toilet Bowl" against Oregon State. The final game of the 1983 season was held at Autzen Stadium in a rainstorm, and the two pathetic teams played to a scoreless tie.

Club seating, a large master suite, and luxury boxes were built in 1981, 1988, and 1993, which boosted seating capacity to 41,698, still leaving the stadium as the third-smallest in the Pac-10. The Casanova Center (1993) and the Moshofsky Center (1998) outside the west end, while providing much-needed facilities for the athletic department, nevertheless made a bad parking situation worse. Life for the green and yellow was improving, however. In 1994, they went 9–4 and represented the conference against Penn State in the Rose Bowl. When Rich Brooks, coach during the previous eighteen years, left for the NFL, Oregon showed its gratitude by naming the field after him, notwithstanding his 46 percent win-loss record.

Mike Bellotti replaced Brooks and kept the ball rolling with a succession of winning seasons and bowl games. Quarterback Akili Smith was the third pick in the 1998 NFL draft, and Autzen Stadium got lights and a high-tech sound system the next year. Almost overnight, it had become one of the loudest and most feared venues on the West Coast. Oregon's little big house gained such a reputation due to rabid quacker-backers who were sometimes rude to visiting teams and fans. As the spotlight shone brighter, their behavior seemed to get uglier.

In 1999, with the Duck football program on the rise, AD Bill Moos announced plans to spend $80 million to renovate and expand the stadium with luxury boxes and an additional 12,000 seats on the south side. But a public relations fiasco broke loose when

UO joined the Worker Rights Consortium, an organization harshly critical of labor conditions in Nike's overseas factories. Nike, the world's biggest athletic apparel maker, had been co-founded by Bill Bowerman (then Oregon's track coach) and Phil Knight (one of his runners), and the company had long given shoes, uniforms, and money in support. In response to the WRC matter, Knight's $30 million pledge was angrily yanked before Moos and others hastened to apologize enough to get it reinstated. The Autzen Stadium construction project is scheduled for completion in 2003.

Ball State Stadium (Ball State)

Basketball and baseball were established sports at Ball State before football got off the ground. Coach Paul "Billy" Williams, who also served as AD for thirty-eight years, sent his first team onto Ball Recreation Field in 1924. That facility would be home to BSU for the next forty-three seasons and would eventually have 9,000 seats. While the Cardinals seldom left Indiana or adjoining states, they were competitive in their own sphere. The 1949 team, under coach John Magnabosco, went 8–0, and Tim Brown, who played at Ball State in the late 1950s, became quite a running back for the Philadelphia Eagles. And Ray Louthen's 1965 team won every regular-season game before being tied by Tennessee State in the small-college Grantland Rice Bowl.

Rather than renovate and expand Ball Recreation Field, the university chose to build a new stadium on the north side of campus. The curtain rose on Ball State Stadium (seating capacity of 16,319) on October 21, 1967, when the Cards pummelled Butler 65–7. The stadium, which had no lights, was home to the 1976 MAC champs in just their second year in the league. Probably the most exciting game in the stadium's history took place in 1993 when Toledo held a 30–3 lead late in the third quarter. BSU proceeded to score four touchdowns, the last as time expired, and Matt Swart's extra point kick made it 31–30.

In 1995, coming off three straight seasons in which average attendance fell below 10,000, the university spent $12 million to ex-

—Courtesy of Ball State sports information department

pand the east side of the stadium by 5,200 seats. The Cardinals were the subject of ridicule from mid-1998 to mid-2000 as they dropped twenty-one games in a row. Compounding their misery, BSU alumnus David Letterman tossed a number of barbs on his late-night television show. The streak ended at an away game, but back in Muncie the next week, the red and white won again, which prompted a mob of students to tear down the goal posts and deposit them in a nearby pond.

Ball State Stadium underwent major improvements following the 2000 season. The north end was enclosed and the south end got more seats, making room for 30,000 fans. The outer facade was enhanced, as was the press box. Club seating and luxury boxes were built on the west side, and a new home locker room and weight room went up in the south end. Using low ticket prices, creative marketing, and help from the Muncie business community, Ball State is doing all it can to remain viable in NCAA Division I-A football.

Romney Stadium (Utah State)

E. L. "Dick" Romney began working at Utah State in 1919. He coached the baseball team for ten years, the basketball team for twenty-two years (winning an AAU national title), track for twenty-four years, and football for twenty-nine years. He was also AD for thirty-one years and spent a decade as commissioner of the Mountain States Conference. Rather early in Romney's tenure, the university named its football stadium after him.

Sheer longevity would make Romney the winningest coach in USU history, but John Ralston, another Hall of Famer, had some fine teams as well. In 1960 and 1961, the Aggies won eighteen games and played in the Sun and Gotham bowls, aided in large part by two-time all-America defensive lineman Merlin Olsen, who went on to a sterling career with the Los Angeles Rams.

Campus growth compelled Utah State to plan a new football stadium. The student body voted to pay fees covering construction of the new Romney Stadium and also the Smith Spectrum for hoops and volleyball. The stadium, oddly assymetrical with all seats between the 15-yard lines, was first used on September 14, 1968, when the Ags beat New Mexico State 28–12 before 9,217 fans, but the dedication game was postponed until 1969. Although light-years from the traditional college football powers, Romney Stadium was in a nice setting in the Cache Valley of northern Utah with mountains visible in every direction.

Attendance has always fluctuated depending on whether Brigham Young (or, to a lesser extent, Utah) visits Logan. Three times in the stadium's history, average attendance has fallen below 10,000 per game. After going 7–3–1 in 1979, USU chose to expand the 20,000-seat facility by adding a south-end horseshoe with room for 10,000 more fans. The neighboring Cougars and Utes played in Romney Stadium in 1996, and both games were sellouts; the blue and white lost to BYU and defeated Utah. In 1997, 4,000 prime seats on the west side were upgraded from wooden bleachers to the chairback variety, and the press box was renovated. The most recent change to the stadium came prior to the 1999 season, when new scoreboards were built in the north and south ends, and extra bleachers raised seating capacity to 35,257. Other than a 1–10

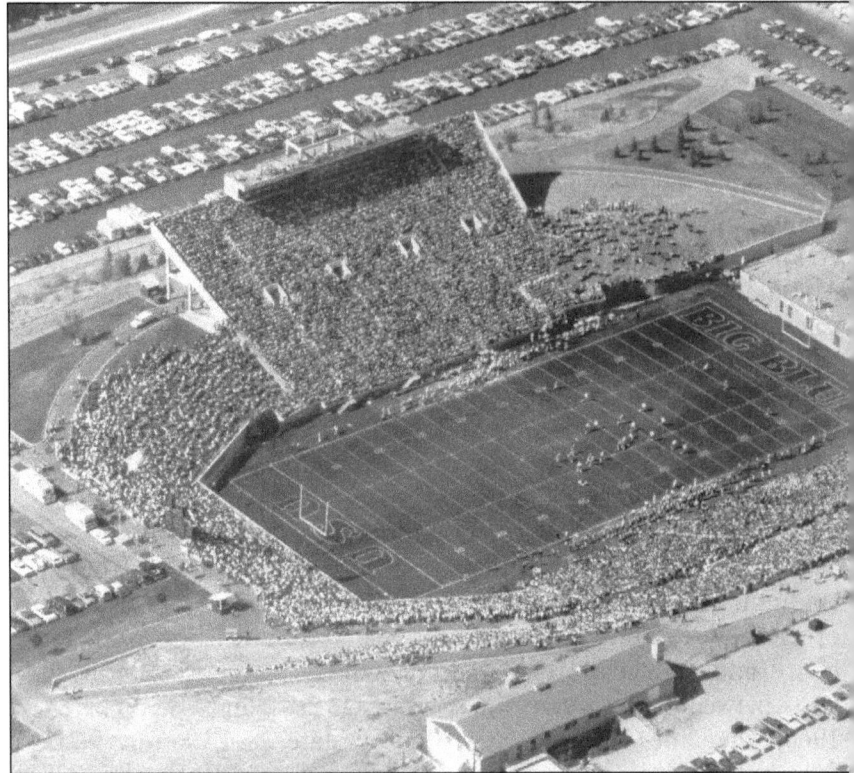

—Courtesy of Utah State sports information department

record in 1984, the Aggies are never really bad. Still, they have had eight coaches over a twenty-eight-year span, and that is one season fewer than Dick Romney held the job, albeit in a much less cutthroat era.

Groves Stadium (Wake Forest)

Since its founding in the 1830s, Wake Forest University had been located in the eastern North Carolina village of Wake Forest. Home games were occasionally played in larger towns such as Charlotte, Greensboro, and Winston-Salem, even after 20,000-seat Groves Stadium was built in 1940. While coach D. C. "Peahead"

Walker had bowl teams in 1945 and 1948, there was uncertainty at Wake Forest, and football was not the issue. In 1956, after eight years of discussion and planning, the university picked up and moved 100 miles west to Winston-Salem. The Groves family, longtime benefactors, made another financial donation to ensure that their name would also be connected to the new stadium, but with more pressing needs, it remained a dream for nearly two decades.

In the meantime, the Deacons used Bowman Gray Stadium. That 16,000-seat horseshoe facility was one of the most unique in the history of American sports. It was a football field surrounded by a quarter-mile track in which stock car racers like Junior Johnson and Richard Petty plied their noisy trade. Bowman Gray Stadium was less than ideal for the black and gold, and the Atlantic Coast Conference fathers urged them to get out as soon as possible. Brian Piccolo, undoubtedly Wake Forest's most famous football player, spent three years in the odd facility. He was a fine runner who gained over 1,000 yards and scored 111 points in 1964 and played alongside Gale Sayers in the Chicago Bears' backfield before succumbing to cancer.

With continued membership in the ACC at stake, Wake Forest began a fundraising drive to build a new stadium. Local philanthropist Charles Babcock donated a seventy-seven-acre plot of land a mile east of campus, and ground was broken in 1967. Groves Stadium, costing $4 million, had a five-level press box on the west side, lights, a grass surface, and two sets of stands with room for 31,500 fans. It was dedicated on September 14, 1968, when the Deacons lost to North Carolina State 10–6. The team went 2–7–1 that year, but AD Gene Hooks had to be pleased with the new stadium.

Wake Forest is a school with scant football history. The Deacons had gone almost thirty years without cracking the top twenty and accordingly had been in few big games. One exception was in 1979 when John Mackovic's No. 18 team hosted No. 13 Auburn and rallied from an 18-point halftime deficit to win. The biggest crowd Groves Stadium has ever seen came the following season when North Carolina visited Winston-Salem and won before 37,411 fans. Most of the overflow sat on "Deacon Hill," a grassy area in the south end.

—Courtesy of Wake Forest sports information department

The appearance and utility of Groves Stadium improved in the late 1990s with a $1.5 million renovation. And $8 million Bridger Field House in the north end has added new locker rooms, offices, and other amenities. But long-suffering Wake Forest fans have doubts about the administration's commitment to winning and believe their school is content to emulate Duke, Vanderbilt, Rice, and those in the Ivy League. The alternative to remaining mired in losing and mediocrity is to throw a ton of money at the football program and cut corners academically to get some blue-chip players. It would be an uphill and expensive battle with no guarantee of success, and Wake Forest is unlikely to make such an attempt.

KSU Stadium (Kansas State)

Like so many other schools after World War I, Kansas State built a football stadium to honor its fallen heros. Memorial Stadium, a 22,500-seat facility, lasted forty-six seasons, but a Big 6 title in 1934 was the best the Wildcats could do during that stretch. The nondescript land-grant college on the Kansas plains had some bad teams; between 1937 and 1967, there were just two winning seasons. No victories, nineteen losses, and a single tie constituted K-State's football results in 1965 and 1966, so it must have seemed an act of hubris when plans were made to build a new stadium on the northern edge of campus. The students voted not to help pay for it, so AD Ernie Barrett went after state and corporate money. He raised $1.6 million, which covered design and construction of 35,000-seat KSU Stadium. It was inaugurated on September 21, 1968, when Vince Gibson's Cats defeated Colorado State 21–0. Memorial Stadium was not razed but lived on as a site for intramurals, with academic and administrative offices below the stands.

KSU Stadium got artificial turf and was expanded in 1970 with 4,000 more seats on the east side and 3,000 more on the west. New locker rooms and offices were built in the north end two years later. Life in Manhattan was less than a dream, as the purple and white lost with numbing regularity. It is indicative that Kansas State could not boast a consensus all-American until 1977 when linebacker Gary Spani won that honor, and the school's first bowl game came five years later.

Lights were installed at the stadium in 1983, but the losing continued unabated. Average attendance bottomed out at 19,000 in 1986 when the Wildcats started a twenty-six-game losing streak. It was the worst of times, and some pundits even suggested that the Big 8 kick K-State out of the conference and bring in the University of Arkansas. Coaches came and went, so no one was surprised when Bill Snyder, a former assistant at Iowa, went 1–10 in 1989, his first year on the job. Things would be different this time, however. President Jon Wefald promised Snyder improved athletic facilities and was good on his word. A four-year, $2 million project enhanced or created new facilities aiming to bring in and retain quality players. One part of that effort was a layer of artificial turf, and the new field was named to honor Kansas State benefactor Dave Wagner. A $3.3 million, five-level press box (including twenty-one luxury boxes) was erected on the west side in 1993, when Snyder's team went 9–2 with a victory over Wyoming in the Copper Bowl.

The Cats' renaissance had begun in earnest. They were winning and winning big, although some critics regarded their nonconference schedule as loaded with creampuffs. From 1995 to 1998, they won forty-one games and played in the Holiday, Cotton, Fiesta, and Alamo bowls. The 1998 team came within a hair of winning the national crown; Snyder was named coach of the year, and no fewer than eight players—Michael Bishop (second in Heisman Trophy voting), David Allen, Martin Gramatica, Jeff Kelly, Jarrod Cooper, Mark Simoneau, Darnell McDonald, and Ryan Young—made at least third-team all-America. It was an unprecedented turnaround in which the Wildcats had gone from chumps to champs, from the outhouse to the penthouse in less than a decade. As a result, KSU Stadium, the "purple palace," grew to a seating capacity of 50,300 (including thirty-one more luxury boxes) at a cost of $12.8 million, and there are blueprints for another 20,000 seats. Wefald, the man who took a big risk and saw it pay off, had this to say: "We had nothing. No tradition, no history, no body of believers. It took a lot of hard work, team effort, and luck."

Hughes Stadium (Colorado State)

They were called the Colorado A&M Aggies during Harry Hughes' thirty-one-year (1911–41) reign as head coach. And they played at 10,000-seat Colorado Field in the southeast corner of campus. The season that old-timers remember most fondly was 1949, when Bob Davis' team, full of World War II vets, went 9–1 and two-way lineman Thurman "Fum" McGraw had his second straight all-American season.

By the early 1960s, they were the Colorado State Rams, but a twenty-six-game losing streak made Ft. Collins an inhospitable place for players, coaches, and fans. When the university began planning a 30,000-seat football facility two miles to the west, campus politicos attempted and largely succeeded in combining the disparate issues of stadium construction with racism and the Vietnam War. Colorado Field had a second life as a track venue named after Jack Christiansen, who had played football and baseball and run track for CSU in the early 1950s. The new stadium, three miles from campus, with forty rows on the east side and sixty on the west, had grassy areas in both end zones for the occasional overflow crowd. If not the Taj Mahal of college football, it was nevertheless an attractive stadium well worth the $3 million investment. Named in honor of Hughes, it was first used on September 28, 1968, when North Texas beat Colorado State 17–12 before 22,000 fans. Because the green and gold were fairly awful in 1968, the first victory did not come until the following season.

Few major changes have been made at Hughes Stadium in its three and a half decades of existence. West-side seats between the 30-yard lines got the VIP upgrade in 1980, and lights were added in 1998, although portable lights had permitted night games as early as 1991. Plans have been formulated to expand the stadium for the first time. If the athletic department can set up the financing, Hughes Stadium will grow to a seating capacity of 40,000 by 2004 with luxury boxes, artificial turf, and a renovated press box.

As for the school's football fortunes, there has been bad (a total of two wins in 1987 and 1988) and good (three appearances in the Holiday Bowl and one in the Liberty Bowl in the mid- and late 1990s). Running back Lawrence McCutcheon, defensive lineman

—Courtesy of Colorado State sports information department

Bubba Baker, and defensive back Greg Myers did well in the pros, and Sonny Lubick won national coach-of-the-year honors from *Sports Illustrated* when his team went 10–2 in 1994. A record crowd of 39,107 filled Hughes Stadium that year to see the Rams lose to Utah. CSU fans have been highly gratified to see their team go toe-to-toe with the University of Colorado, even when that "home" game is played in Denver's Mile High Stadium. With 76,000 people in attendance, it generates a big payday for both schools.

Aillet Stadium (Louisiana Tech)

A 5,000-seat concrete-and-wood facility had served as Louisiana Tech's home field since the mid-1930s. The Bulldogs did well there, winning numerous championships in the Gulf States Conference. The founder of that league was Joe Aillet, Louisiana Tech's coach from 1940 to 1966 and athletic director from 1940 to 1970.

Even for a remote little town like Ruston, however, the stadium was inadequate. Toward the end of Aillet's tenure, the university decided to replace it with something more fitting. Tech Stadium had a seating capacity of 23,000, a grass surface, and eight banks of lights 150 feet above the field. It was unveiled on September 28, 1968, when Louisiana Tech beat East Carolina 35–7. The junior quarterback for the red and blue was Terry Bradshaw. While some good players had passed through Ruston before and others (like Roger Carr, Fred Dean, William Roaf, and Tim Rattay) would follow, Bradshaw is surely the most luminous star. He was the first pick in the 1970 NFL draft and went on to help the Pittsburgh Steelers win four Super Bowls.

Bradshaw was gone when Louisiana Tech hit the heights. From 1971 to 1974, the Bulldogs went 44–4 and won a pair of small-college national championships under coach Maxie Lambright. In 1972, the stadium was named in honor of Aillet, who had died the previous year. President F. Jay Taylor's goal was to leave behind what he called the "mandated mediocrity" of small-college football, so changes had to be made. In 1985, the stadium's press box got a third level with club seating for 200 fans. The schedule was

— Courtesy of Louisiana Tech sports information department

upgraded considerably, which meant taking a few beatings over the years (such as 66–3 by Florida State in 1988, 73–3 by Houston in 1991, and 56–3 by Alabama in 1993), but the Bulldogs usually acquitted themselves well. They expressed a willingness to "play anybody, anywhere," partly because their little stadium precluded hosting big-time opponents. After sections were added to the corners of Aillet Stadium in 1989, bringing seating capacity to 30,600, Louisiana Tech was finally a Division I-A school.

The Bulldogs cracked the top twenty-five for the first time in 1999, despite playing just three home games in which attendance averaged 20,000. The Charles Wyly Athletic Center was erected in the south end of the stadium in 2000, providing sports medicine facilities and coaches' offices.

Dix Stadium (Kent State)

Kent State University, situated on the hilly banks of the Cuyahoga River, does not have the most dazzling football history.

—Courtesy of Kent State sports information department

The Golden Flashes have lost more than they have won, so the high points are few. In 1954, with running back Lou Mariano leading the way, they went 8–2 and played in the long-defunct Refrigerator Bowl. Home field, near the middle of campus, was Memorial Stadium. It was built in 1950 for just $75,000 and expanded twice. Although the team had but one victory in 1968 and brought up the rear in the Mid-American Conference, the university made plans for a new stadium (and later an adjoining track and basketball fieldhouse) a mile to the east. Nearly 17,000 seats in the old place were transported and reused in the new one, which originally retained the name of Memorial Stadium. It was soon renamed for Robert Dix, a longtime member of Kent State's Board of Trustees. Dix Stadium cost $3.5 million and had a seating capacity of 20,000. There was a curved west side with a two-level press box on top and locker rooms and offices below, and a straight and much smaller east side. The stadium was first put to use on September 13, 1969, when the Flashes beat Dayton, with running back Don Nottingham gaining 275 yards. A crowd of 8,172 looked on.

The dedication game did not come until the opener of the next season, and by that time KSU had experienced its defining moment. On May 4, 1970, not far from the site of the old stadium, a demonstration against the Vietnam War turned deadly when a contingent of the Ohio National Guard shot and killed four students, left one paralyzed, and injured eight others. With Kent State placed in an international spotlight, few people cared about something as mundane as football, but life went on. The 1972 team, coached by Don James (who later won a national championship at Washington) took the MAC crown and a spot in the Tangerine Bowl. And the 1973 team was even better, going 9–2 under the captaincy of Jack Lambert. A linebacker noted for agility, mobility, and hostility, he went on to a Hall of Fame career with the Pittsburgh Steelers. A record crowd of 27,363 attended the 1973 Kent State–Miami game.

Like several other schools, KSU had to expand its stadium in the early 1990s to maintain NCAA Division I-A status. So seating was constructed in the north and south ends, making room for 30,520 fans, although the new sections are seldom needed. With two winless seasons in the 1980s and two more in the 1990s, tickets to Kent State home games are not a hot commodity. Sometimes fewer than 3,000 people show up to support a program that manages to send a surprising number of players to the NFL. Still, the university continues to improve Dix Stadium. Lights were added in 1996, followed by artificial turf in 1997 and a new scoreboard in 1998, and a $3 million expansion/renovation project is under discussion. The stadium, which is not strictly for football, hosted the 2001 collegiate field hockey championship.

Rynearson Stadium (Eastern Michigan)

Elton Rynearson, who played football at Eastern Michigan, later coached the team in three stints for a total of twenty-six seasons. His glory years were from 1925 to 1938 when the Hurons twice went 8–0 and never lost more than two games. Rynearson, who was AD until 1963, later would be honored by the university he served for so long. During Rynearson's coaching days, Walter Briggs got involved in EMU athletics. An Ypsilanti native who had grown rich in the auto-body business, Briggs bought the Detroit

Tigers in 1938. He expanded their stadium, which he named after himself and which also became home to the Detroit Lions. Briggs was definitely a man whose name was writ large in sports and industry in the Motor City. He gave $150,000 to Eastern Michigan to improve its football, baseball, and basketball facilities on the south side of campus. The football field was renamed Briggs Stadium, and the Hurons would play there for three more decades.

Rynearson died in 1967, by which time Briggs Stadium simply had to be replaced. Athletic director F. L. "Frosty" Ferzacca pushed for a new stadium on EMU's 182-acre west campus, and he got a $1.4 million, 15,500-seat facility which was dedicated on October 25, 1969, with a 17–7 loss to Tampa. Rynearson Stadium was expanded prior to the 1974 season for the use of an ill-fated pro tenant, the WFL's Detroit Wheels. Lights and 5,000 south-end seats were added, and Dan Boisture, coach of the Hurons for the prior seven seasons, became coach of the Wheels, but the team and league were soon as dead as a proverbial doornail.

Life was not so easy for EMU, either. They joined the MAC in 1976, but average attendance fell below 10,000 for eleven straight years, showing a dearth of loyalty among students, alumni, and local people. In stark contrast, Ypsilanti was almost a suburb of Ann Arbor, home of the Michigan Wolverines, who played in the biggest stadium in the country with never an empty seat. Still, there were bright spots for the green and white as they moved up the ladder from small-college football to I-AA status and finally to I-A. The 1987 team went 10–2, won the MAC title, and beat San Jose State in the California Bowl. There were some stars along the way, too. Lineman John Banaszak and defensive back Ron Johnson were Super Bowl teammates with the Pittsburgh Steelers in the 1970s; running back Rodney Slater went on to become secretary of transportation in the Clinton administration; and quarterback Charlie Batch made it with the Detroit Lions.

In 1991 (when the Hurons became the Eagles), artificial turf was installed at Rynearson Stadium, and it got a $13 million do-over the next year. That consisted of 10,000 new seats on the east side, an expanded west-side press box, a new scoreboard, and other fan amenities. In 1998, $30 million was spent on a basketball arena/convocation center at the south end of the stadium. It also houses EMU's athletic administration and football staff.

Rynearson Stadium's attendance record of 25,009 came at the 1995 UNLV game, which the Eagles won 51–6.

Bronco Stadium (Boise State)

Boise State was a junior college in 1947 when Lyle Smith became AD and football coach. His teams' first forty games were all

—Courtesy of Boise State sports information department

victories, and that was reason enough to erect 10,000-seat Bronco Stadium 200 yards south of the Boise River. The top player from those JC days was Dave Wilcox, who went on to the University of Oregon and later the San Francisco 49ers.

After becoming a four-year institution and a member of the Big Sky Conference, Boise State needed a better facility. The old place was razed and a new one went up in the same spot in 1970. Also known as Bronco Stadium, it cost $2.3 million, had artificial turf, lights, a rubber 400-meter track, a west-side upper deck, and room for 14,500 fans. It was dedicated on September 11, 1970, when BSU defeated Chico State 49–14. Four years later, it was expanded for the first time as a matching east-side upper deck and north and south bleachers raised seating capacity to 22,600.

The Broncos, who had come close to winning the NCAA's Division I-AA title several times, finally reached that pinnacle in 1980 with coach Jim Criner and running back Cedric Minter leading the way. In the spring of 1981, the field at Bronco Stadium was named in honor of Lyle Smith, who had retired after nearly a half-century of service. The next change at the stadium came in 1986 when a new layer of artificial turf was installed. Athletic director Gene Blaymaier chose to forego the usual green and instead use blue, Boise State's primary color. The blue field received plenty of national attention. Some people loved it and others hated it; some found it distinctive and a point of pride, while others were mortified. Anecdotal stories continue to circulate about diving birds that mistake it for a body of water.

The NCAA's track and field championships were held there in southern Idaho in 1994 and again in 1999. Between those two meets, longtime track coach Ed Jacoby retired and thus the track was named for him. Curved extensions of Bronco Stadium's two upper decks were built in 1997, raising seating capacity to 30,000 as BSU moved up to Division I-A status. And with a bigger stadium, the university moved into the bowl business. The Humanitarian Bowl has been won thrice by Boise State, in 1999 when the hometown Broncos beat Louisville, in 2000 when they beat Texas–El Paso, and in 2002 when they beat Iowa State. That was an ideal close for two of the most popular figures in recent BSU football history—coach Dirk Koetter moved on to Arizona State, and record-setting quarterback Bart Hendricks ended his college career.

Cajun Field (Louisiana–Lafayette)

Until 1999, the University of Louisiana–Lafayette was known as Southwestern Louisiana, and its mascot was originally the Bulldog, not the Cajun. In the early years, two men had a big impact on the football program. Chris Cagle, a great run-pass-kick combination in the 1920s, went on to the U.S. Military Academy and was a three-time all-American with the Cadets. Predating Cagle was Clement McNaspy, who spent twenty-five years in Lafayette as a chemistry and physics professor and AD, football, track, and basketball coach and was later known as "the father of Southwestern athletics." When the university built a football/track stadium in 1940, it was named for McNaspy.

A campus landmark, McNaspy Stadium had lights and very steep stands. It was made primarily of bricks and doubled as a dormitory. The Bulldogs played there for thirty-one seasons, and even after they moved out, the west stands lasted another three decades as the field and track were used for soccer and intramurals.

The final football season at McNaspy Stadium was a good one. Russ Faulkinberry's team went 9–3, won the Gulf States Conference title, and played in the Grantland Rice Bowl, just the second bowl game in school history. As part of a plan to move all

—Courtesy of Louisiana–Lafayette sports information department

intercollegiate athletic facilities to a location one and a half miles south of campus, a $3 million stadium was erected in 1971. It had a seating capacity of 31,000 with a second deck on the west side. Surrounded by bayous and wetlands and the meandering Vermilion River, the stadium was two feet below sea level, so a special drainage system with four 60-horsepower pumps was needed to make the field playable. The stadium, which had no formal name at first and was known simply as "the swamp," was christened on September 25, 1971, with a 21–0 defeat of Santa Clara.

In the early 1970s, the SWL basketball team was having a nice run of success. Some local sportswriters began calling them the "Ragin' Cajuns," and the name soon applied to football and other sports. The administration and athletic department went along, happy to acknowledge their setting in the land of the Acadians—the French-Canadians who had moved to Louisiana in the late eighteenth century. And in 1984, the stadium finally got a name. What else but Cajun Field?

Fans in Lafayette were privileged to see Brian Mitchell strut his stuff from 1986 to 1989. He put up some amazing numbers, becoming the first player in major college football to gain over 3,000 yards on the ground and over 5,000 in the air and had the most touchdowns rushing (47) of any quarterback. Mitchell went on to a long career as a versatile offensive player with the Washington Redskins and Philadelphia Eagles. The north and south ends of Cajun Field, usually a grassy expanse where students could spread out, were full when Alabama came to town in 1990. Drawing such a major opponent to Lafayette is not easy, and a record 36,133 fans crammed in to see the Crimson Tide roll over the red and white. And in 1996, that record was broken when a crowd of 38,783 assembled to watch quarterback Jake Delhomme lead the Cajuns to a 29–22 upset of Texas A&M.

Kibbie Dome (Idaho)

Neale Stadium, an all-wood structure, was Idaho's home beginning in the 1937 season. The Vandals, then members of the Pacific Coast Conference, must have been that league's version of the redheaded stepchild. Remote and short on money and population, UI usually brought up the rear, but they regularly met stalwarts like UCLA, California, Southern Cal, and Stanford. It was not uncommon for games in tiny Moscow to be played under blizzard conditions. Still there were some football legends of the Palouse: offensive lineman Jerry Kramer, linebacker Wayne Walker, defensive back Jim Norton, and running back Ray McDonald all went on to fine pro careers.

—Courtesy of Idaho sports information department

Idaho had been nudged out of the PCC and was playing a much easier schedule when Neale Stadium burned in an act of arson following the 1969 season. The people at Washington State University—just eight miles to the west in Pullman—graciously allowed UI to use Martin Stadium in 1970 while a new facility was being built upon the ashes of the old one. Architect Gene Cline designed a 16,000-seat stadium to be named after William Kibbie, an Idaho alumnus who had made his fortune in hydroelectric construction. Kibbie gave $300,000 to help get the project going. It was first used on October 9, 1971, when the Vandals beat Idaho State 40–3.

The stadium was not yet complete. Artificial turf was installed in 1972, and it was domed three years later. A barrel-arch roof was set over the field and stands with such ingenuity that it won an award from the American Society of Civil Engineers. The Kibbie Dome, which had no seating (or possibility thereof) in the east and west ends, was 400 feet from side to side and 144 feet from the field to the underside of the roof. It had a 300-meter unbanked track and served as the school's basketball arena. Costing a total of $7.8 million, it was dedicated on October 11, 1975, when Idaho and Boise State fought to a 31–31 tie.

Locker rooms were in a nearby gymnasium until 1982, when the university spent $4.5 million on an east-end addition to the Kibbie Dome. No seats were added, however. That was the first year Dennis Erickson coached the Vandals, and they went 9–4 and reached the NCAA I-AA playoffs. Idaho became something of a powerhouse at that level, holding the No. 1 spot for several weeks in the 1993 season.

The silver and gold wanted to get back into the big time, relatively speaking. The NCAA granted provisional I-A status in 1996, but the stadium issue would have to be resolved. The Kibbie Dome was barely half the minimum size of 30,000 ostensibly needed to qualify, but there were waivers and wiggle room aplenty. In the meantime, Chris Tormey's 1998 team went 9–3, won the Big West title, and beat Southern Mississippi in the Humanitarian Bowl. It was a matter of necessity and swallowed pride for Idaho to take the next step. WSU, long a cooperative neighbor, agreed to rent 37,400-seat Martin Stadium, thus enabling UI to exceed the 17,000 fans per game needed to stay in the top level of college football. A two-year agreement was signed and then extended. Actually, the numbers worked out so that Idaho could play one game on campus per season while a solution was sought.

A $10 million expansion of the Kibbie Dome's east end began in 2001, but it made no change in seating capacity. The cost of a new outdoor stadium is estimated at $30 million, so the current setup is considerably more cost-effective, even if the Vandals must travel to another school's stadium—in another state, no less—for a "home" game. The Kibbie Dome, which sits idle on most Saturday afternoons in the fall, has another claim to fame, though. It hosts the Lionel Hampton Jazz Festival each February, drawing more than 30,000 spirited music fans to Moscow.

Veterans Stadium (Temple)

President Charles F. Beury believed Temple should be more of a player in the rough-and-tumble world of intercollegiate football, so he raised $350,000 to build a 22,000-seat stadium nine miles from campus. Originally named for Beury, Temple Stadium served as home for the Owls from 1928 through the mid-1970s. The high point of those years was in 1934 when Pop Warner was coach and Dave Smukler and Pete Stevens carried Temple to a 7–1–2 record and a Sugar Bowl loss to Tulane. The low point came in the 1950s when the university de-emphasized football, started playing an Ivy League–type schedule, and still managed to lose twenty-one straight games.

Temple was an afterthought to Philadelphia officials who, in 1964, began planning for a big pro stadium several miles to the south. The Philadelphia Eagles and the Philadelphia Phillies needed a new home, so the city erected Veterans Stadium for $50 million, double the projected cost. Designed by Hugh Stubbins and Associates, it was a seven-tier "octorad" with 65,352 seats for football and 3,000 fewer in its baseball configuration. Veterans Stadium, built in the era of circular concrete multi-purpose facilities (as in Houston, Pittsburgh, St. Louis, and Cincinnati), opened in 1971 to rave reviews, although it would soon become the stadium that players, fans, and media loved to hate. Set in the in-

— Courtesy of Temple sports information department

dustrial flatlands of south Philly, it could be a desolate place when the winds whipped off the nearby Delaware River. The Eagles had one Super Bowl season (1980), the Phillies played World Series games there in 1980, 1983, and 1993, and the Vet hosted major league baseball's all-star game in 1976 and 1996.

Temple first played there in 1976, as old Temple Stadium was converted into a venue for baseball, softball, and soccer. One of the Owls' most thrilling games at Veterans Stadium came before a near-capacity crowd against Penn State in 1976. After a rousing comeback, they lost 31–30 when a last-second two-point conversion failed. The fact that Temple was even playing Penn State and national champion Pittsburgh was indicative of a football revival; the Owls had a sparkling season in 1979 when coach Wayne Hardin led them to a 10–2 record with a win over California in the Garden State Bowl, finishing No. 17.

But they were soon struggling again, with 1–10 records in 1989, 1992, 1993, 1995, and 1996. And Veterans Stadium was no place for college football. Average attendance of 18,000 indicated that fans simply did not seem to give a hoot about the Owls. Even with $74 million in improvements in the mid-1980s, the stadium still had insoluble shortcomings. The most frequent gripes pertained to its rock-hard artificial turf. After just thirty years of use, Veterans Stadium seemed older than the Liberty Bell. Scheduling conflicts were constant, and because the Eagles and Phillies called the shots, Temple was occasionally forced into the mortifying alternative of playing some home games at Franklin Field on the University of Pennsylvania campus.

The Big East was not happy and kicked Temple out of the conference, citing a "sustained failure to meet the minimum criteria expected of all members." Then, fortuitously, city and state politicians came to the rescue. Pittsburgh's Three Rivers Stadium was replaced in 2001 by a new baseball stadium for the Pirates and a new football stadium for the Steelers (which Pitt would share), and Philadelphia followed suit. If all goes well, the city will have two modern single-purpose facilities valued at $1 billion by 2004, and Temple, along with the Eagles and Phillies, will be out of Veterans Stadium.

Boyd Stadium (Nevada–Las Vegas)

One of the youngest of NCAA Division I-A schools, Nevada–Las Vegas originated in 1957. To contrast with the more stately flagship university in Reno, UNLV adopted the Rebel as its mascot, complete with the Confederate battle flag, although Nevada had not even the slightest connection to the side that lost the Civil War. The Rebel moniker remains, but the CSA baggage was jettisoned long ago.

UNLV first fielded a football team in 1968, and home games were played at Cashman Field and Butcher Memorial Field, a pair of high school stadiums that sometimes hosted outdoor boxing matches. That did not really suit an upward-looking football program. So Las Vegas Stadium went up, several miles east of campus and the city's glittering casinos, at a cost of $3.5 million. The 15,000-seat horseshoe had an open north end, and its first rows were exceedingly close to the field. Set in a desert valley with purple mountain ranges, the stadium was dedicated on October 23, 1971, when the Rebs lost to Weber State 30–17.

There were a couple of sellouts in 1974 when coach Ron Meyer and running back Mike Thomas carried the team to a 12–1 record and challenged for the Division II national title. UNLV moved up to Division I-A status in 1978 when the stadium was expanded all the way around, raising seating capacity to 32,000. At that time, it was renamed the Las Vegas Silver Bowl, but only until 1984. Then Sam Boyd, a hotel and gaming mogul, donated $1 million for the installation of retractable artificial turf, so the stadium was named for him. The 1984 team was a fine one, with quarterback Randall Cunningham and running back Ickey Woods, but when UNLV was busted for rules violations, their 11–2 record (with a defeat of Toledo in the California Bowl) became 0–13.

The post-season pantheon got a new member in 1992 with the inaugural Las Vegas Bowl, in which the Rebels have played twice—beating Central Michigan in 1994 and Arkansas in 2000. Boyd Stadium had a pro tenant in 1994, the Las Vegas Posse of the Canadian Football League. And seven years later, the Las Vegas Outlaws of the XFL had an even shorter life.

UNLV, meanwhile, fell into mediocrity and worse. The Rebels were hapless losers in the late 1990s, with just six victories in a

—Courtesy of UNLV sports information department

four-season span. The only good news was a record crowd of 40,091 (possible because of 8,000 bleacher seats in the north end) at the 1996 Wisconsin game and punter Joe Kristosik becoming the school's first consensus all-American in 1998. The athletic department was in a budget deficit, but something had to be done. Prior to the 1999 season, $18 million was invested in Boyd Stadium. The old press box was razed and a new three-level facility with sixteen luxury boxes went in. The raggedy artificial turf was removed and a grass field was installed, and a new facade, expanded concourses, and other structural changes made it a much more pleasant place for football fans. Furthermore, UNLV convinced John Robinson to head the team, bringing immediate credibility. Robinson, who had coached USC for twelve seasons (including the 1978 national championship) and the Los Angeles Rams for nine, paid quick dividends, going from 0–11 to 8–4 in just two years.

Despite its recent makeover, Boyd Stadium faces an uncertain future. There have been proposals regarding a domed stadium in downtown Las Vegas, and if that comes to pass, AD Charles Cavagnaro wants the Rebels to play in it.

Kelly-Shorts Stadium (Central Michigan)

Beginning in 1949, the Central Michigan Chippewas played at Alumni Field, a football/baseball facility on the north side of campus. Bleachers provided seating for a few thousand fans. CMU's best season there was in 1956 when running back Jim Podoley paced the team to a 9–0 record. Alumni Field is today a well-manicured baseball park known as Theunissen Stadium, because the university needed new digs for its football program. Work started almost immediately after the final home game of the 1971 season. Shorts Stadium, named after Perry Shorts, a Central Michigan alum, banker, and donor, cost $2.2 million and was the first college stadium in the state to have artificial turf. Legend said it was built atop an old Chippewa burial ground, and it would soon get a reputation as the windiest football arena in the Mid-American Conference. With a seating capacity of 20,086, Shorts Stadium was dedicated on November 4, 1972, when CMU beat

196 HOME FIELD

—Courtesy of Central Michigan sports information department

Illinois State 21–17 on the strength of three touchdown passes by quarterback Gary Bevington.

Two years later, coach Roy Kramer's Chips went 12–1 and defeated Delaware in the Camellia Bowl, winning the Division II national crown. Their home was renamed Kelly-Shorts Stadium in 1983 to honor Bill Kelly, who had coached the team from 1951 to 1966. The stadium, which did not have lights, got a $140,000 scoreboard in the south end in 1986. After CMU trounced rival Western Michigan when visiting Kalamazoo in 1989, WMU students rioted; so following another win over the Broncos in Mt. Pleasant the next season, CMU students returned the favor. The maroon and gold made it into post-season play in 1990 and 1994 but lost rather badly in the California Raisin and the Las Vegas bowls, respectively.

The locker room complex at the north end of Kelly-Shorts Stadium was renovated in 1996, and bigger changes came two years later. The Christman Construction Company, which had built the stadium in 1972, erected the generically named Indoor

Athletic Complex nearby and 10,000 more seats and a new press box (including eight luxury boxes) on the west side of the stadium for $28 million. Although CMU was already among the attendance leaders in the MAC, athletic director Herb Deromedi felt it was best to reach the 30,000-seat benchmark to help ensure NCAA Division I-A status.

One of the more notable games in the history of Kelly-Shorts Stadium happened in 2000 when conference champ Western Michigan came to Mt. Pleasant as a 34-point favorite. Coach Mike DeBord's team had lost seven straight, but they took an improbable 21–17 victory. Cannon shots blasted through the frigid air as the Chippewas and their fans celebrated.

Commonwealth Stadium (Kentucky)

More than 120 years ago, the first college football game ever held in the South took place on the University of Kentucky campus. Oddly enough, the Wildcats (who had yet to embrace the game) were not participants, but that spot soon became their home. Not until 1916 was it named Stoll Field, in honor of Richard Stoll, a judge and former UK player. Eight years later, a stadium was erected and named for Price McLean, a player who had recently died as a result of injuries sustained in a game. The stadium was first used for night football in 1929; with Lexington in the heart of bluegrass country, people enjoyed watching the horses run at Keeneland racetrack in the afternoon, and this way they could do both on a Saturday in the fall. The stadium was expanded in 1948 and again in 1959 to a seating capacity of 37,500.

The street which ran alongside McLean Stadium was Euclid Avenue, also known as Avenue of Champions. But most of the champs were of the roundball variety. Adolph Rupp's basketball teams far overshadowed football at Kentucky, and Alumni Gym and its successor, Memorial Coliseum, were next-door neighbors. Rupp so dominated the scene that he may have caused UK's greatest football coach to depart. Bear Bryant was hired in 1946 to head a program that had known scant success. He lifted the Cats to unprecedented heights as they played in the Orange, Sugar, and

Cotton bowls in consecutive seasons. In 1950, with quarterback Vito "Babe" Parilli and all-America lineman Bob Gain leading the way, they went 11–1, won the Southeastern Conference crown, ended Oklahoma's thirty-one-game winning streak (in the above-mentioned Sugar Bowl) and finished No. 7 in the nation. But when Bryant returned to Alabama, his alma mater, as he may have been destined to do anyway, Kentucky fell back into the pack. Only Vanderbilt has a worse winning percentage in SEC play.

UK was in the midst of eight straight losing seasons in 1967 when defensive back Nat Northington ran onto Stoll Field in a game against Ole Miss. Although Northington was soon injured and quit the team, he was the first black player in a conference that put off integration as long as possible. The stadium, half a century old, was beyond modernization, so an eighty-six-acre experimental farm on the south side of campus was chosen as a site for the new one. Commonwealth Stadium—so named because Kentucky is one of four states claiming that status—was designed by the Finch-Heery Company of Atlanta and cost $12 million. It had double decks on the north and south sides and a seating capacity of 57,800. The press box, locker rooms, and field were scarcely ready when the first game was played on September 15, 1973, in which the Cats beat Virginia Tech 31–26.

— Courtesy of Kentucky sports information department

Coach Fran Curci sparked hope for a resurgence of the blue and white when his 1976 team went 9–3, shared the SEC title, and beat North Carolina in the Peach Bowl. It was their first bowl game since the Bear was in charge. And the following season, they were even better as quarterback Derrick Ramsey and defensive end Art Still paced them to a 10–1 mark with a No. 6 ranking, but NCAA probation kept UK home during the bowl season. They have not been so close to the top since, not even when Tim Couch was slinging passes. With Couch (the top pick in the 1999 NFL draft) at quarterback, Kentucky never won more than seven games.

The Wildcats' lair was simply not intimidating to opponents, but attendance was strong and UK had to keep up with its SEC brethren, some of whose stadiums had gone from merely big to huge. So Commonwealth Stadium grew prior to the 1999 season. The east and west ends were filled in, ten luxury boxes were built in each corner, and a new front entrance and two videoboards enhanced the look and feel of the facility, which had room for 67,530 fans. But more than 70,000 were there for the first game in the expanded stadium, an embarrassing 56–28 blowout at the hands of in-state rival Louisville.

Indian Stadium (Arkansas State)

Arkansas State was still a junior college in the mid-1920s when Kays Field opened. Named after C.V. Kays, the school's first president, it was a modest football/track facility in the southwest corner of campus, set near the gentle slopes of the Ozark Mountains. Kays Field became the first lighted college football stadium in the state of Arkansas in 1929 and eventually grew to have 8,000 seats. There, Richie Woit gained more than 3,700 yards rushing in the early 1950s and linebacker Bill Bergey (1965 to 1968) honed his skills in preparation for a stellar career with the Cincinnati Bengals and Philadelphia Eagles. The 1970 team, coached by Bennie Ellender and competing in the Southland Conference, rolled to an 11–0 record, including a defeat of Central Missouri in the Pecan Bowl, winning the Division II national championship. The game was on national television at a time when that meant a captive—and thus large—audience. Such coverage is still precious for the Indians, who are among the most obscure programs in major college football.

ASU was only aspiring to such status then, and the key was building a decent stadium. Kays Field had been inadequate for some time, so the university raised $2.5 million, more than half of it from friends and alumni, to do just that. A tract of land to the northwest was chosen, and construction began following the 1973 season. With lights, a grass field, and an extra deck on the west side, Indian Stadium had 16,343 seats. Although mud still abounded and the press box was just half finished, it was unveiled on September 28, 1974, when Louisiana Tech took a 21–7 victory. On dedication day five weeks later, the Tribe beat Northeast Louisiana. While the stands at Kays Field were torn down, it continues to serve Arkansas State students as a 360-meter walking track and a place for soccer and rugby matches.

In 1975, the stadium's second season, the Indians again prevailed against every challenge and had an 11–0 record. Jerry Muckensturm was one of several players from that team who went on to pro success. Bleachers in the south end raised seating capacity to 18,709 in 1980, and similar north-end bleachers and an east-side upper deck brought it up to 33,410 in 1991. In a quarter-century, average attendance at Indian Stadium has vacillated between 8,000 and 17,000. The biggest crowd was in 1997 when 29,465 fans witnessed an exciting 36–35 defeat of Central Arkansas.

It has been interesting to see Arkansas State deal with the forces of history and political correctness regarding the Indian mascot. Several state legislatures up north or out west have virtually mandated the elimination of Native American team names, but not Arkansas. The tradition is taken seriously in Jonesboro, although some of the more offensive aspects have been eliminated or modified over the years. Freshman students beat a drum for twenty-four hours before home games, some fans arrive at the stadium wearing headdresses and war paint and brandishing faux tomahawks, and, most notably, there is the "Indian Family." This consists of three students, representing a chief, a brave, and a princess, who ride in on horseback. They seek to personify school spirit, but in a stately and dignified way. The authenticity of their dances, symbols, and costumes have supposedly won the approval of Cherokee and Osage people in eastern Arkansas.

Aloha Stadium (Hawai'i)

Otto "Proc" Klum coached Hawai'i to back-to-back unbeaten seasons in 1924 and 1925, although just three of those games were against college teams from the mainland. Largely on the strength of that showing, Honolulu Stadium was built. The 25,000-seat wooden facility reflected the islands' vibrant sports culture for nearly fifty years when such players as Tommy "Grass Shack" Kaulukukui, Harry Kahuani, Charles Araki, and Randy Ingraham starred for the Rainbow Warriors, but there was more. Honolulu Stadium was home to the Hawai'i Islanders minor league baseball team, not to mention boxing matches, stock car races, and concerts. Babe Ruth played there, Joe Louis fought there, and Elvis Presley sang there. The Hula Bowl, among the first post-season college all-star games, began at Honolulu Stadium in 1947.

By the 1970s, the old place, beloved though it was, had seen better days. So the city erected another facility away from the Manoa Valley campus, one that would also have a multiplicity of uses. Aloha Stadium, costing $27 million, was built in Honolulu's Halawa district. It had 50,000 seats (including four mobile grandstands), lights, artificial turf, a west-side press box, and amenities comparable to most NFL stadiums of the time. UH first used it on September 13, 1975 in a 43-9 loss to Texas A&I before 32,247 spectators. Everything that had been done at Honolulu Stadium was brought over to Aloha Stadium, and new events began; the NFL's Pro Bowl found it a most pleasant home, the Aloha Bowl was founded in 1982, and the Oahu Bowl began in 1998. Sometimes the latter two were held on the same day. But attendance at both bowl games was weak, and after the 2000 season they departed for the mainland—the Aloha to San Francisco and the Oahu to Seattle. The Hula Bowl was played there from 1976 to 1998 before moving to War Memorial Stadium on the island of Maui. Aloha Stadium has not been significantly altered in its quarter-century of life, and no changes are likely in the near future.

The Rainbow Warriors began playing a tougher schedule in the late 1970s when they moved up to the NCAA's Division I-A and became part of the Western Athletic Conference. They cracked the top twenty for the first time in 1981 and played in their hometown bowl games twice. In 1989, the green and white went 9–3–1 and fell to Michigan State in the Aloha Bowl. The second instance was more surprising. The 1998 team was winless, attendance was down, and the athletic department was losing money hand over fist. Then June Jones, a player at Hawai'i in the early 1970s, was hired. Former head coach of the Atlanta Falcons and San Diego Chargers, Jones wrought a minor miracle: UH went 9–4 and beat Oregon State in the 1999 Oahu Bowl. Six players, led by quarterback Dan Robinson, made all-WAC and Jones won three national coach-of-the-year awards.

Hawai'i football remained in the news following that Cinderella season because AD Hugh Yoshida announced the school was nixing the rainbow name and logo which had been adopted in 1923. The rainbow was widely recognized as a symbol of homosexuality, an issue concerning which Hawai'i is perhaps the most liberal of the fifty states. The gay community was up in arms, claiming homophobia in paradise, but Yoshida and several coaches and players said the rainbow had long been a source of on-field ridicule. Henceforth, they were just the Warriors, and a new logo was unveiled—the letter "H" edged in a traditional Hawai'ian design known as kapa.

Trice Stadium (Iowa State)

Although he was an Iowa graduate (and the Hawkeyes' first all-American), Clyde Williams left his mark at Iowa State, too. He founded the basketball program, coached football, and, as athletic director, oversaw construction of the university's football/track stadium in 1914. It was renamed in Williams' honor after he died in 1938. Expanded several times up to a capacity of 36,000, Williams Field was an oddly shaped facility with 75 percent of its seats on the east side and north end.

The Cyclones did not win too often, but there were exceptions. The 1938 team, with quarterback Everett "Rabbit" Kischer and lineman Ed Bock, went 7–1–1, and the 1959 team was a bunch of overachievers who won seven games and lost three. But Iowa State, a member of the Big 6, the Big 7, the Big 8, and now the Big 12, has never won a conference title or finished a season in the top ten. The red and gold, the cause of such low expectations over the years, was too often other schools' favorite homecoming opponent. The Cyclones' first-ever bowl game came in 1971 when they lost to LSU in the Sun Bowl. The next season, they had three fine players—quarterback George Amundson, running back Mike Strachan, and linebacker Matt Blair—and somehow got invited to the Liberty Bowl with a .500 record.

With Williams Field falling apart, AD Lou McCullough turned his attention to a thirty-acre tract in the southeast corner of campus. Groundbreaking was in October 1973, and Cyclone Stadium was ready less than two years later. Due both to Ames being the northernmost city in the conference and the stadium's design, the wind-chill factor could be daunting to players and fans alike. It had artificial turf, no lights, and two decks on the east and west sides with 42,500 seats. If somewhat basic, the stadium was also cheap at $7.6 million. The first game, on September 20, 1975, was a 17–12 defeat of Air Force.

Bleachers were added in both end zones the next year, elevat-

—Courtesy of Iowa State sports information department

ing seating capacity to over 48,000. But more people could fit in when the occasion arose by sitting on grassy hillsides in the stadium's four corners; a record crowd of 54,475 was there for the 1990 Nebraska game. A $750,000 scoreboard went up in the south end in 1994, and the Jacobson Athletic Building was built in the north end two years later, providing offices and new locker rooms. After two decades of artificial turf, grass was installed at Cyclone Stadium, and portable lights permitted night games. In 1997, a new press box was built atop the west upper deck at a cost of $10.6 million. One level of it plus the old press box were devoted to twenty-three luxury boxes. ISU was also doing a gradual upgrade of its peripheral athletic facilities in hope of remaining or becoming competitive. In 1995 and 1996, Troy Davis gained over 4,000 yards rushing, but the team won just five games. In 2000, however, quarterback Sage Rosenfels led them to nine wins, the first time that had happened since 1906. Cyclone fans, long starved for success, were ecstatic.

When the stadium was built in 1975, there had been a move to have it named to honor Jack Trice. Iowa State's first black athlete, Trice also was an admirable and ultimately tragic figure. In 1923, in only his second varsity game, he suffered injuries to his collarbone and lungs that killed him within days. Classes were suspended, and 4,000 students and faculty gathered on campus for his funeral service. Some fifty years later, Trice had not been forgotten. While the stadium initially was not named for him, pressure remained on the university and athletic department to offer some recognition. Beginning in 1984, the Cyclones played on Trice Field, and a statue of him in thoughtful repose was placed outside the stadium. However, people still felt that was inadequate for a man of such historical significance. Finally in 1997, the Board of Regents voted to name the stadium for him. "It is clear that Jack Trice, for a large majority of students and others associated with Iowa State, exemplifies ... dedication, commitment, enthusiasm and giving one's all to an important cause," said president Martin Jischke. "Universities have precious few opportunities to recognize heroic qualities. This is one of those opportunities."

On the strength of a 9–3 record in 2000, ISU decided the time had come to further expand Trice Stadium. So $14 million was spent to build 7,400 seats in the south end, forming a horseshoe.

Louisiana Superdome (Tulane)

Tulane University is located on the former site of the Etienne de Borets sugar plantation in New Orleans. The Green Wave was doing quite well under coach Clark Shaughnessy, going 17–1–1 in 1924 and 1925, so the university erected a 20,000-seat steel stadium on the north side of campus which would become one of the most glorious venues in the history of college football. When Tulane Stadium opened on October 23, 1926, the Auburn Tigers managed a narrow 2–0 win. Shaughnessy left, but with players like running back Bill Banker and end Jerry Dalrymple, Tulane won twenty-eight games in a three-year span, and only a loss to Southern California in the Rose Bowl prevented them from winning the 1931 national championship.

The good times kept rolling when Tulane won the 1934 Southeastern Conference title and played in the inaugural Sugar Bowl right there on campus. The Green Wave beat Temple 20–16, the New Year's Day game was a financial success, and plans were soon made to expand the stadium. It became a horseshoe, then a bowl, then double decks were added and finally double decks in

— Courtesy of Tulane sports information department

the end zones. A crowd of 73,000 was there in the Sugar Bowl following the 1939 season when Tulane lost to Texas A&M, and a whopping 85,000 filled it up in 1949 when Oklahoma and North Carolina played. If the locker rooms were inadequate and parking was at a premium, the place nevertheless abounded in character. Lights were added in 1957, and (after Tulane pulled out of the SEC due to academic issues) artificial turf was installed in 1970.

Despite the occasional appearance of such stars as Eddie Price and Tommy Mason, Tulane had fallen on hard times. The athletic department was running a deficit, and football, put on an austerity program, often had to use true student-athletes. Attendance at the big stadium was poor, with the main exception being when LSU visited. Simultaneously, things were happening that would drastically change the New Orleans sports scene. Dave Dixon, a TU alum and entrepreneur, had been intrigued by Buckminster Fuller's conceptual design of a domed stadium, a full decade before Houston's Astrodome was built. Dixon wanted to bring pro football to the Crescent City and had sponsored some NFL exhibition games at Tulane Stadium. In 1966, he persuaded Louisiana Congressmen Hale Boggs and Russell Long to help pass an antitrust exemption which allowed the NFL-AFL merger to go through. In gratitude, the league awarded New Orleans a franchise, to be named the Saints, who would play home games at Tulane Stadium. Furthermore, Governor John McKeithen provided the political muscle within the state (in the form of a constitutional amendment) financing Dixon's dream—a huge domed stadium in downtown New Orleans. The city needed a facility for conventions, shows, and other events, but pro football was the catalyst. Problems and controversies delayed groundbreaking until 1971, and construction took four years.

For eight seasons, the Green Wave played at Tulane Stadium on Saturdays and the Saints on Sundays. The most memorable moment for the Saints was in 1970 when Tom Dempsey kicked a record 63-yard field goal against the Detroit Lions. Notre Dame beat Alabama for the national championship in the 1973 Sugar Bowl, and Tulane's final game on campus was a 26–10 loss to Ole Miss. The last big event there was on January 12, 1975, when the Pittsburgh Steelers defeated the Minnesota Vikings in the Super Bowl. Five years later, Tulane Stadium, the scene of countless great games dating back to 1926, met the wrecking ball and made way for student dormitories.

So the Green Wave (as well as the Sugar Bowl and the Saints) traded in campus football for a futuristic building downtown. Costing $163 million, the Louisiana Superdome rose 273 feet into the New Orleans skyline and resembled a gigantic spaceship. Just a short cab ride from Bourbon Street and the Mississippi River, it was an exceptionally versatile arena that would serve the city well for years to come. It had 76,791 seats for football, which was actually a decrease from Tulane Stadium. The Green Wave first used the Superdome on September 20, 1975, beating Mississippi 14–3 before a crowd of 50,000 in climate-controlled splendor. The next two decades were notable mostly for coaching turnover, obscurity, and losing, with three 1–10 seasons. But in 1998, quarterback Shaun King was at the helm as Tulane ran the table, going 12–0 with a Liberty Bowl win over Brigham Young. That team averaged 45 points per game and finished No. 7, TU's highest ranking in sixty years.

The Superdome was also home to the NBA's New Orleans Jazz from 1975 to 1979 before they left for Salt Lake City. It has been the site of four NCAA Final Fours (three for the men and one for the women) and five Super Bowls, not to mention a papal mass, the 1988 Republican National Convention, and a bewildering array of other events. The stadium, described rather hyperbolically by LSU architecture professor Gerald McLinden as "the most usable public building ever designed in the history of man," underwent $22 million in renovations in 1996. A proposal to rename it for ex-Governor John McKeithen was turned down because the Saints—who are not its owners but mere tenants—may sell naming rights. But team owner Tom Benson will not settle for that. He insists that the Saints need a new stadium and has discussed the issue with NFL commissioner Paul Tagliabue and high-level political leaders. Benson's boys, perennial losers, are likely to be out of the Superdome by 2006, at a new stadium in the distant suburbs and possibly as far away as Mississippi. The impact that would have on Tulane football (which runs an annual deficit of $3.5 million) is anybody's guess, but it highlights once again the dangers of a college program getting tied up with the pros; it is never an equal partnership.

Roberts Stadium (Southern Mississippi)

During the Great Depression, in the poorest state in the union, times were beyond hard. What is now the University of Southern Mississippi needed a football stadium, and local men needed work. So Louis Faulkner, head of Hattiesburg's committee for unemployment relief, gathered laborers and donated materials and equipment. Faulkner Field, with wooden west-side bleachers capable of holding 4,000 fans, was ready on October 29, 1932. The Southerners (renamed the Golden Eagles in 1972) defeated Spring Hill 12–0 in the first game there.

Faulkner Field, which was lighted in 1934, got its first expansion following the 1938 season. Coach Reed Green's players worked for 20 cents an hour to build some east-side stands and a dormitory underneath. The players, bantering as they worked, likened their setting to Alcatraz and thus called it "the rock," and the name stuck. A decade later, since the Great Depression was over, as was World War II, the university could afford to hire a construction company to further expand the stadium (with a dorm under the west-side stands) to a seating capacity of 15,000. The project included a scoreboard and new lighting system, all for $440,000. Faulkner Field remained essentially the same for another twenty-five years while the black and gold found football

—Courtesy of Southern Mississippi sports information department

success, albeit on a small scale. They had two appearances in the Sun Bowl and two in the Tangerine Bowl, losing in each instance, but they won the college-division national championship in 1958 and 1962 under coach Thad "Pie" Vann.

It was not easy to get major schools to travel to Mississippi's piney woods region and play in a small, aging stadium. Southern Miss had to build a new facility, so the team went on the road for two years. "Home" games were played in such cities as Jackson, Biloxi, Mobile, and New Orleans while Faulkner Field was razed and Roberts Stadium went up on the same spot. M. M. Roberts was a lawyer and member of the Board of Trustees. He had a degree from USM—having played on the 1914 and 1915 teams—as well as from Mississippi State and Mississippi, ostensibly the state's major schools. The stadium that bore Roberts' name cost $6.3 million, had double decks east and west, and was still known as "the rock." It was dedicated on September 25, 1976, when a capacity crowd of 33,000 saw Ole Miss take a 28–0 win. The only major change at Roberts Stadium has been the construction in 1999 of the 55,000-square-foot Fairchild Athletic Complex in the north end.

USM has won some notoriety over the years as a giant-killer, but they still must leave Hattiesburg to play in such games. The 1981 team, coached by Bobby Collins, briefly cracked the top ten and finished with a 9–2–1 record. Some excellent players have gone through the program, most notably Ray Guy, who had a fourteen-year career with the Oakland Raiders and is widely considered the greatest punter the game has ever seen, and quarterback Brett Favre, a three-time MVP with the Green Bay Packers. The current coach, Jeff Bower, was the team's quarterback when they were road warriors in 1974 and 1975.

Malone Stadium (Louisiana–Monroe)

What is now the University of Louisiana at Monroe began life as a junior college. In that sub-category of college football, the Indians had some good teams, appearing in five bowl games and winning the 1935 JC national championship. Home games were at

— Courtesy of Louisiana–Monroe sports information department

Brown Stadium, a modest 3,400-seat football/track facility on the north side of the campus, which is bisected by the Ouachita River.

After ULM became a four-year school in 1951, the schedule gradually got tougher and the Indians ventured farther afield than Louisiana, Mississippi, and Arkansas. In 1967, walk-on running back Joe Profit became the first black player at an erstwhile European-American college in the Bayou State. Profit gained over 2,000 yards during his career there, was the seventh player chosen in the 1971 draft, and went on to become the CEO of five companies.

Brown Stadium simply would not suffice for a football program striving to reach Division I-A status. Coach and athletic director John David Crow led the drive to build a bigger and more modern place just to the east. Indian Stadium cost $6.6 million and originally consisted of just west-side stands with room for 12,000 spectators. It was dedicated on September 16, 1978, when ULM beat Arkansas State 21–13. East-side stands were erected the following year, raising seating capacity to 20,000. In 1980, the university honored James Malone, the coach from 1934 to 1953, by renaming the stadium. Fans of the maroon and gold were happy to see the 1987 team, led by quarterback Stan Humphries, win the Division I-AA national championship with a 43–42 defeat of Marshall. Humphries nearly reached an even higher peak seven years later when his San Diego Chargers fell to the San Francisco 49ers in the Super Bowl.

Desirous of getting back into I-A competition, ULM built a precipitously steep east-side upper deck at Malone Stadium in 1993, just topping the requisite 30,000-seat mark. The central "Indian Skybox" and nine individual luxury boxes have been added for the football-viewing pleasure of boosters. The biggest crowd in stadium history was in 1998 when Louisiana Tech went to Monroe; 28,725 fans saw the Bulldogs take a 44–14 victory.

Aggie Memorial Stadium (New Mexico State)

Joe Quesenberry was one of four brothers who played football at New Mexico State between 1910 and 1914. He died soon after in World War I, and when the university set up a new athletic facility in 1933, it was named Quesenberry Field. Bleachers with room for 6,800 spectators were built in 1950, and it became Memorial Stadium in honor of NMSU students who had fought in the Spanish-American War, World War I, and World War II. The Aggies, who have a long though fairly modest gridiron history, enjoyed two straight good seasons in 1959 and 1960. Coach Warren Woodson exploited the talents of quarterback Charley Johnson and running back Pervis Atkins to go 8–3 and 11–0, winning the Sun Bowl twice. Despite the ever-growing roster of bowl games, New Mexico State has not reached post-season play since. At any rate, that spurt of success was enough to merit expansion of Memorial Stadium to a seating capacity of 12,000 in 1962.

Some New Mexico State alumni, desirous of a new stadium, began a decade-long grassroots fundraising campaign in the mid-1960s. But the AD during most of that time was Lou Henson, the school's basketball coach, and little was accomplished. To be fair, however, NMSU had a small athletic budget, so it was not an easy matter. Finally, the state legislature stepped in and supplemented the money raised by the alumni to a total of $4 million. A 30,343-

—Courtesy of New Mexico State sports information department

seat stadium with curved east and west stands was designed by Craig Protz and built over an eighteen-month span by Ray Ward & Son. It had lights and a berm-style grass field. The Board of Regents named it Aggie Memorial Stadium—this time to honor students and alumni who had served in more recent conflicts like Korea and Vietnam. The stadium, on the eastern edge of campus, was dedicated on September 16, 1978, with a 35–32 defeat of Texas–El Paso.

But it was rough going in Las Cruces. Between 1984 and 1991, the Aggies never won more than two games. Average attendance fell below 10,000 at one point, and a twenty-seven-game losing streak brought dubious national attention. When victory came at last (against Cal State–Fullerton), New Mexico State students tore down the goal posts. Aggie Memorial Stadium has been sold out only four times, always against UTEP, which brings many of its fans forty-five miles up Interstate 25. NMSU had a fine running back in the late 1990s, Denvis Manns. He gained over 1,000 yards all four seasons and was the third Division I-A player to do that; the first two, Tony Dorsett of Pittsburgh and Amos Lawrence of North Carolina, did it against stiffer competition, though. And the Ags had just a 10–34 record with Manns in the backfield.

Mountaineer Field (West Virginia)

The earliest West Virginia football teams had a hardscrabble existence, playing in a glorified cow pasture and the infield of a harness track. In the mid-1920s, during a four-year span when the blue and gold lost but three games, they were rewarded with a new stadium. Mountaineer Field was a 35,000-seat horseshoe nestled in a hollow between some railroad tracks and the Monongahela River. It would be home for fifty-five seasons, a place where such luminaries as Joe Stydahar, Sam Huff, and Bruce Bosley performed. Probably the greatest WVU team in the history of what is now called Old Mountaineer Field came in 1953. Art Lewis' squad went 8–2 and was upset by Georgia Tech in the Sugar Bowl, ending up No. 10.

By the 1970s, the stadium was aging fast. Inspection by a Morgantown city engineer showed leaks and structural cracks; extensive repairs were needed soon or a new stadium would have to be built. After some lobbying of the state legislature down in Charleston, $22 million was appropriated for a new facility. Five sites were discussed, and the one chosen was an abandoned golf course near the university's medical center. Gates/Finch-Heery designed a 50,000-seat, curved double-decker with artificial turf and a nice press box and locker rooms—a far cry from Old Mountaineer Field. There were numerous problems during the eighteen-month construction project (done by Huber, Hunt & Nichols), and a few bells and whistles were quietly abandoned. New Mountaineer Field was dedicated on September 6, 1980, with a 41–27 defeat of Cincinnati before a sellout crowd. Pregame ceremonies included John Denver doing a riveting rendition of "Country Roads," the state's unofficial anthem.

Not only was there a new stadium but a new coach. Don Nehlen took over a program with four straight losing seasons and began the slow process of building a national power. He stayed at West Virginia for twenty-one years, and during that time Mountaineer Field was expanded twice, in the south end (1985) and in the north end (1986), raising seating capacity to 63,500. Nehlen's 1988 team was led by freewheeling quarterback Major Harris, twice a Heisman Trophy finalist. They routed Penn State at home and won all eleven games before losing to Notre Dame in the Fiesta Bowl. No. 3 entering that game, WVU finished No. 5. It was the same story in 1993. The Mountaineers, by then members of the Big East, ran the table. That included a defeat of Miami in Morgantown before a record crowd of 70,222, but they lost decisively to Florida in the Sugar Bowl. While their dream of winning a national title was again smashed, they still came in at No. 8. Nehlen led the Mountaineers through 2000 but never again approached the summit. His teams played in four more minor bowls and lost them all.

A number of improvements have been made in and around

—Courtesy of West Virginia sports information department; photo by Mike Hardy

Mountaineer Field, most notably twelve luxury boxes in 1994 and a $2 million scoreboard in 2000. Following Nehlen's retirement, a wave of appreciation and sentiment seemed to roll down from the Alleghenies, and some people urged that the stadium be renamed in his honor. But those individuals were engaged in wishful thinking, since AD Ed Pastilong had his eyes affixed to the bottom line. In other words, the stadium's name was for sale to the highest bidder. Pastilong, a native of the state and a member of the WVU football team in the mid-1960s, was not unaware of the heritage pertaining to the Mountaineer Field name, which covers two facilities dating back nearly eighty years. "If an opportunity presented itself, we would very much consider it," he said. "It would be 'blank' Stadium/Mountaineer Field. It's been done throughout the country, so we're very receptive to that."

Carrier Dome (Syracuse)

One person was killed and 100 injured when a set of bleachers collapsed during a Syracuse home football game in 1906. That tragedy made the need for a new stadium all the more evident. John Archbold, the former president of Standard Oil and the university's biggest philanthropist, put up $400,000 to erect a stadium on a hill in the heart of campus in 1907. Archbold Stadium originally held 20,000 seats, although crowds as large as 46,000 sometimes gathered. The stadium was one of the finest of its time, even drawing comparisons to the Roman Colosseum. Lighted in 1929, it served the Orangemen for seventy-two seasons amid the cold, snow, and rain of New York's Finger Lakes region.

Other than two-time all-America lineman Joe Alexander, SU had few stars in those early seasons. But things began to change after Ben Schwartzwalder was hired in 1949. Schwartzwalder, a World War II hero, broadened the scale of scheduling and recruiting, and soon Syracuse was the Beast from the East. Having gone six decades without a bowl game, the Orangemen played in the Orange and Cotton bowls twice each in the 1950s and won the 1959 national crown. Two men from those glorious days deserve special mention, and both were running backs. Jim Brown played from

—Courtesy of Syracuse sports information department; photo by Stephen Parker

1955 to 1957 (as well as lettering in track, basketball, and lacrosse) and went on to a career with the Cleveland Browns that most football historians say was the greatest ever. And Ernie Davis, a sophomore on the aforesaid national championship team, won the 1961 Heisman Trophy but never played a down of pro football, because he was stricken with leukemia and died shortly thereafter.

Almost as suddenly as the good times came on, Syracuse was in decline. Archbold Stadium was a small, depressing place, beyond repair. Some black athletes revolted against perceived inequities, and Schwartzwalder's teams could no longer compete. At one point, the Syracuse administration considered following the example of the University of Chicago in the 1930s and dropping intercollegiate sports altogether. Soon after the 1978 season—in which SU had a 3–8 record—Archbold Stadium was torn down and construction began on a new facility. The 1979 team played "home" games in stadiums belonging to the New York Giants, the Buffalo Bills, and Cornell University. In the meantime, the Carrier Dome was being erected. Melvin Holm, chairman of the Board of

Trustees and a Carrier Corporation executive, was the key figure in the almost unheard-of concept of corporate naming rights for a college athletic facility. The company gave $2.75 million, out of a total of $28 million, for that creative if not insidious bit of advertising. (Unlike subsequent arrangements, there was no time limitation on the Carrier name; it would last as long as the building itself.) What the university got was a domed structure that has proven to be a splendid economic engine, one that hosts a variety of events besides sports year-round. With room for 33,000 fans in basketball and nearly 50,000 in football, it had an inflated fiberglass roof supported by a latticework of cables. It featured artificial turf, of course, and thirty-eight luxury boxes. A new era began on September 20, 1980, when a capacity crowd saw SU's 36–24 defeat of Miami of Ohio.

The Orangemen struggled their first seven years in the dome, losing more than winning, but coach Dick McPherson's plans came to fruition in 1987. With quarterback Don McPherson (no relation) leading the way, Syracuse went 11–0–1, tying Auburn in the Sugar Bowl. They finished up No. 4, the best since Ernie Davis was playing. Another Syracuse quarterback, Donovan McNabb, won some fame of his own, starting an NCAA-record forty-nine games, and was taken by the Philadelphia Eagles as the second pick in the 1999 NFL draft.

The Carrier Dome, looking like a fluffy marshmallow as it towers above other campus buildings, has been a success in every way, bringing prominence and recognition beyond the fondest dreams of Jake Crouthamel, athletic director since 1978. The university and the city of Syracuse are justifiably proud of the arena, which got a new 220-ton roof in 1999 at a cost of $14 million.

Bulldog Stadium (Fresno State)

Ratcliffe Stadium, a 13,000-seat facility erected in the 1930s, was home to the football and track teams of Fresno State and local high schools. That is where the Raisin Bowl was played in the late 1940s, and the Bulldogs continued using it after a new campus was built on the east side of town in 1955. In the heart of California's

San Joaquin Valley, FSU labored in anonymity, through good seasons and bad.

In 1975, the university announced plans to erect its own football stadium on a plot of land adjacent to the northwest corner of campus, but progress was slow. Local residents fought it tooth and nail, protesting the environmental impact and methods of fundraising. They lost the legal battle, however, and construction began next to the Fresno State baseball park, which had been built in 1966. Bulldog Stadium, with a field thirty-seven feet below ground level, cantilevered lights, and 30,000 seats, cost $7 million and was ready on November 15, 1980. The Dogs, who had been averaging just 9,000 fans per game at Ratcliffe Stadium, drew 25,684 that day to witness a 21–14 defeat of Montana State.

The coach was Jim Sweeney. He had been at FSU in 1976 and 1977, spent two years as an assistant with the Oakland Raiders, and then returned to college ball. Sweeney coached the next seventeen seasons in Fresno, and when he was through, the field was named in his honor. Playing in the Pacific Coast Athletic Conference, the Big West, and then the WAC, Fresno State won at least ten games in 1982, 1985, 1988, 1989, and 1991 and beat such Pac-10 teams as Oregon, Oregon State, Southern Cal, Arizona, Washington State, and California. A number of fine players came out of the program, the most prominent of them being receiver Henry Ellard (who went on to a long career with the LA Rams) and Sweeney's son, Kevin. In the mid-1980s, he became one of the most prolific passers in college football history, with nearly 11,000 yards in the air. The most significant player in recent FSU history is surely quarterback David Carr, the first pick in the 2002 NFL draft, by the Houston Texans.

Bulldog Stadium was just a year old when it hosted the inaugural California Bowl. That game, in which the red and blue played five times, lasted until 1991, the same year Bulldog Stadium was expanded to a seating capacity of 41,031. Changes consisted of new stands in the north and south ends, reconfiguration of seats on the east side, and the addition of twenty-two luxury boxes. FSU football, which generated twenty-four NFL draft picks in the 1990s, gets little recognition from the media, pollsters, or bowl representatives. Nevertheless, the athletic department dreams of the time when Bulldog Stadium will require another 30,000 seats.

Vanderbilt Stadium (Vanderbilt)

Dr. William Dudley, the dean of Vanderbilt's medical school for thirty years, also helped organize the NCAA and the Southern Conference and advocated standardization of rules when the game was still subject to regional variations. Vanderbilt's first football facility was named after Dudley back in 1892. It lasted until 1922, when a 20,000-seat stadium was erected on the west side of campus. Retaining the name of Dudley Field, it was christened with a scoreless tie against Michigan. Dan McGugin, who coached the Commodores for three decades, allegedly roused his team prior to that game with Civil War references.

Vandy had a powerful football program in those days, boasting eighteen straight winning seasons and intersectional victories against teams like Ohio State, Minnesota, and Texas. Only

—Courtesy of Vanderbilt sports information department

a 7–2 loss to LSU in Nashville prevented the black and gold from winning the 1935 SEC title—and they have never again come so close. Similarly, a two-point loss to Alabama in 1937 kept them out of the Rose Bowl. The stadium, which was expanded three times to a seating capacity of 34,000, was lighted in 1954 and got artificial turf in 1970. But the Commodores were in trouble long before then. They suffered at least one shutout every year from 1952 to 1966 and averaged just six points per game in one malodorous season. Vanderbilt had few truly outstanding players and became the Southeastern Conference's favorite whipping boy. Other than a 14–10 upset of No. 2 Alabama in 1969, the biggest thing to happen at Dudley Field was when President John F. Kennedy spoke to a crowd of 33,000 in 1963.

The Commodores had won just nine games in five seasons when AD Roy Kramer decided something had to change. The stadium was too small and lacked the amenities athletes and fans had come to expect. A fundraising campaign netted $10.1 million, and the Foster & Creighton Construction Company was employed to build a new facility. Well, not entirely new, because parts of the east and west stands, each weighing 400 tons and holding 6,000 seats, were preserved and raised ten feet by hydraulic jacks. The work was done in just nine months, resulting in a 41,000-seat stadium with artificial turf and a press box eight times larger than its predecessor. Vanderbilt Stadium (the field was still named for Dudley) was dedicated on September 12, 1981, with a 23–17 defeat of Maryland.

In the 1980s, Vanderbilt had three quarterbacks—Whit Taylor, Kurt Page, and Eric Jones—who had more than 6,000 yards in total offense during their careers. The 1982 team went 8–4 and played in the Hall of Fame Bowl, the stadium was nearly full for every home game, and the fans dared to dream big. The very next year, however, the losing resumed, eighteen straight years of it. Vandy is by far the SEC leader in graduation rates (80 percent) of its football players, but only eight were drafted by NFL teams in the 1990s, none of them in the first round. Amid the madness of the SEC facilities arms race, only VU has not expanded its stadium. A new scoreboard in the north end and installation of a grass field have been the only significant changes.

The competition got tougher in 1998 when the Tennessee Oilers/Titans moved to Nashville and rented Vanderbilt Stadium for a year. It also hosted the inaugural Music City Bowl before the bowl game and Bud Adams' team moved into a new $292 million coliseum (originally named for Adelphia before that company was nabbed in the corporate scandals of 2002). Vanderbilt then took a difficult step. The 2000 game with Tennessee, the regular-season closer for over half a century, was shifted to the fancy new pro stadium overlooking the Cumberland River. It drew more than 68,000 fans, most of them wearing orange, and made more money for both VU and UT than a campus game would have. The university has expressed a willingness to play other games there, as well.

Humphrey Metrodome (Minnesota)

They called it "the old brickhouse" because, in addition to wood, concrete, and steel, it contained over a million bricks. Minnesota's Memorial Stadium was built to honor the 3,527 UM students, faculty, and staff who had fought in World War I, 98 of whom died. Costing $572,000, the classic horseshoe was in the heart of campus, with fraternity row right across the street. A 440-yard track stood between the stands and the football field, and there were no lights; in a fifty-eight-season lifespan, Memorial Stadium never hosted night games. It had 52,736 permanent seats, although crowds as large as 66,000 were known to gather, not including the intrepid souls who watched from atop nearby telephone poles. The Gophers had already faced North Dakota, Haskell, Michigan, and Iowa State in the stadium before it was dedicated on November 15, 1924, against Illinois, with famed running back Red Grange. UM took a 20–7 victory.

Bronko Nagurski, whose name is still synonymous with raw, brute force, played there in the late 1920s. And in Minnesota's golden decade, coach Bernie Bierman led them to seven Big 10 titles and no less than five national championships between 1934 and 1941, and halfback Bruce Smith won the Heisman Trophy in the latter year. The Gophers played just eight games in each of those glorious seasons but were never in a bowl game. They had become the dregs of the conference in the late 1950s and then surprised everyone by winning the 1960 national crown (despite a Rose Bowl loss to Washington). Quarterback Sandy Stephens and lineman Bobby Bell took them back to Pasadena the next year and beat UCLA 21–3. Who knew they would go more than forty years without another outright Big 10 championship and disappear from the top-ten rankings? Who knew trouble was brewing due to the arrival of pro sports in the Twin Cities? The Minnesota Vikings began playing football and the Minnesota Twins began playing baseball at Metropolitan Stadium in suburban Bloomington in 1961, and coincidentally or not, the Gophers' for-

—Courtesy of Minnesota sports information department

tunes—as well as attendance figures at Memorial Stadium—went down. The nadir was in 1975, when they barely drew 31,000 fans per game.

The stadium had not received the sort of loving maintenance it deserved. A blue-ribbon task force determined that Memorial Stadium needed at least $10 million of work but still doubted UM could win in the old, outdoor, on-campus facility. The task force responded to political and financial interests determined to erect a municipal domed football/baseball facility. Minneapolis' downtown business community played a crucial role in pressuring legislators and members of the Board of Regents to go along with a plan that was oriented, first and foremost, to the Vikings and Twins. It was a decision that many UM football fans would come to rue. Groundbreaking for the Hubert H. Humphrey (former senator and vice president from Minnesota) Metrodome was in 1979, and the Regents voted in March 1981 to move, signing a thirty-year lease. The last game played at Memorial Stadium was in November of that year, a five-point loss to Wisconsin. The stadium, however, did not meet the wrecking ball until 1992. There were protests, proposals to use the structure for other purposes, and a host of legal maneuvers doomed to failure. A somber ceremony which included the UM alumni band playing "Taps" preceded the razing of Memorial Stadium. Its bricks were later sold for $10 apiece.

The Metrodome, meanwhile, was a $75 million building covered by ten acres of Teflon-coated fiberglass with 63,669 seats in football mode. There were 115 luxury boxes for the monied crowd. Critics, and there were many, called the stadium as sterile as an operating room. The Metrodome, which would host two NCAA Final Fours, two World Series, and a Super Bowl, was also home to the NBA's Minnesota Timberwolves for three seasons. The Gophers, who may have felt like just another tenant, first played there on September 11, 1982, shredding Ohio 57–3.

The stadium has not been a cure-all for Minnesota's football problems. Four coaches have come and gone, and all had losing records, while Glen Mason is now trying to avoid a similar fate. Although defensive back Tyrone Carter was a consensus all-American in 1999, he was UM's first in over thirty years. Since the novelty wore off, attendance at the Metrodome has hovered around 40,000, again begging the question of why Memorial Stadium, which had exuded collegiate atmosphere, was ever abandoned. With the Vikings and Twins threatening to leave town for a variety of reasons, Gopher fans grew more vocal in their criticism of everything pertaining to home games and waxed nostalgic about the old days. Other schools pointed to Minnesota as a prime example of what not to do. Further impetus came when a university commission advocated football's return to campus. Whether that happens soon—or ever—remains to be seen because the site of the long-lamented brickhouse is now an aquatics center, a luxury hotel, and a parking garage. And to make matters worse, the school suffered a PR disaster that got coverage in such publications as *Sports Illustrated* and the *Chronicle of Higher Education* when an academic fraud scandal resulted in the firing of AD Mark Dienhart and another top official.

Yager Stadium (Miami [Ohio])

When Miami University devoted ten acres of its rustic campus to athletics in 1896, some people grumbled, considering it a waste of perfectly good pastureland. Miami Field, home to the Redskins (renamed the RedHawks in 1996) for eighty-seven seasons, was enclosed by a wooden fence and had a ticket office that resembled a shed but it eventually got brick arches, a set of bleachers, then steel stands with a seating capacity of 15,000. As the years went by, there were occasional calls to renovate, replicate, or relocate, but other things took priority and most alumni favored keeping the stadium as it was in days gone by.

MU, located in the rolling hills of southwestern Ohio, was hardly part of the big-time college football scene, and yet it would come to have a unique niche. Not because the red and white went 32–1–1 from 1973 to 1975 with three MAC titles and three Tangerine Bowl wins over Florida, Georgia, and South Carolina (finishing No. 15, No. 10, and No. 12, respectively), although that was impressive. No, what amazes football cognoscenti is how the school turned out so many great coaches. Some were players, some were assistants, and others were head coaches, all of them going on

—Courtesy of Miami sports information department

to greater fame elsewhere. Only the biggest names include Earl Blaik, Weeb Eubank, Paul Brown, Sid Gillman, Paul Dietzel, Woody Hayes, Ara Parseghian, and Bo Schembechler. They won enough games, coach-of-the-year awards, and college and pro championships to compile an unmatched legacy. At one point, five of the Big 10's head coaches were Miami products. Thus it is called "the cradle of coaches." The man who really rocked the cradle was Gillman, who had a passion for football and conveyed it to players and coaches for over half a century—at Miami and Cincinnati, and then with the Los Angeles Rams, San Diego Chargers, and Houston Oilers before becoming an executive with the Dallas Cowboys, Oakland Raiders, and Chicago Bears.

Miami Field may have been on the fringe of campus in 1896, but it was surrounded by dorms and academic and administrative buildings by the early 1980s. Sentiment weighed heavily on students and alumni regarding the oldest stadium in NCAA Division I-A. President Paul Pearson and AD Richard Shrider agreed that MU needed a new stadium, and it should be on the north side of campus in the Four Mile River valley. After the last game played at Miami Field, a 23–0 defeat of Central Michigan on November 6, 1982, a few nostalgic fans lingered in the dusk. Other than a memorial gateway meticulously preserved and moved to the new facility, it was razed to make way for a biological sciences building. Miami Field's replacement cost $13.5 million and had 25,183 seats, more than half of them on the west side. It was named in honor of Fred Yager, who had attended the school in 1911 and 1912 before dropping out and eventually making it big in the stock market. Yager's estate (he died in 1974) supported the stadium project as well as medical and fine arts buildings on campus. The Redskins ran onto the virgin field for the first time on October 1, 1983, as an overflow crowd looked on. They suffered a two-point loss to Western Michigan, however.

In 1996, new end-zone stands brought seating capacity at Yager Stadium up to 30,012 at a cost of $350,000. While it is too early to tell whether Randy Walker will merit inclusion in Miami's pantheon of great coaches, his 1998 team went 10–1. Despite that record, the RedHawks did not receive a bowl invitation.

Marshall University Stadium (Marshall)

Fairfield Stadium, built in 1928, served as home field to Marshall University and Huntington High School. It would grow from 10,000 seats to 18,000 over a sixty-three-year lifespan. But the Ohio River flooded the city with grim regularity, sometimes affecting the stadium. The Thundering Herd had its share of good and bad seasons. Running back Jackie Hunt scored twenty-seven touchdowns in 1940 (a collegiate record that would stand for years), and the 1947 team played in the Tangerine Bowl. However, from mid-1965 to mid-1969, MU was horrible, winning three games, losing thirty-eight, and tying one. Like many other schools at the time, it suffered racial unrest, drug problems, and war protests. The debt-ridden football program was put on probation by the NCAA, which found 140 recruiting violations, and Fairfield Stadium was in poor shape, all of which prompted the Mid-American Conference to unceremoniously throw Marshall out. A few disgusted alumni and people on campus suggested pulling the plug on football altogether.

As if things could not get worse, there followed the greatest tragedy in the history of college sports. On the rainy, foggy evening of November 14, 1970, the green and white were returning home after a loss to East Carolina. The DC-9 passenger jet carrying them crashed at Tri-State Airport, killing all seventy-five on board—players, coaches, administrators, fans, and crew. That stunning, shocking event came just six weeks after a similar catastrophe hit Wichita State, with thirty-one dying. The two schools shared an agony no others could imagine but went in different directions with vastly different results. The Shockers kept trying to play a big-time schedule, losing games, losing money, and finally losing the desire to carry on. The WSU program ended in 1986.

Success came in small doses for the Herd in the first few years after the plane crash. A new coach, Jack Lengyel, was hired, and he made do with freshmen, sophomores, and walk-ons. MU took a calculated gamble, stepping down to Division I-AA before becoming competitive again. The 1984 team had a winning record, and soon West Virginia Governor Arch Moore signaled a willingness to help Marshall finance a new stadium on the east side of campus.

— Courtesy of Marshall sports information department

Ground was broken in the summer of 1990, and it was ready eighteen months later. Marshall University Stadium cost $30 million and had 28,000 seats evenly divided between east and west sides. There was artificial turf, twenty luxury boxes, and a south-end scoreboard measuring 37' x 54'. The stadium was first put to use on September 9, 1991, when the Herd beat New Hampshire 24–23 before 33,116 fans.

A $2 million donation by the widow of James Edwards convinced school officials to name the field in his honor in 1993, the year after MU won the first of two I-AA national championships. But the great times had just begun. Between 1991 and 1999, Marshall won an astounding 108 games. The 1996 team went 15–0 and laid claim to being the best in I-AA history, so it was obviously time to rejoin the big boys. The MAC let them back in, and they proceeded to dominate. Randy Moss, an electrifying receiver, came in fourth in Heisman Trophy voting in 1997, and quarterback Chad Pennington was fifth in 1999 (when the Thundering Herd had its first top-ten finish). Amid four straight appearances by the team in the Motor City Bowl, Marshall University Stadium was expanded by 10,000 seats in the south end prior to the 2000 season. It is already the biggest and best stadium in the MAC, and there are tentative plans to go up to a seating capacity of 55,000. If melancholy has lingered at MU since 1970, the lives that were lost have been validated in some measure by the football program rising from ashes to glory.

UB Stadium (Buffalo)

The State University of New York at Buffalo, which fancies itself the University at Buffalo, started using Rotary Field in 1923. The stadium was peculiar, in that one end zone stood six feet higher than the other, so the teams were always playing either uphill or downhill. Football was suspended during World War II and resumed in 1946 when the Bulls moved most of their games to Civic Stadium, which was later renamed War Memorial Stadium. Constructed by the WPA in 1938, it was not the most aesthetically pleasing facility, but it was big and served many purposes. Minor league baseball (the Buffalo Bisons), pro football (the Buffalo Bills) and stock car racing were just a few of the things that took place at "the old rockpile."

UB was splitting time between Rotary Field and War Memorial Stadium when the 1958 team, coached by Dick Offenhammer, went 8–1. The Bulls were invited to play in the Tangerine Bowl, but Orlando's city fathers were clinging to the last vestiges of Jim Crow. They asked Offenhammer not to bring black players to the game, and he declined, missing the school's one and only bowl offer. In the early 1960s, quarterback John Stofa and defensive tackle Gerry Philbin starred at Buffalo before getting on with their pro careers. Philbin was with the New York Jets when they beat the Baltimore Colts in the third Super Bowl.

While the Bulls had not suffered a losing season in nearly a decade, the pot was boiling. Attendance was weak, there were financial problems, and the 1970 team had a 2–9 record. Their 16–0 defeat of Holy Cross at Rotary Field was televised nationally—a first—but ABC refused to show the UB marching band's halftime

—Courtesy of Buffalo sports information department

protest of the Vietnam War, and major repercussions followed. The football program was summarily dropped.

It began again seven years later on a non-scholarship basis. Despite predictable trials and tribulations, the blue and white persevered and twice moved up to higher divisions and thus tougher competition. They left Rotary Field for good in 1985 when a 4,000-seat stadium was erected on Buffalo's north campus. A new and bigger place went up eight years later at a cost of $23 million. Built originally for the 1993 World University Games, UB Stadium had 16,500 seats, lights, a grass field, and a 400-meter track. With end-zone bleachers and twelve luxury boxes, it was expanded to a seating capacity of 31,000 in 1999. That year, the Bulls became full-fledged members of the NCAA's Division I-A and the Mid-American Conference. In both 1999 and 2000, they had the dubious honor of being the lowest-ranked team in the nation by *Sports Illustrated*. ADs Nelson Townsend and Bob Arkeilpane deserve credit for having created something from virtually nothing, but the achievement is precarious because a relatively large investment has been made, and there is no guarantee that UB can ever become one of the few schools with a profitable athletic program. As a result, stadium naming rights are now being solicited. And not everyone is happy about the resumption of football at Buffalo. Arkeilpane has noted that the faculty's attitude toward intercollegiate athletics ranges from grudging acceptance to outright hostility.

Rutgers Stadium (Rutgers)

The 100 or so spectators did not realize they were witnessing an event of major historical import. But there on College Field in New Brunswick, New Jersey, Rutgers hosted Princeton in the first intercollegiate football game. The date was November 6, 1869. It scarcely resembled modern-day football, as the two teams of twenty-five men each battled under rugby-like rules. Rutgers won 6–4 (one point was given per score), but the Tigers returned the favor at home nine days later. College Field, now a gymnasium parking lot with a statue commemorating that famous game, was

—Courtesy of Rutgers sports information department; photo by Larry Levanti

home to Rutgers football until 1892, when Neilson Field was erected nearby.

It had a lifespan of nearly fifty years, and while many poignant athletic moments transpired there, surely the most significant involve Paul Robeson, one of the earliest black football players. He dealt with raw racism from teammates and opponents but eventually won their respect and became an all-American in 1917 and 1918. Robeson graduated Phi Beta Kappa and went on to become a renowned actor, singer, scholar, and most of all, an outspoken civil rights activist. Paul Robeson, a man of deep courage and integrity, is surely Rutgers' most distinguished alumnus; the university has named three buildings after him, and he has been honored posthumously in countless other ways.

Robeson had left the realm of sports far behind when Rutgers decided to replace deteriorating Neilson Field. A 256-acre tract of land a few miles up the Raritan River was purchased and would later comprise one of the university's satellite campuses. Athletic director George Little was the dynamic force behind the construction of Rutgers Stadium. Roughly two-thirds of the $1.2 million and all of the labor was provided by the WPA, the $411 billion program that helped lift the U.S. out of its economic woes. An unlighted football field surrounded by a track, Rutgers Stadium had 23,000 seats. Beginning in 1938, the Scarlet Knights spent fifty-five seasons there and secured 168 victories. There were a couple of undefeated teams (1961 and 1976), but the biggest game ever at the stadium was in 1969 when a record crowd of 31,000 saw Rutgers and Princeton replay their game of a century earlier. The visiting Tigers fell 29–0.

In 1976, the New Jersey Sports and Exposition Authority built Giants Stadium as part of the Meadowlands Sports Complex in nearby East Rutherford. Although it was a pro facility (home to the New York Giants and New York Jets) first and foremost, Rutgers was enticed to play as many as three home games there for each of the next twenty-one seasons. Coinciding with that, the athletic department chose to junk the Ivy League–type schedule and play some stiffer competition. It was a major change in philosophy and one that would meet determined opposition from some students, faculty, and alumni. At any rate, the Scarlet Knights stopped playing Lafayette (after seventy-two games) in 1975, Lehigh (seventy-four games) in 1977, Columbia (forty-nine games) in 1978, and most painful of all, Princeton (seventy-one games) in 1981. The state of New Jersey gave $3 million in 1984 for a makeover of Rutgers' facilities, but with scant results. The Scarlet Knights won barely one-third of their games in the remainder of the twentieth century despite being in a heavily populated state with lots of football talent.

As a member of the Big East Conference since 1991, Rutgers had to make some changes, and it got help from the aforementioned New Jersey Sports and Exposition Authority. Led by Bob Mulcahy (soon to be the school's athletic director), that entity spent $28 million to raze "old" Rutgers Stadium and build "new" Rutgers Stadium on the same spot. The Scarlet Knights played all their 1993 home games at Giants Stadium while construction was underway. The new facility had no track (the NJSEA also built Rutgers new soccer and track stadiums), two upper decks, lights, and room for 41,500 fans. It was inaugurated on September 3, 1994, with a 28–6 defeat of Kent State. Those who climb to the top claim they can see the hills of Pennsylvania to the west and downtown Manhattan to the east.

Papa John's Cardinal Stadium (Louisville)

In 1923, Parkway Field opened at the south end of the University of Louisville campus. Not far from Churchill Downs, it was a three-purpose facility: horseracing, minor league baseball, and college football. While the names of the ponies that ran there have been lost in the mists of time, the Louisville Colonels (and such major leaguers as Babe Ruth, Ted Williams, and Jackie Robinson) played at Parkway Field in the spring and summer, and UL's football team used it in the fall for over three decades.

Early in Frank Camp's twenty-three-year tenure as coach, the Cardinals had a player who would later be a gridiron god. Louisville won twelve games and lost twenty-two from 1951 to 1954, but it would have been much worse without quarterback

—Courtesy of Louisville sports information department

Johnny Unitas. He went on to become one of the all-time greats with the Baltimore Colts. And one of Unitas' young teammates was also quite special. Lenny Lyles broke the color barrier there in 1954, averaged 7 yards per carry on offense, played defensive back, and rejoined Unitas in Baltimore.

During Lyles' senior year, 1957 (when the team went 9–1 with a victory in the Sun Bowl), UL left Parkway Field for Fairgrounds Stadium, a new 20,600-seat facility two miles southeast of campus. Again sharing space with the local minor league baseball club, the Cards made it home for forty years. The rather weird-looking stadium was expanded to a seating capacity of 37,500 and got artificial turf in 1973, at which time it was renamed Cardinal Stadium, but few people were truly happy with it. Some were calling for a football-only stadium even in the 1960s. The biggest crowd in the history of Cardinal Stadium was in 1991 when 40,457 saw the Tennessee Volunteers win 28–11. Over the years, a new press box, a new set of locker rooms, and a facelift or two only made it tolerable to UL fans.

Coach Howard Schnellenberger led the 1990 team to a 10–1–1 record, including a 34–7 spanking of Alabama in the Fiesta Bowl. They finished No. 14, the highest in Louisville history. That helped spark a drive to finance a new stadium. Mayor Jerry Abramson was for it, and so was president Donald Swain, but high rollers did not achieve the goal so much as a grass-roots campaign among alumni, citizens, and football fans in northern Kentucky. Private donations came to $28 million (out of an eventual $63 million) before corporate and governmental entities got involved. There were problems and controversies galore, weather delays, and even a strike, and at times it may have seemed hopeless, but perseverance paid off. Luckett & Farley designed and Huber, Hunt & Nichols built a horseshoe-shaped stadium on the site of a former railroad yard south of campus. It had twenty-eight luxury boxes, natural grass grown on a synthetic base, 42,000 chairback seats, an athletic complex in the north end, and a UL football museum named for Unitas. Some people were amused when Papa John's Pizza paid $5 million for naming rights. Others found it merely unappetizing or hard to swallow.

The inaugural game at Papa John's Cardinal Stadium was on September 5, 1998. Louisville's opponent was the University of

Kentucky, making its first visit in eighty-three years. Quarterback Tim Couch threw seven touchdown passes as the Wildcats humiliated the Cards 68–34. UL's first win there came three weeks later when they beat Boston College 52–28. By all accounts, Louisville now has a superb football stadium, one that with a set of upper decks could hold 80,000 fans and conceivably draw a pro team to the city.

Rice-Eccles Stadium (Utah)

In the early years of the twentieth century, Utah played home football games at Cummings Field, an expanse of dirt cleared of sagebrush. Byron Cummings, for whom the rustic stadium was named, was a professor who lent his energy to organizing Ute athletics. Cummings Field was improved over the years and grew to a seating capacity of 10,000, but its ad hoc nature ensured its demise. When the 1926 team, coached by Ike Armstrong, went 7–0 and allowed its opponents to score just 23 points, the time was ripe. Construction of a new stadium began in the spring of 1927,

—Courtesy of Utah sports information department

and it was ready the following season. Costing $133,000, Ute Stadium was a 20,000-seat facility made of timber and concrete. Sitting on the southwest corner of the campus in Salt Lake City, it was dedicated on October 1, 1927, when the Utes beat Colorado Mines 40–7. In 1947, Armstrong was nearing the end of his twenty-five-year tenure when the stadium got another 10,000 north-end seats. Utah was nothing special in the late 1950s, but they had a running back, Larry Wilson, who went on to a Hall-of-Fame career as a defensive back with the St. Louis Cardinals.

In 1972, Utah alumnus Robert Rice gave $1 million to help renovate the stadium. The track was taken out, artificial turf was put in, new lighting was installed, and the place got a much-needed facelift. In gratitude, the university renamed it Rice Stadium. Ten years later, a set of stands was built in the south end, raising seating capacity to 32,500, although the BYU game that year drew a record crowd of 36,250. The 1994 team, led by all-America defensive lineman Luther Elliss, was one of the best in school history—they went 10–2, beat Arizona in the Freedom Bowl, and finished No. 10.

Athletic director Chris Hill used that success, along with the news that Salt Lake City had won the right to hold the 2002 Winter Olympics (notwithstanding the bribery scandal that shone a harsh light on a city known for righteous behavior), to accelerate a long-held dream of replacing the antiquated and crumbling stadium. Spencer Eccles, a Utah graduate, announced that his family's foundation was giving $10 million in the effort, and the Salt Lake City Olympic Committee gave another $8 million, which was a good start on the $50 million required. The Layton Construction Company worked within that budget and tight time constraints to raze the old stadium (except for the south stands, circa 1982) and build a new one with 45,634 seats. It had a grass field, seventeen luxury boxes, a fancy scoreboard, and a modern and spacious press box. Named Rice-Eccles Stadium, it was christened on September 12, 1998, when the Utes beat Louisville 45–22 before a crowd of 44,112.

The stadium elevated Utah to so-called "mid-major" status, and teams from the Pac-10, Big 12, Big 10, and ACC have shown a new willingness to visit. Rice-Eccles Stadium got 5,000 temporary seats prior to the Olympics because the opening and closing ceremonies would be held there. Furthermore, the University of Utah campus served as the athletes' village, home to skiers, skaters, lugers, bobsledders, hockey players, and other cold-weather jocks from around the world.

Princeton Stadium (Princeton)

Harvard, Yale, and Princeton were the big three in the early decades of college football, each winning several putative national championships. The Crimson built a massive stadium in 1903, while the Bulldogs and Tigers followed suit eleven years later. Edgar Palmer, a loyal and wealthy Princeton alumnus, desired to honor his father, Stephen, a former member of the Board of Trustees. So he underwrote the construction of a 41,000-seat facility on the southeast corner of campus, close to newly created Lake Carnegie. It was a concrete horseshoe with a track, a pair of Gothic entrance towers, and an exterior characterized by tall, narrow arches. The first game at Palmer Stadium was on October 24, 1914, when Princeton beat Dartmouth 16–12.

A place redolent with tradition, suitable to such an old and prestigious university, Palmer Stadium was where Bill Roper's teams won the national title in 1920 and 1922 and where Fritz Crisler's teams won a version of it in 1933 and 1935, although they played a strictly eastern schedule at a time when the balance of power in college football was shifting in a westerly and southerly direction; Michigan had a stronger claim in 1933 and Minnesota and Southern Methodist in 1935. It was where Dick Kazmaier paced the 1950 and 1951 teams to eighteen straight victories before he was awarded the Heisman Trophy. And it was where Princeton took the high road in 1956 as a charter member of the Ivy League—adhering to tough academics and forswearing athletic scholarships and post-season bowl games.

Little change took place at Palmer Stadium over the years, other than the installation of a rubber track in 1978. For the big games (and there were sellouts as recently as the mid-1960s), bleachers were put up in the south end. But with use and exposure to the elements, it was a crumbling and antiquated building beyond repair. The 461st and final game was on November 23, 1996, a 24–0 loss to Dartmouth witnessed by 16,000 sentimental fans, some of whom took wooden benches and handfuls of turf home as mementos.

The 1997 orange and black played every game on the road, including "home" games against Fordham at Lions Stadium on the campus of the College of New Jersey and Yale at Giants Stadium. In the meantime, the stadium was demolished, AD Gary Walters galvanized the alumni, and architect Rafael Vinoly designed a $45 million facility that included some of the rubble of Palmer Stadium in its foundation. Princeton Stadium had 27,800 seats in two tiers with a set of glassed-in luxury boxes on the north rim. It was much more intimate than its venerable predecessor because there was no track; the Weaver Track and Field Stadium was built just to the south. While some critics said the stadium was "feminized" and lacked gravitas, it won kudos from the *Wall Street Journal* and *New York Times*.

Princeton Stadium was first used on September 19, 1998, when the Tigers beat Cornell 6–0. The Board of Trustees mandated that it serve a wide array of civic as well as athletic purposes, but there has been some difficulty achieving that goal. Walters and other administrators are open about selling naming rights to the stadium, although preferably not to a commercial entity. "It hasn't been the tradition at Princeton to solicit corporations to put their names on individual buildings," he said. "I don't think that's consistent with our approach."

Ford Stadium (Southern Methodist)

Since SMU alumnus Jordan Ownby made the biggest donation in the drive to erect a $223,000 stadium on the southeast corner of campus, it bore his name. The Mustangs first used 22,000-seat Ownby Stadium on September 24, 1926, when they ripped North Texas 42–0. They also won the Southwest Conference championship that year. SMU enjoyed a rapid ascent to prominence as Matty Bell's 1935 team won the national crown despite a 7–0 loss to Stanford in the Rose Bowl. Further glory in Dallas centered around Doak Walker, a three-time all-American who ran, passed, kicked, returned kicks, and was an accomplished defensive back. Walker led the 1947 Ponies to a 9–0–2 record (one of the ties was with Penn State in the Cotton Bowl) and a No. 3 ranking. The next year, Walker, the post–World War II golden boy, won the Heisman Trophy and was largely responsible for SMU moving its home games from Ownby Stadium to the Cotton Bowl. That stadium, which cost $328,000 to erect in 1930, was expanded twice during the Walker era to a seating capacity of over 70,000. Thus, it is still known as "the house that Doak built." In 1949 and 1950, SMU averaged over 60,000 in home attendance, third-highest in the nation.

Two of the top Mustangs in the ensuing decades were quarterback Don Meredith and receiver Jerry LeVias, who, as the first black player in SWC history, dealt admirably with horrific pressure. LeVias was an all-American and came in fifth in Heisman Trophy voting in 1968. The Cotton Bowl was home to SMU and the New Year's Day classic, as well as the annual Texas-Oklahoma game and the Dallas Cowboys since 1960. But the pro team (which had stolen considerable thunder from the Mustangs) got a new place in 1971, Texas Stadium in suburban Irving. SMU, whose average attendance had fallen 50 percent compared to when Doak Walker bestrode the gridiron like a colossus, began splitting time between the Cotton Bowl and the Cowboys' palatial 65,000-seat stadium. And in 1979, the red and blue made the switch complete. Texas Stadium may have been impressive to a high school recruit, but it was still a long way from campus. SMU enjoyed some fine years there, winning forty-one games from 1981 to 1984, coming in Nos. 3, 2, 12, and 8, respectively. In Eric Dickerson and Craig James, they had the greatest running back tandem of all time, two guys who gained a total of 8,198 yards on the ground. The happy times came to a crashing halt, however. The NCAA found evidence of brazen cheating and put the Ponies on probation in 1981, 1985, and again in 1987. They were recidivists, repeat offenders, and college football's governing body made an example of them, administering the "death penalty."

The sport would not resume at SMU until 1989, although some dismayed alumni and faculty favored dropping it altogether. Following a top-to-bottom cleansing of the athletic department, the Mustangs returned to Ownby Stadium (which was too small) and later the Cotton Bowl (too old and too far away), but it was a struggle regaining fans and the competitive edge. Still, a core of SMU faithful would not give up. They advocated raising money to build a new stadium on campus and won the support of AD Jim Copeland and finally the administration. A handsome $20 million donation from Gerald Ford—not the thirty-eighth president, but a banker with two degrees from SMU—got it off to a fast start. The total came to $57 million, which covered demolition of Ownby Stadium and the design and construction of Ford Stadium. Built in the Collegiate Georgian style, its west side was made to resemble the late Ownby. One of a handful of Division I-A stadiums erected since the 1980s, it had 32,000 seats and twenty-four luxury boxes. The open south end, which provided a nice view of Dallas' skyline, left room for future expansion to 45,000 seats. With appropriate fanfare, Ford Stadium opened on September 2, 2000, when a sellout crowd saw Mike Cavan's Ponies beat Kansas 31–17.

Heinz Field (Pittsburgh)

When the Pittsburgh Pirates unveiled Forbes Field in 1909, it doubled as home to the University of Pittsburgh football team. That was handy, since the Pitt campus was next door. Pop Warner's 1916 and 1918 teams won the national championship at Forbes Field, and seats were hard to come by. Thus, the university devoted ten acres to the construction of a new stadium. Mammoth (with room for 69,000 fans), oval-shaped Pitt Stadium was designed by W. S. Hindman and built by the Turner Construction Company and cost $2.1 million. Pittsburgh, the famous city of steel, churned out 3,200 tons of it for use in the stadium. It was a unique multi-purpose venue, housing not only football but track, basketball, baseball, riflery, and gymnastics. The inaugural game was on September 26, 1925, when the Panthers—then coached by Jock Sutherland—defeated Washington & Lee 26–0.

Pitt, never afraid to play a national schedule, had become one of the giants of college football, making four Rose Bowl appearances between 1927 and 1936 and winning the 1937 national title

An Illustrated History of 120 College Football Stadiums 241

—Courtesy of Pittsburgh sports information department; photo by William McBride

with star running back Marshall Goldberg. The 1938 game with Fordham drew a record crowd of 68,918. Despite the occasional appearance of great players like Joe Schmidt and Mike Ditka, however, the blue and gold had begun to decline. Average attendance at Pitt Stadium fluctuated between 13,000 and 48,000. Clearly, the stadium had been overbuilt, and plans for expansion by another 30,000 seats were put away. The Pittsburgh Steelers, longtime tenants at Forbes Field, moved over to Pitt Stadium in 1963 and remained there until Three Rivers Stadium (home to both the Steelers and Pirates) was built in 1970. The university did little to adapt its stadium to changing times, with these exceptions: artificial turf and aluminum benches in 1970, lights in 1987, and a new scoreboard in 1995.

The Panthers had suffered nine straight non-winning seasons, including three 1-9s, before the arrival of coach Johnny Majors in 1973. He stayed in Pittsburgh four years and, not coincidentally, so did running back Tony Dorsett. Together, they lifted the program to a level not seen or imagined in four decades. It all culminated in the 1976 team going 12-0 with a Sugar Bowl defeat of Georgia and winning the national championship. Dorsett set a collegiate career record with 6,082 yards gained and won the Heisman Trophy. More high times followed with quarterback Dan Marino (who later threw for over 61,000 yards with the Miami Dolphins) and a boatload of other No. 1 draft picks. They went 33–3 from 1979 to 1981 with victories in the Fiesta, Gator, and Sugar bowls before another dropoff occurred. It was getting harder to entice top players to even visit a stadium that had come to be seen as a dinosaur, at least in the eyes of some.

Simultaneously, the Pirates and Steelers, who won six titles at Three Rivers Stadium in the 1970s, were beginning to feel the same way. Pitt had played a few home games there over the years. Voters turned down a 1997 referendum to build two new stadiums for the pros, but politicians such as Governor Tom Ridge and Mayor Tom Murphy knew what was best. After some extremely contentious debate, they cobbled together a financial plan that would preserve the city's pro sports heritage. Almost as an afterthought, the Panthers were brought into the deal. AD Steve Pederson ignored the pleas to keep on-campus football and Pitt Stadium itself and pushed for inclusion. A petition signed by many of Pitt's greatest living players could not slow the project's momentum. Pitt Stadium was demolished in February 2000, and Three Rivers Stadium (where the Panthers played that season) met the same fate twelve months later. To one side on the north shore of the Allegheny, $262 million PNC Park was built for the Pirates, and on the other, a $284 million facility was built for the Steelers. The idea of naming it for Art Rooney, the late owner of the Steelers, was quashed because the franchise sought the sweetest corporate offer, which turned out to be $57 million over twenty years from Heinz, a local company best known for ketchup. Heinz Field has 65,000 seats, 127 luxury boxes, and a plethora of high-tech features to keep players and fans happy. With the two stadiums, post-industrial Pittsburgh was again transforming itself, or so it was hoped.

In place of Pitt Stadium, the university erected a basketball arena/convocation center and student housing. Pederson, chancellor Mark Nordenberg, and other officials have made a bold move, and only time will tell whether it was the right one. Pittsburgh did not spend a single dollar for Heinz Field, so they rent it on

Saturdays each fall. The Panthers' first game there was a 31–0 defeat of East Tennessee State on September 1, 2001.

Rentschler Field (Connecticut)

For more than three decades, the University of Connecticut played home games at Gardner Dow Field, named for a player who had died during a 1919 game against New Hampshire. In 1953, it was replaced with Memorial Stadium, a 16,200-seat facility on the west side of the campus in Storrs. The Huskies, longtime members of the Yankee Conference, played a schedule consisting mostly of other New England schools. Except for a smattering of stars (such as quarterbacks Pete Petrillo and Matt DeGennaro and running backs Walt Trojanowsky and Eric Torkelson), UConn was content to keep its dreams of football grandeur in check.

It is hard to say when the university began thinking in terms of the big time. Perhaps in 1987 when Gampel Pavilion was built just east of Memorial Stadium; eventually, both the men's and

— Courtesy of Connecticut sports information department

women's basketball teams would win national championships. Perhaps it was the formation of the Big East Conference in 1991. Or perhaps it was the arrival of Lew Perkins as AD, a job he had held previously at Wichita State and Maryland. Perkins saw what anybody else could see, that Memorial Stadium was a quaint throwback to the 1950s, albeit sufficient for the program as it then stood. Connecticut, the state with the highest per capita income, was fertile ground for fundraising, or "development" as it is now called. And Perkins had allies in chairman of the UConn Board of Trustees Lewis Rome, president Philip Austin, and Governor John Rowland. Heavy hitters, every one.

First, there was a plan to build a new stadium on campus, but it fell through. Once the two basketball teams started using the Hartford Civic Center as a home away from home, Perkins figured, why not work a similar deal for football? And since the New England Patriots of the NFL were considering a new stadium in Hartford, UConn became part of the mix, but that, too, went nowhere when the Patriots backed out. There were futile discussions about a multi-purpose domed stadium in downtown Hartford. Then finally, the blue and white got a break. United Technologies, the parent company of aircraft builder Pratt & Whitney, donated 75 acres at the north end of its 700-acre campus in East Hartford. Rentschler Field—named in honor of P & W founder Frederick Rentschler—was an old airport that had been used by Charles Lindbergh, Amelia Earhart, World War II training pilots, and others. Some environmentalists were aghast at the potential loss of some wetlands and the removal of nine species of rare birds. But fast-track legislation went to Rowland's desk, and he signed it, ensuring that Rentschler Field would be built with $90 million in state and private money. Groundbreaking ceremonies, complete with gold-plated shovels, took place in October 2000. The stadium was to keep the Rentschler name for fifteen years before naming rights could be sold. Ellerbe Becket, a Minnesota firm, was chosen to design a 40,000-seat bowl (with thirty-five luxury boxes) capable of expansion to 50,000. Opening day is scheduled for August 30, 2003, when the Huskies, by then full-fledged NCAA Division I-A members, will host Rutgers.

Perkins, et al., have embarked on what should be an interesting walk down the primrose path. The stadium, it should be noted, will be thirty miles from campus in a remote area. If all goes as planned, and it seldom does, Rentschler Field will be part of a $771 million development project known as Adriaen's Landing. And whether Connecticut, which has little football history and is not to be confused with Florida, Texas, or California in terms of producing talented players, can become one of a handful of schools with a genuinely profitable football program remains to be seen. But Perkins and some dreamy-eyed fans have already spoken of contending for a national championship within ten years.

Index

A—
Abramson, Jerry, 234
Adams, Bud, 221
Ade, George, 49
Aggie Memorial Stadium (New Mexico State), 211-213
Aikman, Troy, 29
Aillet, Joe, 180
Aillet Stadium (Louisiana Tech), 180-181
Air Force (U.S. Air Force Academy), 148-149
Akers, Fred, 121
Akron Municipal Stadium. *See* Rubber Bowl (Akron)
Albert, Frankie, 24
Aldrich, Ki, 77
Alexander, Bill, 4
Alexander, Joe, 215
Allen, David, 178
Allen, Forrest "Phog," 19
Alleva, Tom, 70
Aloha Stadium (Hawai'i), 201-202
Alumni Field (Central Michigan), 195
Alumni Stadium (Boston College), 134-136

Alvarez, Barry, 14
Ameche, Alan, 14
Amundson, George, 203
Anderson, Billy, 87
Anderson, Donny, 119
Anderson, Eddie, 74
Anderson, Qadry, 157
Antrim, Frank, 136
Araki, Charles, 201
Archbold, John, 215
Archbold Stadium (Syracuse), 215, 216
Arizona Stadium (Arizona), 67-69
Arizona State University, 136-139
Arkansas State University, 199-200
Arkeilpane, Bob, 230
Armstrong, Ike, 235, 236
Army (U.S. Military Academy), 45-47
Arrington, LaVar, 145
Atwood and Nash, 62
Auburn University, 107-108
Ault, Chris, 163
Austin, Philip, 244
Autry, Darnell, 56
Autzen Stadium (Oregon), 169-171
Autzen, Thomas, 169-170

247

B—

Babcock, Charles, 175
Bagwell, Al, 150
Bailey, Carl E., 103
Baker & Carpenter, 24
Baker, Bubba, 180
Baker, Ralph, 56
Baker, Terry, 132
Ball State Stadium (Ball State), 171-172
Ball State University, 171-172
Banaszak, John, 184
Banker, Bill, 205
Barber, Red, 81
Barnett, Gary, 56
Barnhart, Mitch, 133-134
Barnhill, John, 103
Barrett, Ernie, 177
Bartow, Gene, 64
Batch, Charlie, 184
Baugh, Sammy, 77
Baylor Stadium. *See* Casey Stadium (Baylor)
Baylor University, 121-123
Beamer, Frank, 159
Beard, Jeff, 108
Beasley, Terry, 108
Beaver, James, 143
Beaver Stadium (Penn State), 143-146
Beban, Gary, 29
Bebb & Gould, 17
Bednarik, Chuck, 31
Bell, Bobby, 222
Bell, Chuck, 92
Bell, Matty, 238
Bellino, Joe, 141
Bellmont, L. Theo, 50
Bellotti, Mike
Benson, Tom, 207
Beres, George, 57
Bergey, Bill, 199
Beury, Charles F., 191
Bevington, Gary, 196
Bible, Dana, 50, 79
Bidwell, Bill, 138
Bienen, Henry, 57
Bierman, Bernie, 221

Biletnikoff, Fred, 129
Bingham, William, 2
Bishop, Michael, 178
Blaik, Earl "Red," 46, 47, 225
Blair, Matt, 203
Blake, Jeff, 150
Blanchard, Felix "Doc," 46
Blaymaier, Gene, 186
Bledsoe, Drew, 98
Bock, Ed, 202
Bockrath, Bob, 67
Boggs, Hale, 206
Boise State University, 185-186
Boisture, Dan, 184
Bork, George, 160
Bosco, Robbie, 155
Bosley, Bruce, 213
Boston College, 134-136
Boulder Bowl. *See* Folsom Field (Colorado)
Bowden, Bobby, 129, 130
Bower, Jeff, 209
Bowerman, Bill, 171
Bowling Green State University, 163-164
Bowman Gray Stadium (Wake Forest), 175
Boyd, Sam, 194
Boyd Stadium (Nevada–Las Vegas), 193-195
Bradshaw, Terry, 180
Brees, Drew, 49
Brewer, Chester, 57-58
Brice, Martha Williams, 94
Bridgers, John, 129
Briggs Stadium (Eastern Michigan), 184
Briggs, Walter, 183-184
Brigham Young University, 153–155
Brockington, John, 27
Brodie, John, 24
Bronco Stadium (Boise State), 185-186
Brooks, Rich, 170
Brooks, Robert, 76
Brown & Root, 126
Brown, Bill, 106
Brown, George, 139

Brown, Jim, 215-216
Brown, Paul, 26, 225
Brown Stadium (Louisiana–Monroe), 210
Brown, Ted, 166
Brown, Tim, 171
Brown, Watson, 64
Broyles, Frank, 104
Brumbelow, Mike, 152
Bryant, Bobby, 93
Bryant, Paul "Bear," 64, 66, 67, 80, 122, 125, 130, 159, 197-198
Bryant-Denny Stadium (Alabama), 65-67
Bukovich, Dan, 100
Bulldog Stadium (Fresno State), 217-218
Burdine, Roddy, 101
Burkett, Jackie, 108
Burrell, Leroy, 112
Butcher, Jade, 147
Butkus, Dick, 33
Butts, Wally, 72
Byrd, H. C. "Curley," 123-124
Byrd Stadium (Maryland), 123-125

C—

Cagle, Chris, 46, 187
Cajun Field (Louisiana–Lafayette), 187-188
California State University, Fresno, 217-218
Camp, Frank, 233
Camp Randall Stadium (Wisconsin), 12-14
Camp, Walter, 5, 6, 7, 159
Campbell Stadium (Florida State), 128-130
Campell, Earl, 51
Cannon, Billy, 52
Cappelletti, John, 144
Cardinal Stadium. *See* Papa John's Cardinal Stadium (Louisville)
Carolina Stadium. *See* Williams-Brice Stadium (South Carolina)
Carr, David, 218
Carr, Fred, 153
Carr, Roger, 180

Carrier Dome (Syracuse), 215-217
Carson, Arch, 11-12
Carson Field (Cincinnati), 12
Carter, Amon, 77
Carter, Harry, 165
Carter, Jimmy, 141
Carter Stadium (Texas Christian), vii, 77-79
Carter, Tyrone, 223
Carter, Virgil, 155
Carter, Wilbert, 165
Carter-Finley Stadium (North Carolina State), 164-167
Cartier Field (Notre Dame), 84
Casey, Bernie, 163
Casey, Carl, 123
Casey, Floyd, 123
Casey Stadium (Baylor), 121-123
Casper, Gerhard, 25
Cassill, Harvey, 18
Cassinelli, Dave, 156
Cavagnaro, Charles, 195
Cavan, Mike, 240
Cawthon, Pete, 117-118
Centennial Field (Florida State), 128
Central Michigan University, 195-197
Chadwick, W. D., 8
Chandler, Wes, 82
Chastain, Brandi, 29
Christiansen, Jack, 178-179
Christman Construction Company, 196-197
Churchill, Winston, 101
Citrus Bowl (Central Florida), 95-97
Claiborne, Jerry, 159
Clemson University, 115-117
Cline, Gene, 190
Clinton, Bill, 63
Coaches Building (Oklahoma State), 16
Cochrane, Kenneth, 110
Cockerham, Steve, 110
Coleman, Horace "Hap," 105
College Field (Rutgers), 230-231
Collier, Marvin, 91
Collins, Bobby, 209
Colorado Stadium. *See* Folsom Field (Colorado)

Colorado State University, 178-180
Commonweatlh Stadium (Kentucky), 197-199
Cooper, Jarrod, 178
Copeland, Jim, 240
Cornell University, 9-11
Corso, Lee, viii
Coryell, Don, 168
Cotton Bowl (Southern Methodist), 239
Couch, Tim, 199, 235
Cozza, Carmen, 7
Criner, Jim, 186
Crisler, Fritz, 237
Crouthamel, Jake, 217
Crow, John David, 210
Crowder, Eddie, 44
Culpepper, Daunte, 96
Cummings, Byron, 235
Cummings Field (Utah), 235
Cunningham, Randall, 194
Cuozzo, Gary, 88
Curci, Fran, 199
Curry, Tim, 149
Curtice, Jack, 152
Curtis, Isaac, 168
Cutcliffe, David, 115

D—
Dale, Carroll, 158
Dalrymple, Jerry, 205
Darden, Colgate, 88
Darnell, Gary, 106
Darrell K Royal–Texas Memorial Stadium. *See* Royal-Memorial Stadium (Texas)
Daugherty, Hugh "Duffy," 37
Davalos, Rudy, 143
Davis, Anthony, 42
Davis, Bob, 178
Davis, Ernie, 216, 217
Davis, Glenn, 46
Davis, Kenneth, 78
Davis, Troy, 204
Davis Wade Stadium at Scott Field. *See* Scott Field (Mississippi State)
Dawkins, Pete, 46
Dayne, Ron, 14
Dean, Fred, 180

DeBerg, Steve, 91
DeBord, Mike, 197
DeGennaro, Matt, 243
DeGroot, Dudley, 91
Delhomme, Jake, 188
Dempsey, Tom, 207
Denny Field (Washington), 16
Denver, John, 213
Deromedi, Herb, 197
Detmer, Ty, 120, 155
Devaney, Bob, 36, 121
Devine, Aubrey, 73
Devine, Dan, 58, 136
Dickerson, Eric, 239
Diehm, L. F. "Tow," 143
Dienhart, Mark, 224
Dietzel, Paul, 52, 93-94, 95, 225
Ditka, Mike, 241
Dix, Robert, 182
Dix Stadium (Kent State), 181-183
Dixon Construction Company, 40
Dixon, Dave, 206
Dobbs, Bobby, 152
Dobbs, Glenn, 87
Dobie, Gil, 16
Dockery, Rex, 157
Dodd, Bobby, 4, 5, 159
Dodd Stadium (Georgia Tech), 3-5
Dodds, DeLoss, 51
Donahue, Terry, 30
Dooley, Vince, 72
Dorais, Gus, 83
Dorsett, Tony, 52, 213, 241, 242
Dowdy, Ron, 150
Dowdy-Ficklen Stadium (East Carolina), 150-151
Dryer, Fred, 168
Dudley, Bill, 88
Dudley Field (Vanderbilt), 219-221
Dudley, William, 219
Duke Stadium. *See* Wade Stadium (Duke)
Duke University, 69-70
Durand, William, 24
Durham, Larry, 152, 153
Dutton, John, 163
Dyche Stadium. *See* Ryan Field (Northwestern)

Dyche, William, 55
Dye, Pat, 121
Dykes, Spike, 119

E—
E. H. Latham Company, 26
Ealey, Chuck, 100
Earhart, Amelia, 244
Easley, Kenny, 29
East Carolina University, 150-151
Eastern Michigan University, 183-185
Eccles, Spencer, 236
Edwards, Earle, 165
Edwards, James, 228
Edwards, LaVell, 154, 155
Edwards Stadium (Brigham Young), 153-155
Edwards, Turk, 97
Eggers & Higgins, 147
Eisenhower, Dwight, 76
Ellard, Henry, 218
Ellender, Bennie, 199
Ellerbe Becket, 244
Elliss, Luther, 236
Elway, John, 24
Emtman, Steve, 19
Engle, Charles "Rip," 144
Enyart, Bill "Earthquake," 132
Erickson, Dennis, 102, 121, 133, 190
Eubank, Weeb, 225
Evans, George "Chick," 160

F—
Fairfield Stadium (Marshall), 226
Fairgrounds Stadium (Louisville), 234
Falcon Stadium (Air Force), 148-149
Fambrough, Don, 20
Faulk, Marshall, 169
Faulkinberry, Russ, 187
Faulkner Field (Southern Mississippi), 208-209
Faulkner, Louis, 208
Faurot, Don, 58
Faust, Gerry, 110
Favre, Brett, 209
Fenimore, Bob, 15
Ferry, Charles, 6
Ferry Field (Michigan), 59, 60

Ferzacca, F. L. "Frosty," 184
Ficklen, James, 150
Ficklen Stadium. *See* Dowdy-Ficklen Stadium (East Carolina)
Finch-Heery Company, 198
Finley, Albert, 166
Fisher, Robert, 2
Fletcher, Howard, 160
Florida Field (Florida), 81-83
Florida State University, 128-130
Floyd, Johnny "Red," 91
Floyd, Ralph, 147
Floyd Stadium (Middle Tennessee), 90-91
Flutie, Doug, 135-136
Folsom Field (Colorado), 42-45
Folsom, Frank, 42, 44
Ford, Gerald, 240
Ford, Mariet, 40
Ford Stadium (Southern Methodist), vii, 238-240
Fortie, Eldon, 154
Foster & Creighton Construction Company, 220
Foster, Louis, 25
Fouts Field (North Texas), 130-132
Fouts, J. Theron, 130
Frank, Clint, 7
Franklin Field (Pennsylvania), 30-32
French, Thomas, 26
Fresno State (California State University, Fresno), 217-218
Fry, Hayden, 75, 131
Fuller, Buckminster, 206
Fulton, B. E. "Shorty," 108

G—
Gabriel, Roman, 165
Gain, Bob, 198
Gamble, James, 12
Gardner Dow Field (Connecticut), 243
Garner, Dwight, 40
Gates/Finch-Heery, 213
Geiger, Andy, 27
Georgia Tech, 3-5
Gerber, Max, 100
Gernsdorff, George Bruno de, 1

Gibbs, Joe, 168
Gibson, Vince, 177
Gill, Slats, 132
Gillman, Sid, 12, 225
Gladchuk, Chet, 113
Glass Bowl (Toledo), 99-100
Glidden Field (Northern Illinois), 160
Goldberg, Marshall, 241
Goldsberry, Blaine, 76
Goldsmith, Fred, 127
Gonson, Harry, 147
Graham, Otto, 56, 162
Gramatica, Martin, 178
Grange, Red, 31, 33, 221
Grant Field. *See* Dodds Stadium (Georgia Tech)
Grant, John W., 4
Grant, U. S., 13
Gray, Mike, 105
Grecni, Dick, 76
Green, Reed, 208
Green, Sammy, 82
Green, Woody, 136
Greene, Herbert, 50
Greene, Joe, 131
Griese, Bob, 49
Griffin, Don, 91
Groves Stadium (Wake Forest), 174-176
Guy, Ray, 209

H—
Hadden, Gavin, 10
Haden, Pat, 42
Hagan, Darian, 44
Hale, I, B., 77
Hall, Galen, 83
Hannah, John, 66
Hardin, Wayne, 141, 192
Hare, Cliff, 107
Hare Stadium. *See* Jordan-Hare Stadium (Auburn)
Harley, Charles "Chic," 26
Harris, Leo, 169
Harris, Major, 215
Harris, Marcus, 120
Harrison, David A., III., 89
Harrison, Robert, 76

Harvard Stadium (Harvard), 1-3
Hatfield, Ken, 127
Hawkins, Alex, 93
Hayes, Woody, 27, 137, 159, 225
Haynes, Abner, 131
Haynes, Mike, 136
Heard, T. P. "Skipper," 52
Heery & Heery, 72
Hein, Mel, 97
Heinz Field (Pittsburgh), 240-243
Heisman, John, 4, 5
Helwig, Craig, 131
Hemingway Stadium. *See* Vaught-Hemingway Stadium (Mississippi)
Hemingway, William, 113
Henderson, Elmer, 86
Hendricks, Bart, 186
Hendricks, Ted "the Mad Stork," 102
Hennings, Chad, 149
Henson, Lou, 211
Herty, Charles, 70-71
Higgins, Bob, 144
Hill, Calvin, 7
Hill, Chris, 236
Hill, Dan, 69
Hill, Darryl, 125
Hill, Jerry, 120
Hindman, W. S., 240
Hoggard, Dennis, 144
Hollingsworth, Jerry, 115
Holm, Melvin, 216-217
Holovak, Mike, 134
Holt, Torry, 166
Holtz, Lou, 95, 104
Holub, E. J., 119
Honolulu Stadium (Hawai'i), 201
Hooks, Gene, 175
Hoover, Herbert, 24
Hornung, Paul, 85
Horvath, Les, 26
Howard, Frank, 116
Howard, John Galen, 38
Huber, Hunt & Nichols, 213, 234
Hudson, Al, 101
Huff, George, 32
Huff, Sam, 213
Hughes, Harry, 178, 179

An Illustrated History of 120 College Football Stadiums   253

Hughes Stadium (Colorado State), 178-180
Hugh Stubbins and Associates, 191
Humphrey Metrodome (Minnesota), 221-224
Humphries, Stan, 211
Hunt & Nichols, 147
Hunt, Jackie, 226
Hunt, Joel, 79
Hunt, Myron, 28
Huskie Stadium (Northern Illinois), 160-161
Husky Stadium (Washington), 16-19
Hutson, Don, 66

I—

Indian Stadium (Arkansas State), 199-200
Indiana University, 146-148
Ingraham, Randy, 201
Iowa State University, 202-204
Isenbarger, John, 147

J—

Jackson, Bo, 108
Jackson, Levi, 37-38
Jacoby, Ed, 186
Jamail, Joe, 52
James, Craig, viii, 239
James, Don, 18, 183
Janikowski, Sebastian, 129
Jefferson, Thomas, 87
Jenkins, Leo, 150
Jennings, Ernie, 149
Jensen, James, 154
Jeppesen Stadium (Houston), 112
Johnson, Bob, 56
Johnson, Charley, 211
Johnson, Jimmy, 102
Johnson, John Henry, 136
Johnson, Junior, 175
Johnson, LeShon, 160
Johnson, Lyndon, 76
Johnson, Ron, 142, 184
Jones, Clifford, 37, 118
Jones, Eric, 220

Jones Field. *See* Floyd Stadium (Middle Tennessee)
Jones, Horace, 90
Jones, Howard, 41
Jones, June, 202
Jones, Marvin, 129
Jones, Robert, 150
Jones SBC Stadium (Texas Tech), 117-120
Jones, Stan, 124
Jordan, Henry, 88
Jordan, Homer, 117
Jordan, Lee Roy, 66
Jordan, Ralph "Shug," 108
Jordan-Hare Stadium (Auburn), 107-108
Justice, Charlie "Choo-Choo," 63

K—

Kahuani, Harry, 201
Kansas State University, 176-178
Kapp, Joe, 40
Kaulukukui, Tommy "Grass Shack," 201
Kays, C. V., 199
Kays Field (Arkansas State), 199, 200
Kazmaier, Dick, 237
Kellar, Mark, 160
Kelley, Larry, 7
Kelly, Bill, 196
Kelly, Jeff, 178
Kelly-Shorts Stadium (Central Michigan), 195-197
Kenan Stadium (North Carolina), 61-63
Kenan, William, Jr., 61
Kennedy, John F., 63, 135, 220
Kent State University, 181-183
Kern, Rex, 27
Keyes, Leroy, 49
Kibbie Dome (Idaho), 188-191
Kibbie, William, 190
Kidd Field (Texas–El Paso), 152
Kidd, John "Cap," 152
Kimbrough, John, 80
Kinard, Terry, 117
King, Shaun, 207
Kinley, David, 32

Kinnick, Nile, 74-75
Kinnick Stadium (Iowa), 73-75
Kischer, Everett "Rabbit," 202
Klum, Otto "Proc," 201
Knight, Phil, 171
Koch, Barton "Botchey," 121-122
Koetter, Dirk, 186
Kramer, Jerry, 189
Kramer, Roy, 196, 220
Kristosik, Joe, 195
KSU Stadium (Kansas State), 176-178
Kush, Frank, 136, 137-138
Kustok, Zac, 57
Kyle, Edwin, 79
Kyle Field (Texas A&M), 79-81

L—
Lambert, Jack, 183
Lambeth Stadium (Virginia), 88
Lambright, Maxie, 180
Lane, Edward, 158
Lane Stadium (Virginia Tech), 158-160
Langford, Ernest, 79
Larson, Gordon, 110
Laval, Billy, 93
Lawrence, Amos, 213
Layton Construction Company, 236
Leaf, Ryan, 98
Leahy, Frank, 85
Legion Field (Alabama–Birmingham), 63-65
Leishman, William, 27-28
Lengyel, Jack, 227
Letterman, David, 172
LeVias, Jerry, 239
Levy, Marv, 141-142
Lewis, Art, 213
Lewis, Bill, 150
Lewis, Carl, 112
Lewis Field (Oklahoma State), 14-16
Lewis, Laymon, 15
Liberty Bowl (Memphis), 155-158
Lindbergh, Charles, 244
Lindenmeyer, Ed, 58
Little, George, 231-232
Lockhart, Carl "Spider," 131
Lombardi, Vince, 137

Long, Chuck, 75
Long, Huey, 52
Long, Mel, 100
Long, Russell, 206
Loria, Frank, 159
Los Angeles Memorial Coliseum (Southern California), 40-42
Louis, Joe, 201
Louisiana State University, 52-54
Louisiana Superdome (Tulane), 205-207
Louisiana Tech University, 180-181
Louthen, Ray, 171
Lubick, Sonny, 180
Lucas, Richie, 144
Luckett & Farley, 234
Luppino, Art, 68
Lyles, Lenny, 234

M—
MacArthur, Douglas, 46
Mackay, John, 161-162
Mackay Stadium (Nevada), 161-163
Mackey, Guy, 48
Macklin Field. *See* Spartan Stadium (Michigan State)
Macklin, John, 37
Mackovic, John, 175
Madden, John, 168
Magnabosco, John, 171
Majors, Johnny, 241
Mallory, Bill, 147
Malone, James, 210
Malone Stadium (Louisiana–Monroe), 209-211
Mann, Charles, 163
Manning, Archie, 114-115
Manning, Peyton, 23
Manns, Denvis, 213
Mariano, Lou, 182
Marinaro, Ed, 11
Marino, Dan, 242
Marion, Brock, 163
Marsh, Mike, 112
Marshall University, 226-228
Marshall University Stadium (Marshall) 226-228
Martin, Ben, 149
Martin, Clarence, 98

Martin, Dan, 98
Martin Stadium (Washington State), 97-98, 190-191
Marz, Charles, 24
Mason, Glen, 223
Mason, Tommy, 206
Matheson, Jack, 105
Maxwell, Joseph, 135
May, Bobby, 127
Maynard, Don, 152
McAfee, George, 69
McAllister, Deuce, 115
McAshan, Eddie, 4
McCallum, Napoleon, 141
McClure, Brian, 164
McCook Field (Kansas), 19-20
McCullough, Lou, 203
McCutcheon, Lawrence, 179
McDonald, Darnell, 178
McDonald, Ray, 189
McDowell, Gene, 96
McFadden, Banks, 115
McGraw, Thurman "Fum," 178
McGugin, Dan, 219
McKale, J. F. "Pop," 67
McKeen, Allyn, 9
McKeithen, John, 206, 207
McKim, Charles, 1
McLean, Price, 197
McLean Stadium (Kentucky), 197
McLinden, Gerald, 207
McMahon, Jim, 155
McMillin, Bo, 146, 147
McNabb, Donovan, 217
McNaspy, Clement, 187
McNaspy Stadium (Louisiana–Lafayette), 187
McNown, Cade, 29
McPherson, Dick, 217
McPherson, Don, 217
McVea, Warren, 112
Meagher, Jack, 107
Meisnest, Darwin, 16
Memorial Stadium (California), 38-40
Memorial Stadium (Clemson), 115-117
Memorial Stadium (Connecticut), 243
Memorial Stadium (Illinois), 32-34

Memorial Stadium (Indiana), 146-148
Memorial Stadium (Kansas), 19-21
Memorial Stadium (Minnesota), 221, 223, 224
Memorial Stadium (Missouri), 57-59
Memorial Stadium (Nebraska), 34-36
Memorial Stadium (Oklahoma), 54-55
Memphis Memorial Stadium. *See* Liberty Bowl (Memphis)
Menefee, Bill, 123
Meredith, Don, vii, 239
Meredith, James, 114
Meyer, Ron, 194
Miami Field (Miami [Ohio]), 224, 226
Miami University (Ohio), 224-226
Michie, Dennis, 46
Michie Stadium (Army), 45-47
Michigan Stadium (Michigan), viii, 59-61
Michigan State University, 36-38
Middle Tennessee State University, 90-91
Mildren, Jack, 55
Miles, Clarence, 158
Miles Stadium (Virginia Tech), 158
Minisi, Anthony "Skip," 31
Minter, Cedric, 186
Mississippi State University, 7-9
Mitchell, Brian, 188
Mitchell, Odus, 130
Moen, Kevin, 40
Montana, Joe, 85
Montgomery, Bill, 104
Moore, Arch, 227
Moore, Herman, 89
Moore, Nat, 82
Moore, Shawn, 89
Moos, Bill, 170, 171
Morgan, Blane, 149
Morris, Teddy, 90
Moseley, Frank, 159
Moses, Haven, 168
Moss, Randy, 228
Motley, Marion, 162
Mountaineer Field (West Virginia), 213, 215
Muckensturm, Jerry, 200
Mulcahy, Bob, 232

Munger, George, 32
Munn, Clarence "Biggie," 37
Murphy, Billy, 156
Murphy, Charles, 90
Murphy, Jack, 168
Murphy, Tom, 242
Murr Center (Harvard), 3
Murray, Fanny, 32
Myers, Gerald, 119-120
Myers, Greg, 180

N—
Nagurski, Bronko, 221
Namath, Joe, 66
Navy (U.S. Naval Academy), 139-141
Navy–Marine Corps Memorial Stadium (Navy), 139-141
Neale, Earle "Greasy," 88
Neale Stadium (Idaho), 190
Neely, Jess, 115-116, 125
Nehemiah, Renaldo, 125
Nehlen, Don, 214, 215
Neilson Field (Rutgers), 231
New Athletic Field. *See* Scott Field (Mississippi State)
New Mexico State University, 211-213
Newport Engineering and Construction Company, 46
Newsome, Ozzie, 66
Neyland, Bob, 22, 23
Neyland Stadium (Tennessee), 21-23
Nguyen, Dat, 81
Nicholson, Jim, 99
Nielsen, Gifford, 155
Nippert, James, 12
Nippert Stadium (Cincinnati), 11-12
Nixon, Richard, 104
Nordenberg, Mark, 242
Norlin, George, 42
Norlin Stadium. *See* Folsom Field (Colorado)
North Carolina State University, 164-167
Northern Illinois University, 160-161
Northington, Nat, 198
Northwestern University, 55-57
Norton, Homer, 80
Norton, Jim, 189

Notre Dame Stadium (Notre Dame), 83-85
Novacek, Jay, 120
Novak, Joe, 161
Nutt, Houston, 104

O—
O'Brien, Davey, 77
O'Quinn, John, 113
O'Rourke, Charlie, 134
Oerter, Al, 20
Offenhammer, Dick, 229
Ohio Stadium (Ohio State), 26-27
Ohio Stadium (Ohio University). *See* Peden Stadium (Ohio), 75
Ohio State University, 26-27
Ohio University, Athens, 75-77
Oklahoma State University, 14-16
Ole Miss, 113-115
Olsen, Merlin, 173
Oosterbaan, Bennie, 60
Orange Bowl (Miami), 101
Oregon State University, 132-134
Osborne Engineering Company, 84
Osborne, Tom, 36
Owen, Bennie, 54
Owens, Jesse, 26
Ownby, Jordan, 238
Ownby Stadium (SMU), vii, 238, 239, 240

P—
Page, Kurt, 220
Paige, Satchel, 101
Palmer, Edgar, 237
Palmer Stadium (Princeton), 237, 238
Palmer, Stephen, 237
Papa John's Cardinal Stadium (Louisville), 233-235
Papit, Johnny, 88
Parilli, Vito "Babe," 198
Parker, Charles, 132
Parkinson, John, 40
Parkway Field (Louisville), 233, 234
Parseghian, Ara, 56, 85, 225
Pastilong, Ed, 215
Paterno, Joe, 144, 145

Payne, Billy, 73
Pearson, Paul, 225
Peden, Don, 75
Peden Stadium (Ohio), 75-77
Pederson, Steve, 242
Pennington, Chad, 228
Pennsylvania State University, 143-146
Percy Field (Cornell), 9
Perkins, Don, 141-142
Perkins, Lew, 244, 245
Perry, Doyt, 163, 164
Perry Stadium (Bowling Green), 163-164
Peterson, Bill, 129
Petrillo, Pete, 243
Petty, Richard, 175
Phelan, James, 47
Philbin, Gerry, 229
Phillips, Jimmy, 108
Piccolo, Brian, 175
Pifferini, Bob, 91
Pinkel, Gary, 100
Pitt Stadium (Pittsburgh), 240, 241, 242
Plummer, Jake "the Snake," 138
Plunkett, Jim, 24
Podoley, Jim, 195
Pont, John, 147
Porter & Bradley, 120
Powell, Chris, 157
Presley, Elvis, 201
Price, Eddie, 206
Price, Mike, 98
Princeton Stadium (Princeton), 237-238
Pritchett, Norton, 88
Profit, Joe, 210
Prothro, Tommy, 132
Protz, Craig, 212
Pruitt, Greg, 55
Public School Stadium (Houston), 111, 112
Purdue University, 47-49

Q—
Qualcomm Stadium (San Diego State), 167-169
Quayle, Frank, 88
Queen Elizabeth, 125
Quesenberry, Joe, 211

R—
Ralston, John, 173
Ramsey, Derrick, 199
Ratcliffe Stadium (Fresno State), 217, 218
Rattay, Tim, 180
Ray Ward & Son, 212
Razorback Stadium. *See* Reynolds Razorback Stadium (Arkansas)
Reagan, Ronald, 155
Reese, Brad, 110
Renfro, Mel, 169
Rentschler Field (Connecticut), 243-245
Rentschler, Frederick, 244
Reser, Al, 133-134
Reser Stadium (Oregon State), 132-134
Reynolds, Bob, 163
Reynolds, Donald, 105
Reynolds Razorback Stadium (Arkansas), 102-105
Rhome, Jerry, 87
Ribar, Frank, 69
Rice, Grantland, 72, 112
Rice, Robert, 236
Rice Stadium (Rice), 125-128
Rice Stadium (Utah). *See* Rice-Eccles Stadium (Utah)
Rice University, 125-128
Rice-Eccles Stadium (Utah), 235-237
Riddick Stadium (North Carolina State), 165, 166
Riddick, Wallace, 164-165
Ridge, Tom, 242
Ritcher, Jim, 166
Roaf, William, 180
Robeson, Paul, 231
Robertson, Corbin, 112
Robertson Stadium (Houston), 111-113
Roberts Stadium (Southern Mississippi), 208-209
Robinson, Dan, 202
Robinson, Eddie, 159

Robinson, Jackie, 29, 233
Robinson, Jerry, 29
Robinson, John, 131-132, 195
Rockne, Knute, 83-84, 85, 122
Roddy Burdine Municipal Stadium. *See* Orange Bowl (Miami)
Rodgers, Johnny, 36
Rogers Field (Washington State), 97, 98
Rogers, George, 94
Rogers, John, 97
Rogers, Richard, 40
Roland, Johnny, 58-59
Rome, Lewis, 244
Romney, E. L. "Dick," 173-174
Romney Stadium (Utah State), 173-174
Rooney, Art, 242
Roosevelt, Franklin, 95
Roper, Bill, 237
Rose Bowl (UCLA), 27-30
Rosenbach, Timm, 98
Rosenfels, Sage, 204
Ross, Bobby, 4, 125
Ross, David, 47
Ross-Ade Foundation, 47, 48
Ross-Ade Stadium (Purdue), 47-49
Rotary Field (Buffalo), 229, 230
Rote, Kyle, vii
Rote, Tobin, 126
Rowland, John, 244
Royal, Darrell, 50
Royal-Memorial Stadium (Texas), 49-52
Rubber Bowl (Akron), 108-111
Rupp, Adolph, 197
Rutgers Stadium (Rutgers), 230-233
Rutgers, the State University of New Jersey, 230-233
Ruth, Babe, 201, 233
Ryan Field (Northwestern), 55-57
Ryan, John, 141
Ryan, Patrick, 57
Rynearson, Elton, 183
Rynearson Stadium (Eastern Michigan), 183-185
Ryun, Jim, 20

S—

Saban, Lou, 96
San Diego Stadium. *See* Qualcomm Stadium
San Diego State University, 167-169
San Jose State University, 91-92
Sanders, Barry, 16, 120
Sanders, Deion, 129
Sanders, Henry "Red," 29
Sands, Tony, 20
Sandstedt, Carl, 79
Sanford Stadium (Georgia), 70-73
Sanford, Steadman, 71
Santee, Wes, 20
Sauer, George, 20
Savitsky, George, 31
Sayers, Gale, 175
Schembechler, Bo, 61, 225
Schmidt, Francis, 77
Schmidt, Joe, 241
Schnelker, Bob, 163
Schnellbacher, Otto, 20
Schnellenberger, Howard, 102, 234
Schoellkopf Field (Cornell), 9-11
Schoellkopf Hall (Cornell), 11
Schuh, Harry, 156
Schwartzwalder, Ben, 215, 216
Scott, Clyde, 103
Scott, Dick, 139
Scott, Don, 8
Scott Field (Mississippi State), 7-9
Scott, Frederic W., 88
Scott Stadium (Virginia), 87-89
Sharpe, Sterling, 94
Shaughnessy, Clark, 205
Shaw, Dennis, 168
Sherrill, Jackie, 9, 81
Shields, W. S., 22
Shields-Watkins Field. *See* Neyland Stadium (Tennessee)
Shorts, Perry, 195
Shorts Stadium. *See* Kelly-Shorts Stadium (Central Michigan)
Shrider, Richard, 225
Shula, Don, 102
Simmons, Ron, 129
Simmons, Sam, 57
Simoneau, Mark, 178

An Illustrated History of 120 College Football Stadiums 259

Singletary, Mike, 123
Sinkwich, Frank, 72
Sipe, Brian, 168
Sisco, Jack, 130
Skelly Stadium (Tulsa), 86-87
Skelly, William, 86
Slater, Duke, 73
Slater, Rodney, 184
Sleight, Elmer, 47
Sloan, Steve, 97
Slocum, R. C., 81
Smith, Akili, 170
Smith, Andy, 38
Smith, Bruce, 159, 221
Smith, Carl, 89
Smith, Charles "Bubba," 37
Smith, Gene, 138
Smith, Howard, 26
Smith, Lyle, 185-186
Smith, Vernon "Catfish," 72
Smith, Zeke, 108
Smukler, Dave, 191
Snavely Carl, 63
Snyder, Bill, 177, 178
Snyder, Meredith P., 40
Soldiers Field (Harvard), 1
Sossamon, Lou, 93
Southern Methodist University, 238-240
Southwestern Louisiana University. *See* University of Louisiana–Lafayette
Spani, Gary, 177
Spartan Stadium (Michigan State), 36-38
Spartan Stadium (San Jose State), 91-92
Sperber, Murray, xi
Spiegelberg Lumber and Building Company, 120
Spurrier, Steve, 70, 82-83
St. John, Lynn, 26
Stallings, Gene, 67
Stanford Stadium (Stanford), 24
Stark, H. J. Lutcher, 50
Stasavich, Clarence, 150
Stassen, Harold, 31
State University of New York at Buffalo, 228-230

Staubach, Roger, 141
Steele, Kevin, 123
Stephens, Sandy, 222
Stevens, Billy, 153
Stevens, Pete, 191
Still, Art, 199
Stillwagon, Jim, 27
Stofa, John, 229
Stoll Field (Kentucky), 197
Stoll, Richard, 197
Stoops, Bob, 55
Strachan, Mike, 203
Strode, Woody, 29
Stull, Bob, 153
Stydahar, Joe, 213
Sullivan, James, 79
Sullivan, Pat, 108
Sun Bowl (Texas–El Paso), 151-153
Sun Devil Stadium (Arizona State), 136-139
Sutherland, Jock, 240
Swain, Donald, 234
Sweeney, Jim, 218
Sweeney, Kevin, 218
Swick, Gene, 100
Swink, Jim, 77
Switzer, Barry, 55
Syracuse University, 215-217

T—

T. C. Thompson and Brothers, 62
Tagge, Jerry, 36
Tagliabue, Paul, 138, 207
Tait, Wasean, 100
Talboom, Eddie, 120
Tangerine Bowl. *See* Citrus Bowl (Central Florida)
Tatum, Jack, 27
Tatum, Jim, 124
Taylor, Charley, 136
Taylor, F. Jay, 180
Taylor, Jim, 52
Taylor, Whit, 220
Taylor, William, 28
Teaff, Grant, 123
Tech Stadium (Texas Tech), 118
Temple University, 191-193
Templeton, Larry, 9

Tensi, Steve, 129
Testaverde, Vinny, 102
Texas A&M University, 79-81
Texas Christian University, 77-79
Texas Stadium, 239
Texas Tech University, 117-120
Thomas, Frank, 66
Thomas, Kevin, 123
Thomas, Lloyd, 91
Thomas, Mike, 194
Thompson, Anthony, 147
Thompson, Jack, 98
Thompson, Robert, 139
Thompson Stadium (Navy), 139
Thorpe, Jim, 2
Tiger Stadium (Louisiana State), 52-54
Tiller, Joe, 49, 121
Tittle, Y. A., 52
Tolliver, Billy Joe, 119
Tomey, Dick, 69
Tomlinson, LaDainian, 79
Torkelson, Eric, 243
Tormey, Chris, 190
Torretta, Gino, 102
Townsend, Nelson, 230
Tressel, Jim, 27
Trice, Jack, 204
Trice Stadium (Iowa State), 202-204
Triplett, Mel, 100
Trippi, Charley, 72
Tripplett, Wally, 144
Trojanowsky, Walt, 243
Tulane University, 205-207
Tunnell, Emlen, 100
Turman Fieldhouse (Mississippi State), 9
Turner Construction Company, 11, 240
Tuttle, Perry, 117
Twilley, Howard, 87
Tyee Center (Washington), 18

U—
U.S. Air Force Academy, 148-149
U.S. Military Academy, 45-47
U.S. Naval Academy, 139-141
UB Stadium (Buffalo), 228-230
UCLA, 27-30
Unitas, Johnny, 234
University at Buffalo, 228-230
University of Akron, 108-111
University of Alabama–Birmingham, 63-65
University of Alabama, Tuscaloosa, 65-67
University of Arizona, Tucson, 67-69
University of Arkansas, 102-105
University of California, Berkeley, 38-40
University of California, Los Angeles, 27-30
University of Central Florida, 95-97
University of Cincinnati, 11-12
University of Colorado at Boulder, 42-45
University of Connecticut, 243-245
University of Florida, Gainesville, 81-83
University of Georgia, Athens, 70-73
University of Hawai'i, 201-202
University of Houston, 111-113
University of Idaho, 188-191
University of Illinois, 32-34
University of Iowa, Iowa City, 73-75
University of Kansas, 19-21
University of Kentucky, 197-199
University of Louisiana–Lafayette, 187-188
University of Louisiana–Monroe, 209-211
University of Louisville, 233-235
University of Maryland, 123-125
University of Memphis, 155-158
University of Miami, 101-102
University of Michigan, 59-61
University of Minnesota, Twin Cities, 221-224
University of Mississippi, 113-115
University of Missouri at Columbia, 57-59
University of Nebraska, Lincoln, 34-36
University of Nevada–Las Vegas, 193-195
University of Nevada, Reno, 161-163

University of New Mexico, 142-143
University of North Carolina at Chapel Hill, 61-63
University of North Texas, 130-132
University of Notre Dame, 83-85
University of Oklahoma, Norman, 54-55
University of Oregon, 169-171
University of Pennsylvania, 30-32
University of Pittsburgh, 240-243
University of South Carolina, 93-95
University of Southern California, 40-42
University of Southern Mississippi, 208-209
University of Tennessee, 21-23
University of Texas at Austin, The, 49-52
University of Texas–El Paso, 151-153
University of Toledo, 99-100
University of Tulsa, 86-87
University of Utah, 235-237
University of Virginia, 87-89
University of Washington, 16-19
University of Wisconsin–Madison, 12-14
University of Wyoming, 120-121
University Stadium (New Mexico), 142-143
Urlacher, Brian, 143
Utah State University, 173-174
Ute Stadium. *See* Rice-Eccles Stadium (Utah)

V—
Van Brocklin, Norm, 169
Van Buren, Steve, 52
Vanderbilt Stadium (Vanderbilt), 219-221
Vanderbilt University, 219-221
Vann, Thad "Pie," 209
Varney, Ed, 136
Varney, Pete, 2
Vaught, Johnny, 113, 115
Vaught-Hemingway Stadium (Mississippi), 113-115
Vermeil, Dick, 91
Veterans Stadium (Temple), 191-193

Vick, Michael, 159
Vinoly, Rafael, 238
Virginia Bridge and Iron Company, 93
Virginia Tech, 158-160
Voigts, Bob, 56

W—
W. A. Cray and Sons, 93
W. S. Lee Engineering Corporation, 69
Wacker, Jim, 78
Wade Stadium (Duke), 69-70
Wade, Wallace, 69
Wadiak, Steve, 93
Wagner, Dave, 177
Wait Field (Tennessee), 22
Wake Forest University, 174-176
Waldo, Dwight, 105
Waldo Stadium (Western Michigan), 105-106
Walker, D. C. "Peahead," 174-175
Walker, Doak, vii, 239
Walker, Herschel, 72-73
Walker, Randy, 226
Walker, Wayne, 189
Walsh & Burney Company, 50
Walsh, Bill, 91
Walters, Gary, 238
War Memorial Stadium (Arkansas), 103, 105
War Memorial Stadium (Buffalo), 228-229
War Memorial Stadium (Wyoming), 120-121
Ward, Charlie, 130
Ware, Andre, 112, 120
Warner, Glenn "Pop," 9-10, 24, 191, 240
Warrick, Peter, 129
Washington Field. *See* Husky Stadium (Washington)
Washington, Gene, 37
Washington, Kenny, 29
Washington State University, 97-98
Watkins, L. Whitney, 36-37
Webster, George, 37
Wefald, Jon, 177, 178
Weger, Mike, 163

Welch, Ralph, 47
Welsh, George, 89
West Virginia University, 213-215
Western Michigan University, 105-106
White, Danny, 136
White, James, 32
White, Randy, 125
Whitmore, Don, 139
Wilcox, Dave, 186
Wilkinson, Bud, 54
Williams, Alfred, 44
Williams, C. C., 20
Williams, Clyde, 202
Williams, Dan, 100
Williams Field (Iowa State), 202, 203
Williams, Froggy, 126
Williams, Paul "Billy," 171
Williams, Ricky, 51-52
Williams, Ted, 233
Williams-Brice Stadium (South Carolina), 93-95
Wilson, Kareem, 76
Wilson, Larry, 236
Wilson, Marc, 155
Wilson, Ralph, 37
Wing, Charles, 24
Woit, Richie, 199
Woods, Ickey, 194
Woodson, Charles, 61
Woodson, Rod, 49
Woodson, Warren, 211
Worker Rights Consortium, 171
Wortham, Wes, 159
WPA, 95, 103, 108, 111, 163, 232
Wright, Louie, 91
Wuerffel, Danny, 83
Wyatt, Bowden, 120

Y—

Yager, Fred, 226
Yager Stadium (Miami [Ohio]), 224-226
Yale Bowl (Yale), 5-7
Yale Field, 5-6
Yarborough, Ryan, 120
Yeoman, Bill, 112
Yoshida, Hugh, 202
Yost, Fielding, 59, 60, 61
Young, Brigham, 153
Young, Ryan, 178
Young, Steve, 155

Z—

Zampese, Ernie, 168
Zarosinski, Dan, 132
Zimmerman, Leroy, 91
Zuppke, Bob, 32, 33

About the Author

Richard Pennington, one of the top sports historians in the Lone Star State, easily discourses on athletics in the context of education, culture, and politics, with an occasional dash of humor. In addition to *Home Field*, he is the author of *Breaking the Ice: Racial Integration of Southwest Conference Football* (McFarland & Co.), *"For Texas, I Will": The History of Memorial Stadium* (Historical Publications), and *Longhorn Hoops: The History of Texas Basketball* (University of Texas Press). A native of Dallas and a 1976 UT graduate, Pennington lives in Austin and works as an editor. His web site is at www.richardpennington.info.

www.ingramcontent.com/pod-product-compliance
Lightning Source LLC
Chambersburg PA
CBHW071702160426
43195CB00012B/1555